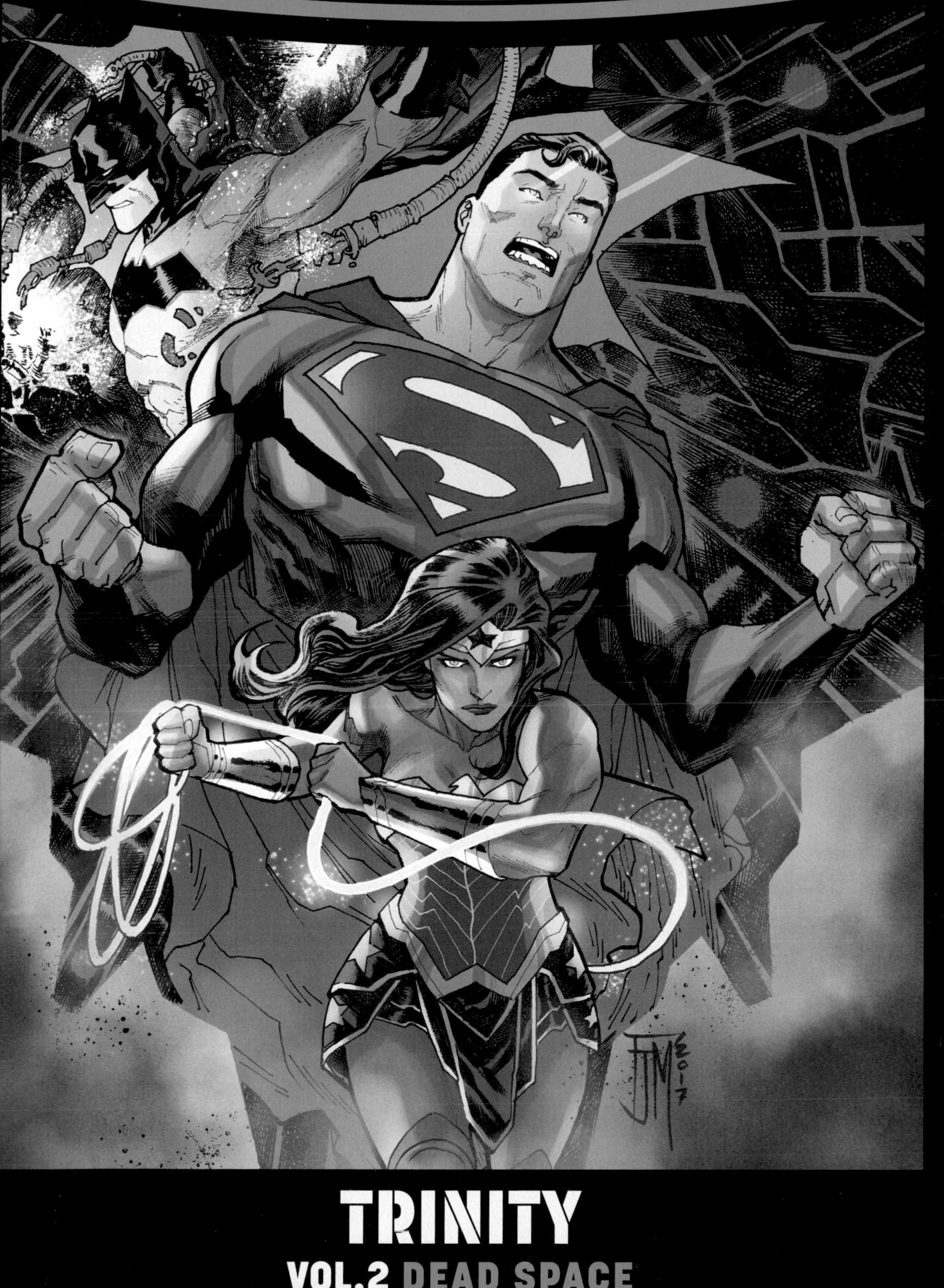

TRINITY

VOL.2 DEAD SPACE

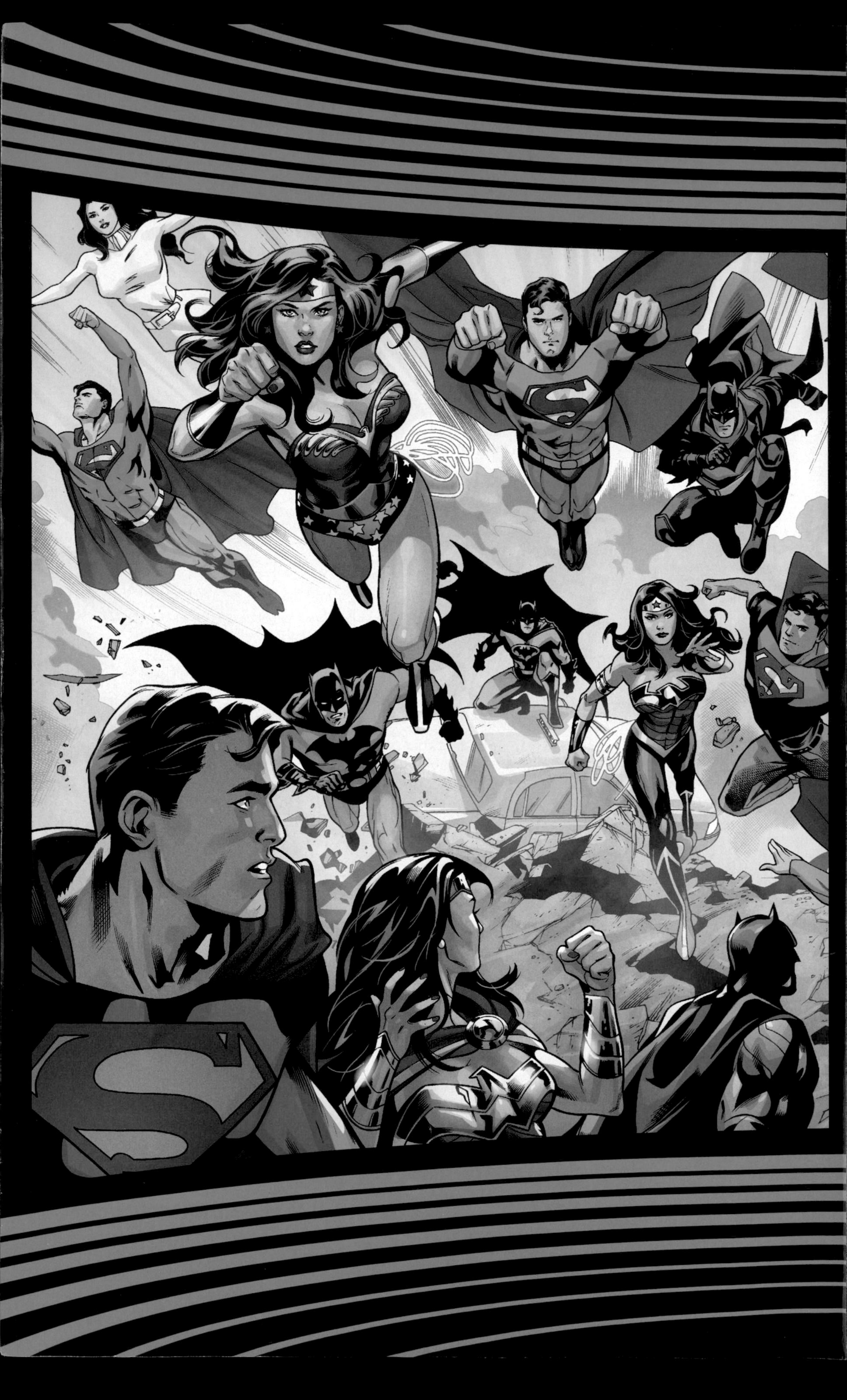

TRINITY
VOL.2 DEAD SPACE

FRANCIS MANAPUL
CULLEN BUNN
writers

FRANCIS MANAPUL
SCOTT HANNA * SCOTT GODLEWSKI * CLAY MANN * EMANUELA LUPACCHINO
MIGUEL MENDONÇA * JOHNNY DESJARDINS * RAY McCARTHY
artists

FRANCIS MANAPUL
WIL QUINTANA * BLOND * BRAD ANDERSON * HI-FI
colorists

STEVE WANDS
TOM NAPOLITANO
letterers

FRANCIS MANAPUL
collection cover artist

SUPERMAN created by **JERRY SIEGEL** and **JOE SHUSTER**.
By special arrangement with the Jerry Siegel family.
BATMAN created by **BOB KANE** with **BILL FINGER**.
WONDER WOMAN created by **WILLIAM MOULTON MARSTON**.

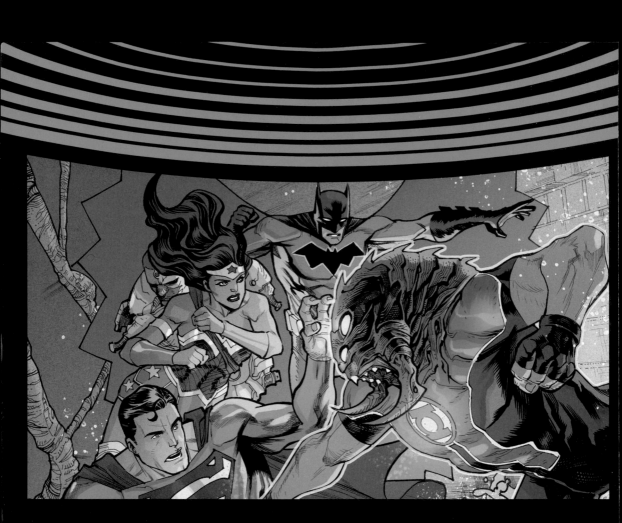

EDDIE BERGANZA, PAUL KAMINSKI Editors - Original Series * **JEB WOODARD** Group Editor - Collected Editions
ALEX GALER Editor - Collected Edition * **STEVE COOK** Design Director - Books

BOB HARRAS Senior VP - Editor-in-Chief, DC Comics * **PAT McCALLUM** Executive Editor, DC Comics

DIANE NELSON President * **DAN DiDIO** Publisher * **JIM LEE** Publisher * **GEOFF JOHNS** President & Chief Creative Officer
AMIT DESAI Executive VP - Business & Marketing Strategy, Direct to Consumer & Global Franchise Management
SAM ADES Senior VP & General Manager, Digital Services * **BOBBIE CHASE** VP & Executive Editor, Young Reader & Talent Development
MARK CHIARELLO Senior VP - Art, Design & Collected Editions * **JOHN CUNNINGHAM** Senior VP - Sales & Trade Marketing
ANNE DePIES Senior VP - Business Strategy, Finance & Administration * **DON FALLETTI** VP - Manufacturing Operations
LAWRENCE GANEM VP - Editorial Administration & Talent Relations * **ALISON GILL** Senior VP - Manufacturing & Operations
HANK KANALZ Senior VP - Editorial Strategy & Administration * **JAY KOGAN** VP - Legal Affairs * **JACK MAHAN** VP - Business Affairs
NICK J. NAPOLITANO VP - Manufacturing Administration * **EDDIE SCANNELL** VP - Consumer Marketing
COURTNEY SIMMONS Senior VP - Publicity & Communications * **JIM (SKI) SOKOLOWSKI** VP - Comic Book Specialty Sales & Trade Marketing
NANCY SPEARS VP - Mass, Book, Digital Sales & Trade Marketing * **MICHELE R. WELLS** VP - Content Strategy

TRINITY VOL. 2 DEAD SPACE

DC Comics, 2900 West Alameda Ave., Burbank, CA 91505
Printed by LSC Communications, Kendallville, IN, USA. 5/18/18. First Printing.
ISBN: 978-1-4012-8050-5

Library of Congress Cataloging-in-Publication Data is available.

PEFC Certified
Printed on paper from sustainably managed forests, controlled sources
PEFC
PEFC/29-31-337
www.pefc.org

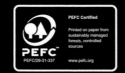

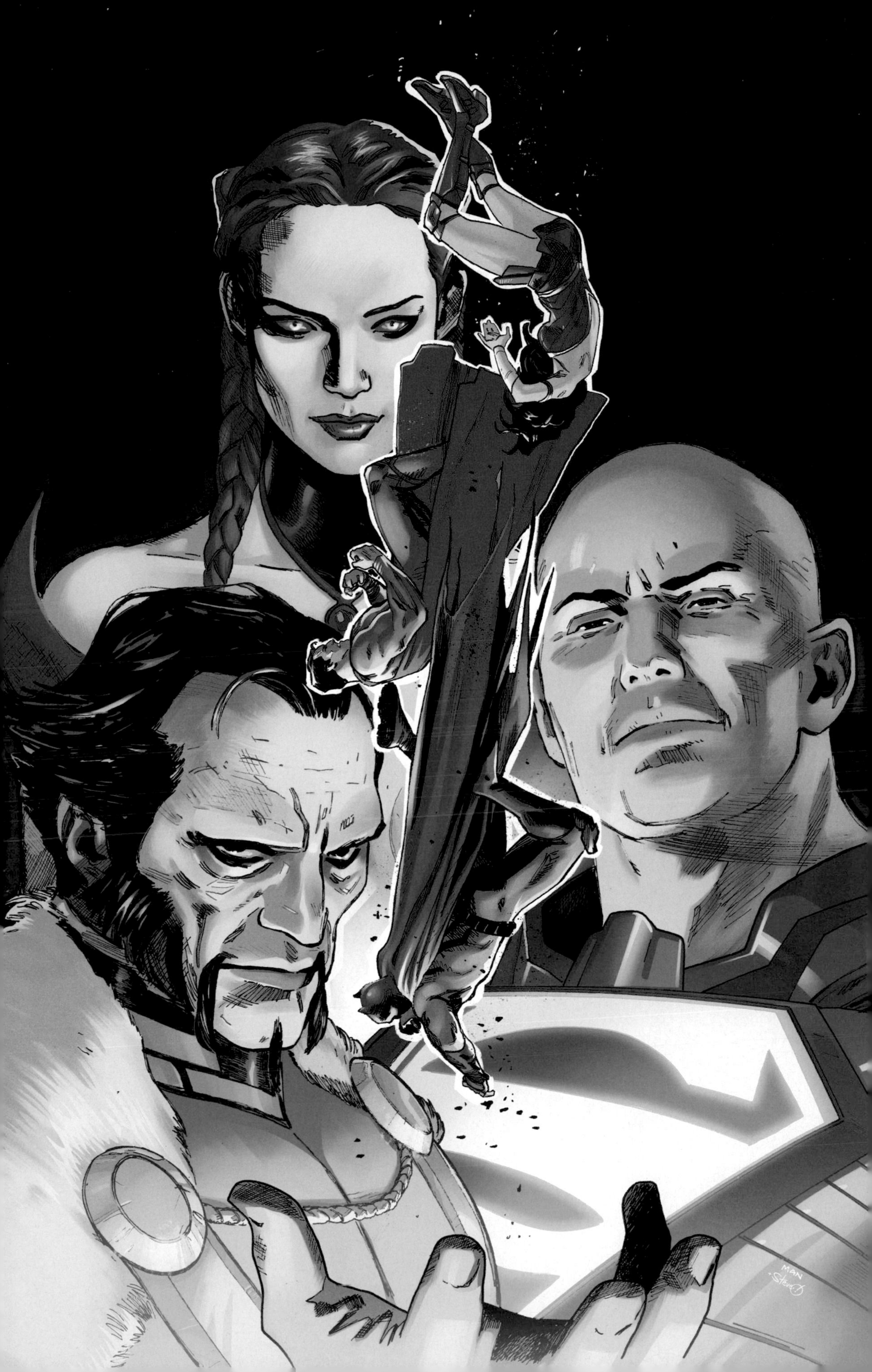

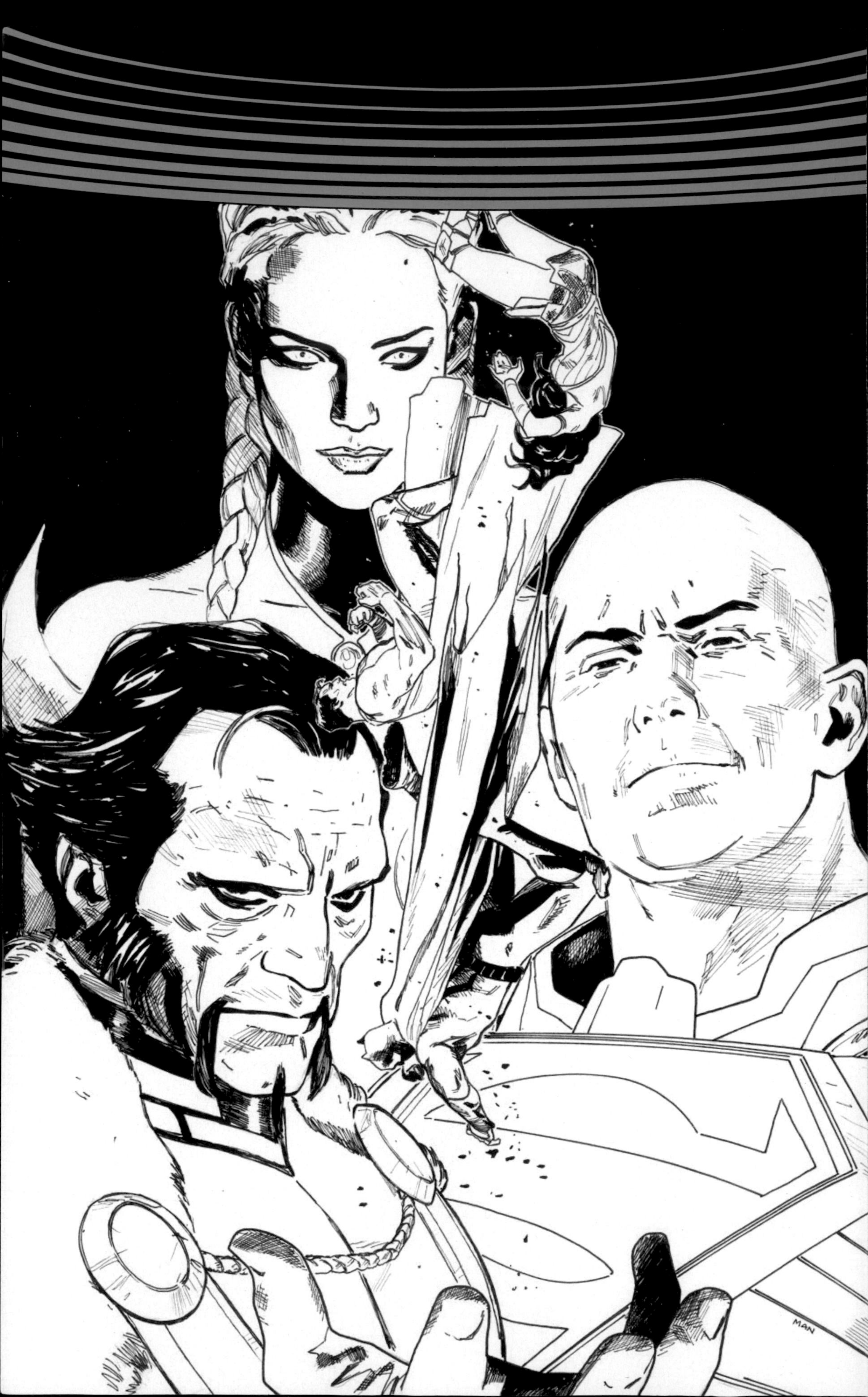
MAN

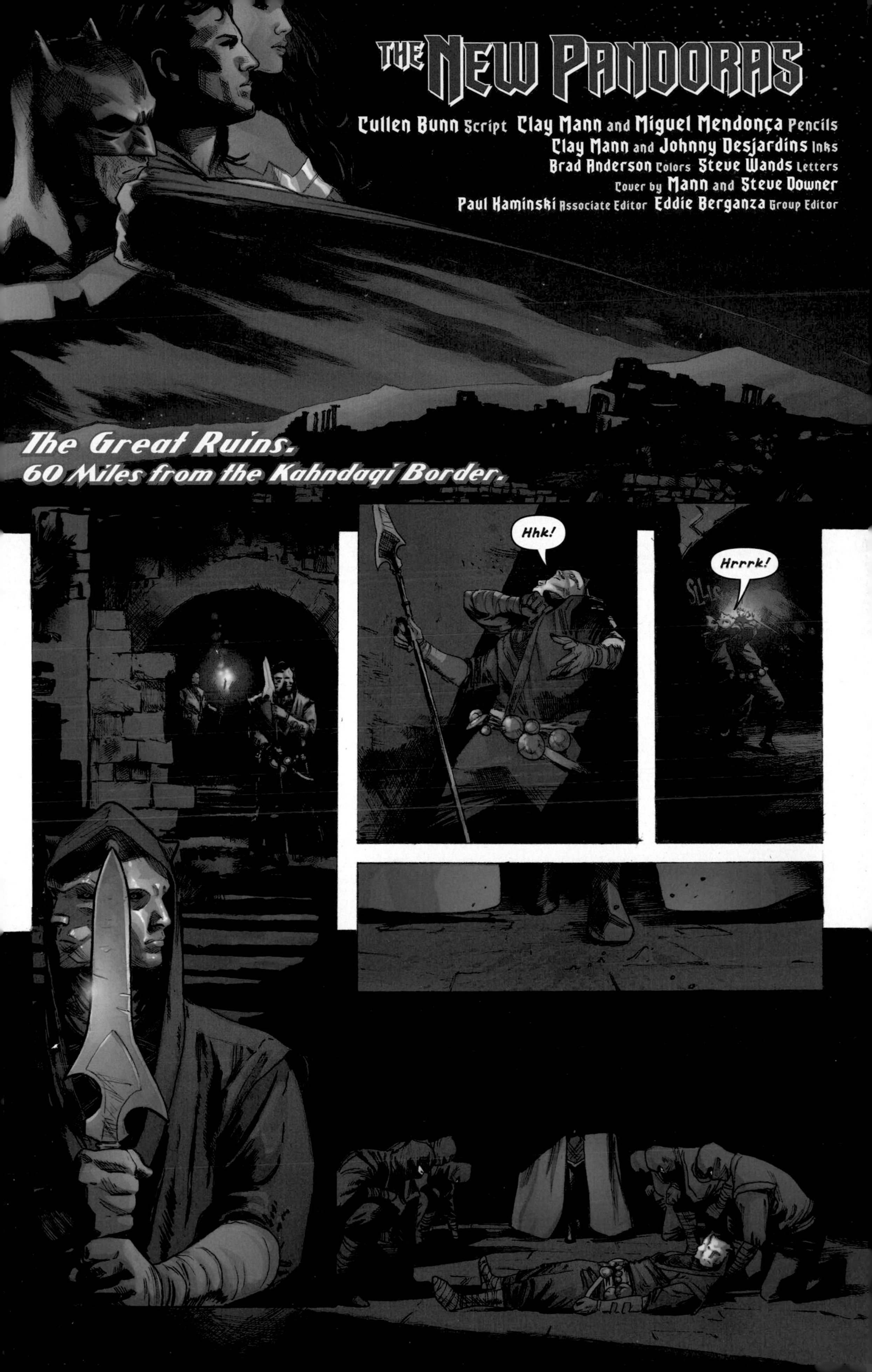
THE NEW PANDORAS
Cullen Bunn Script Clay Mann and Miguel Mendonça Pencils
Clay Mann and Johnny Desjardins Inks
Brad Anderson Colors Steve Wands Letters
Cover by Mann and Steve Downer
Paul Kaminski Associate Editor Eddie Berganza Group Editor
The Great Ruins.
60 Miles from the Kahndaqi Border.
Hhk!
Hrrrk!

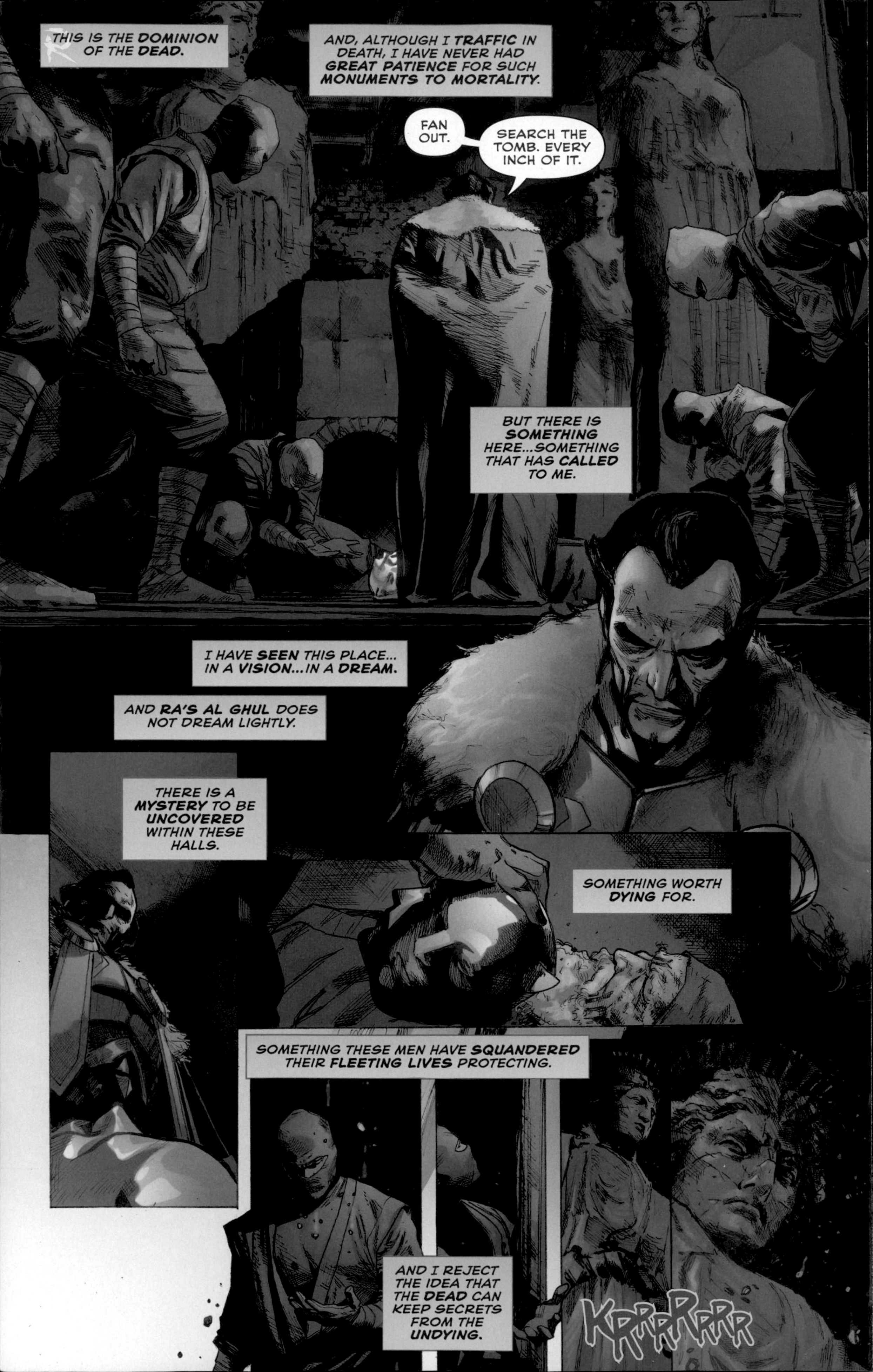
THIS IS THE DOMINION OF THE DEAD.
AND, ALTHOUGH I TRAFFIC IN DEATH, I HAVE NEVER HAD GREAT PATIENCE FOR SUCH MONUMENTS TO MORTALITY.
FAN OUT.
SEARCH THE TOMB. EVERY INCH OF IT.
BUT THERE IS SOMETHING HERE...SOMETHING THAT HAS CALLED TO ME.
I HAVE SEEN THIS PLACE... IN A VISION...IN A DREAM.
AND RA'S AL GHUL DOES NOT DREAM LIGHTLY.
THERE IS A MYSTERY TO BE UNCOVERED WITHIN THESE HALLS.
SOMETHING WORTH DYING FOR.
SOMETHING THESE MEN HAVE SQUANDERED THEIR FLEETING LIVES PROTECTING.
AND I REJECT THE IDEA THAT THE DEAD CAN KEEP SECRETS FROM THE UNDYING.
KRRRRRRR

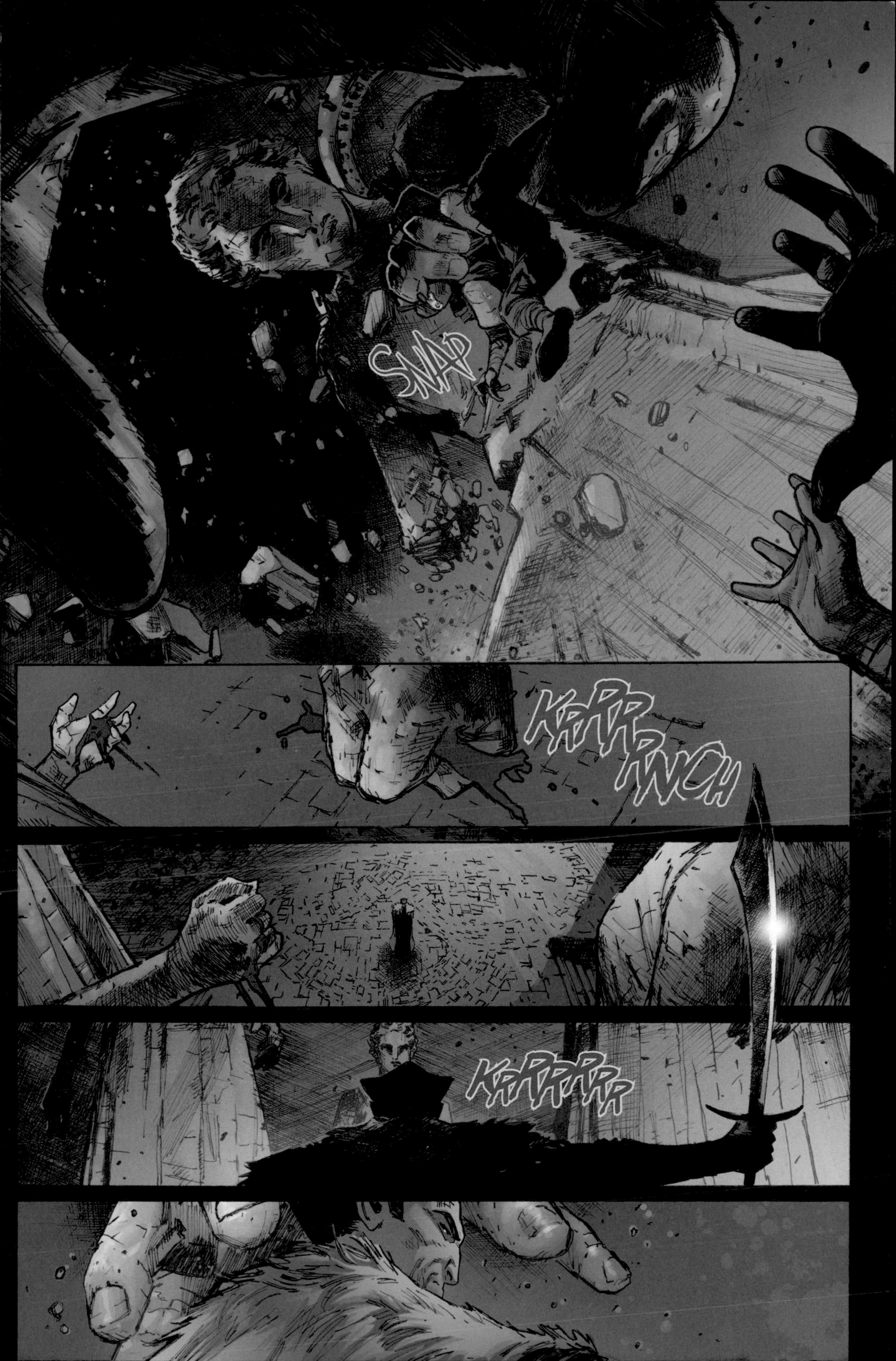
SNAP
KRRRR RNCH
KRRRRRR

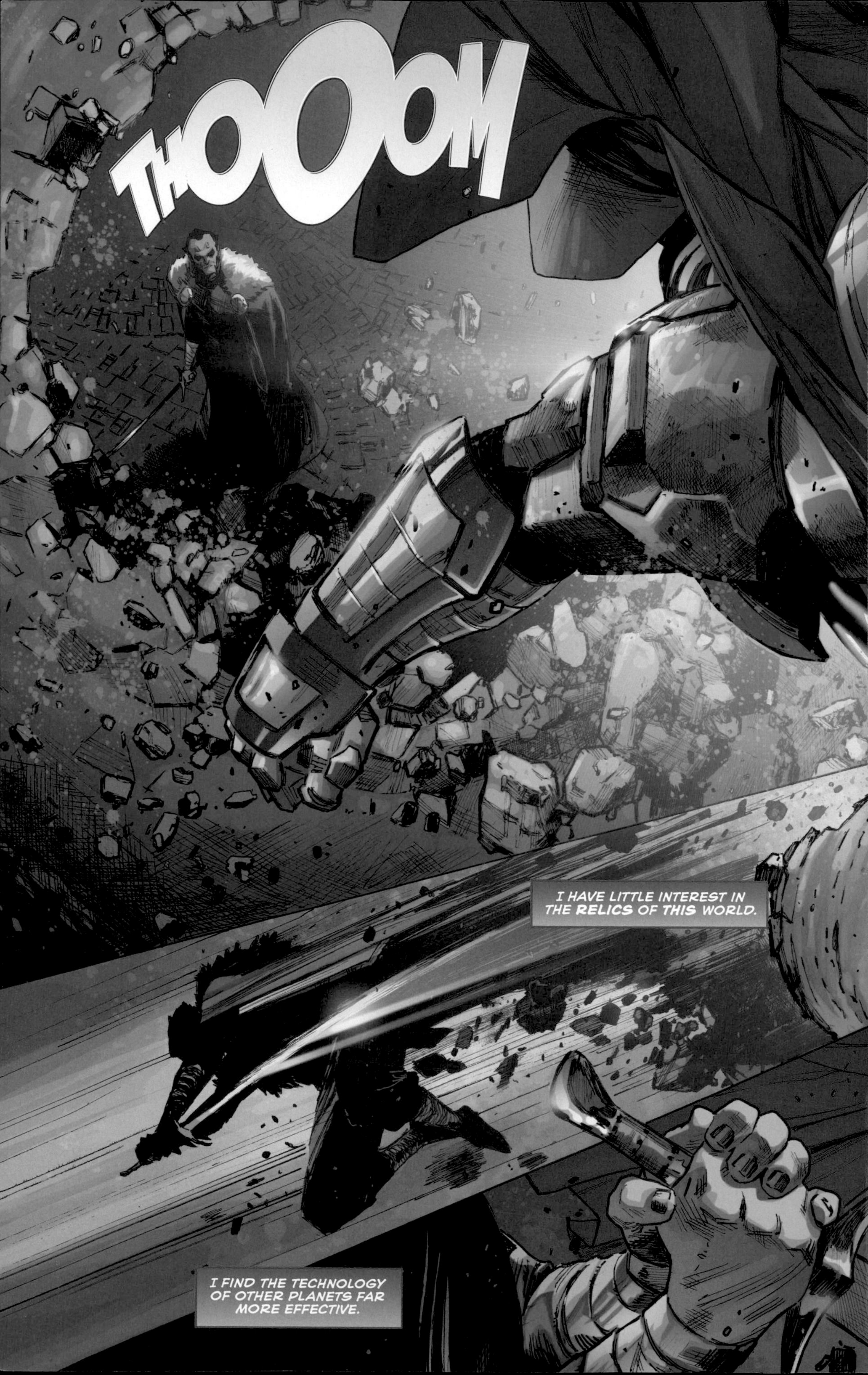
THOOOM
I HAVE LITTLE INTEREST IN THE RELICS OF THIS WORLD.
I FIND THE TECHNOLOGY OF OTHER PLANETS FAR MORE EFFECTIVE.

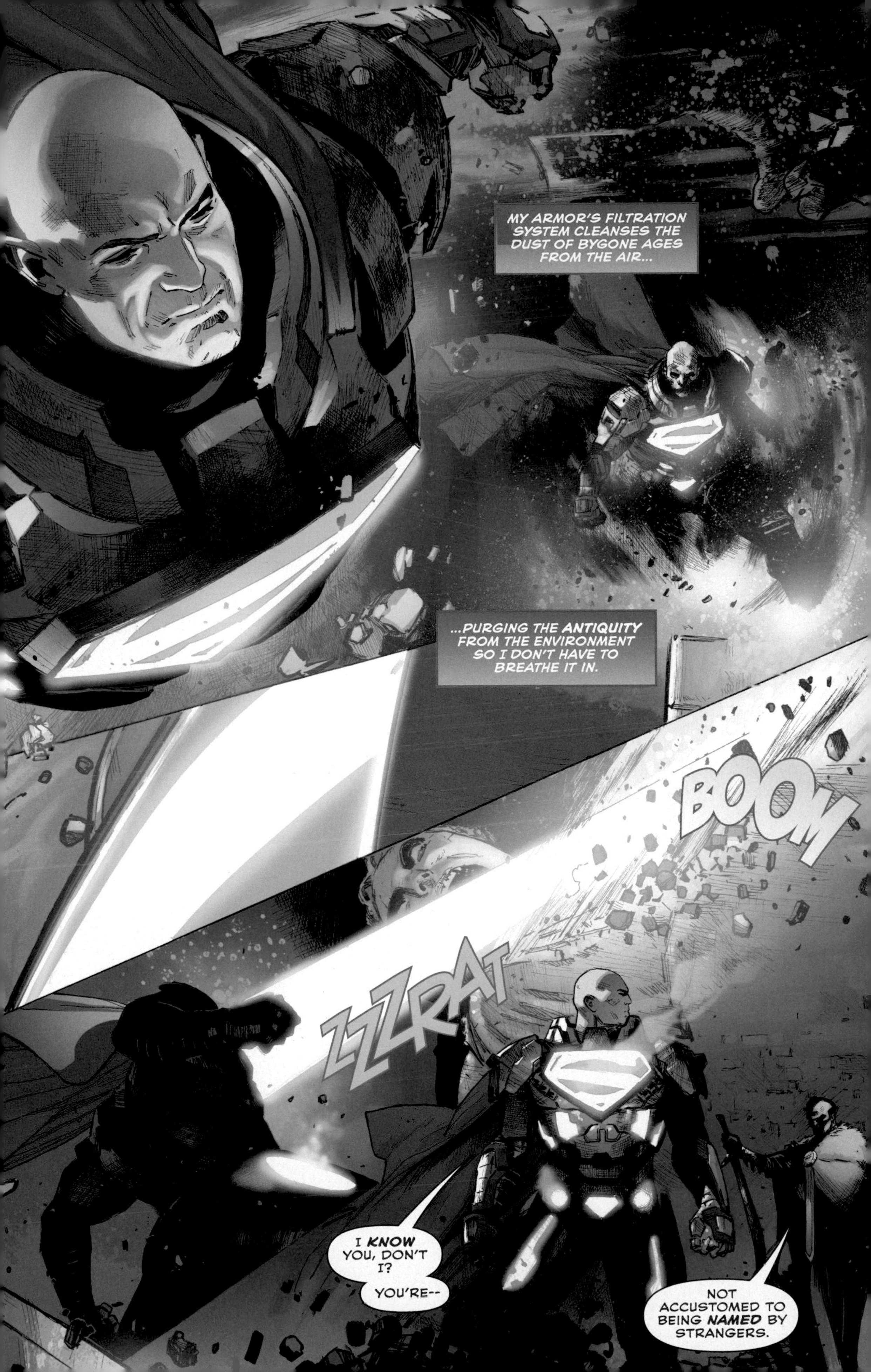
MY ARMOR'S FILTRATION SYSTEM CLEANSES THE DUST OF BYGONE AGES FROM THE AIR...
...PURGING THE ANTIQUITY FROM THE ENVIRONMENT SO I DON'T HAVE TO BREATHE IT IN.
BOOM
ZZZRAT
I KNOW YOU, DON'T I?
YOU'RE--
NOT ACCUSTOMED TO BEING NAMED BY STRANGERS.

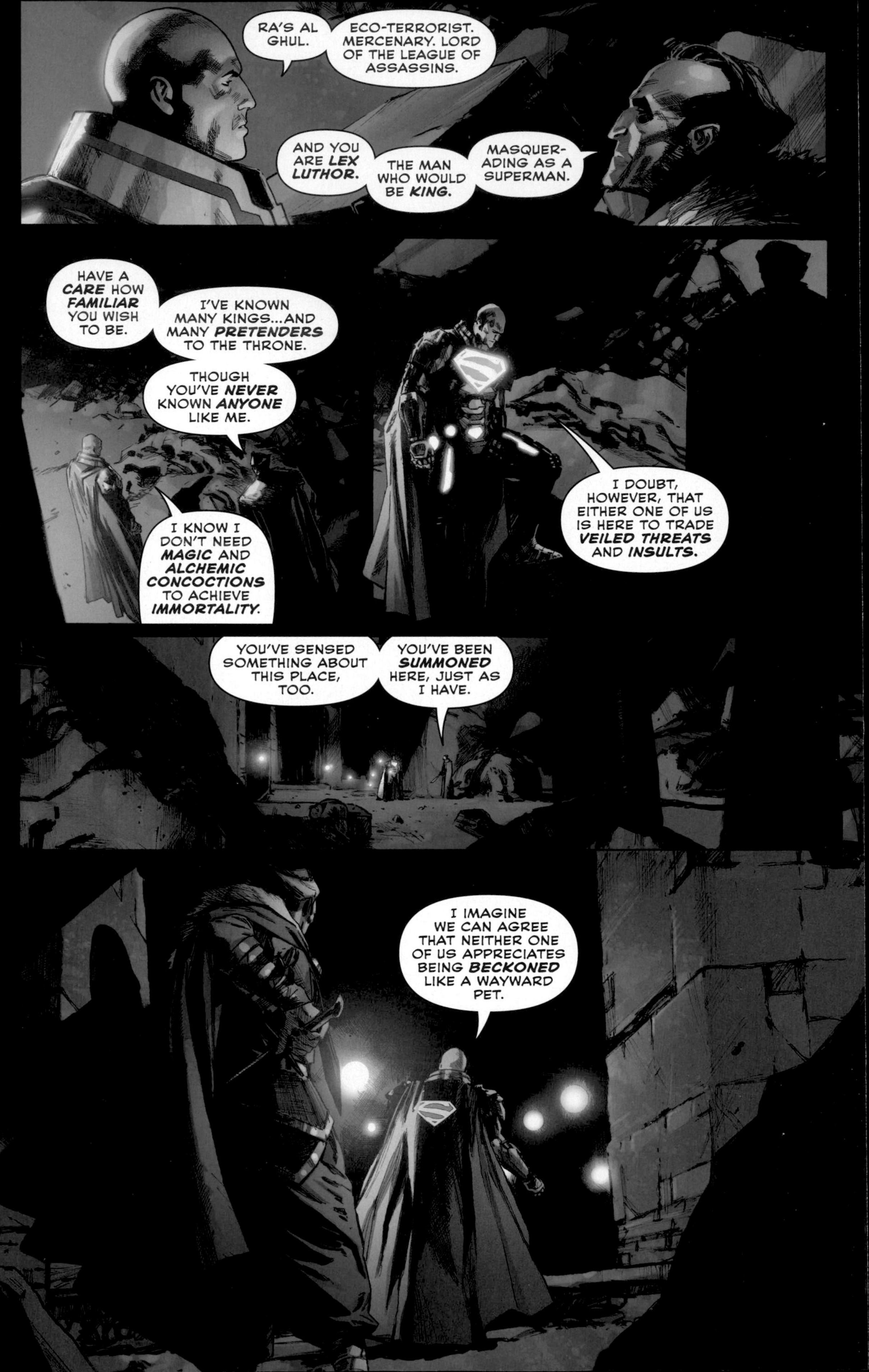
RA'S AL GHUL.
ECO-TERRORIST. MERCENARY. LORD OF THE LEAGUE OF ASSASSINS.
AND YOU ARE LEX LUTHOR.
THE MAN WHO WOULD BE KING.
MASQUERADING AS A SUPERMAN.
HAVE A CARE HOW FAMILIAR YOU WISH TO BE.
I'VE KNOWN MANY KINGS...AND MANY PRETENDERS TO THE THRONE.
THOUGH YOU'VE NEVER KNOWN ANYONE LIKE ME.
I KNOW I DON'T NEED MAGIC AND ALCHEMIC CONCOCTIONS TO ACHIEVE IMMORTALITY.
I DOUBT, HOWEVER, THAT EITHER ONE OF US IS HERE TO TRADE VEILED THREATS AND INSULTS.
YOU'VE SENSED SOMETHING ABOUT THIS PLACE, TOO.
YOU'VE BEEN SUMMONED HERE, JUST AS I HAVE.
I IMAGINE WE CAN AGREE THAT NEITHER ONE OF US APPRECIATES BEING BECKONED LIKE A WAYWARD PET.

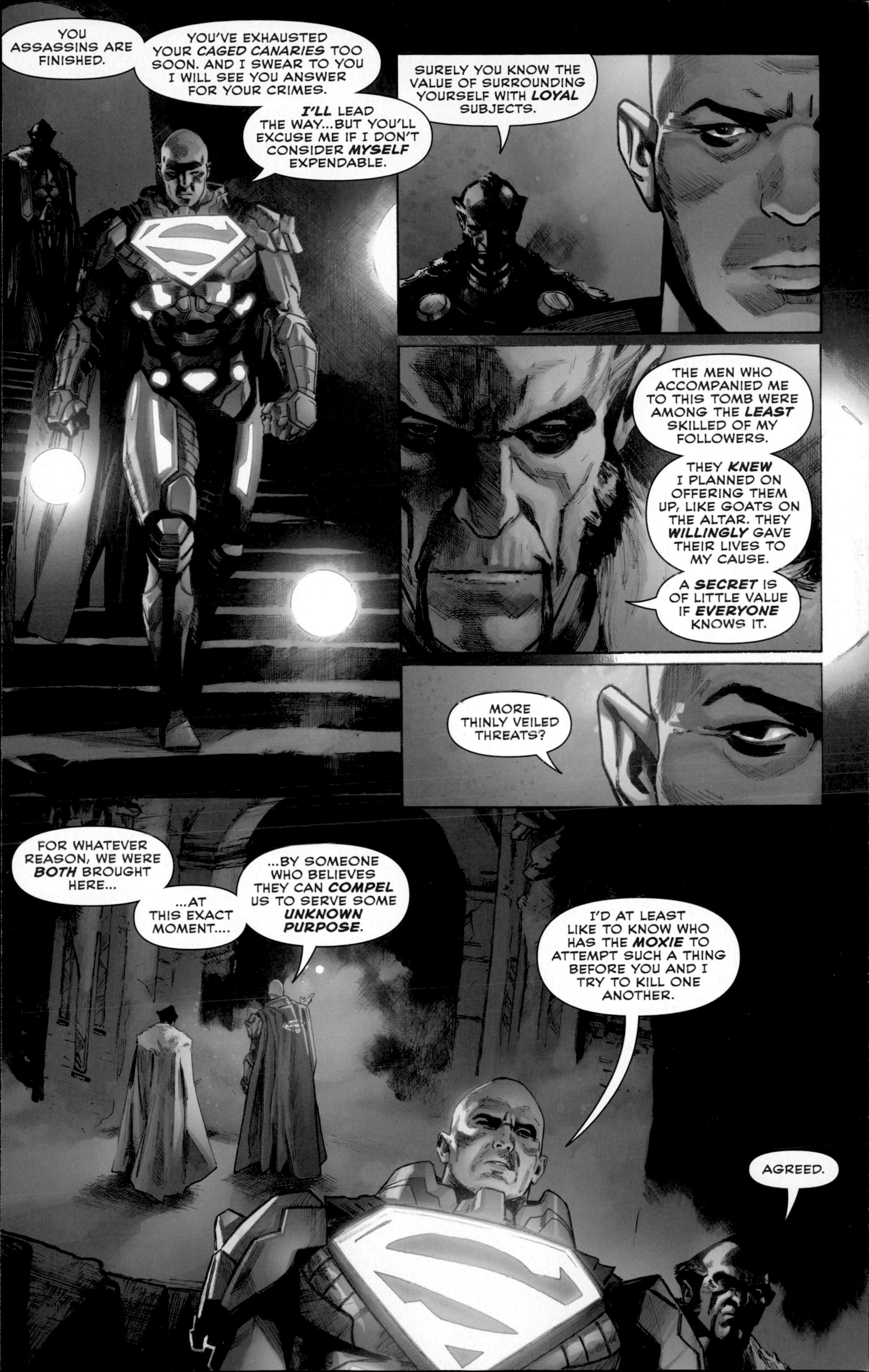
YOU ASSASSINS ARE FINISHED.
YOU'VE EXHAUSTED YOUR CAGED CANARIES TOO SOON. AND I SWEAR TO YOU I WILL SEE YOU ANSWER FOR YOUR CRIMES.
I'LL LEAD THE WAY...BUT YOU'LL EXCUSE ME IF I DON'T CONSIDER MYSELF EXPENDABLE.
SURELY YOU KNOW THE VALUE OF SURROUNDING YOURSELF WITH LOYAL SUBJECTS.
THE MEN WHO ACCOMPANIED ME TO THIS TOMB WERE AMONG THE LEAST SKILLED OF MY FOLLOWERS.
THEY KNEW I PLANNED ON OFFERING THEM UP, LIKE GOATS ON THE ALTAR. THEY WILLINGLY GAVE THEIR LIVES TO MY CAUSE.
A SECRET IS OF LITTLE VALUE IF EVERYONE KNOWS IT.
MORE THINLY VEILED THREATS?
FOR WHATEVER REASON, WE WERE BOTH BROUGHT HERE...
...AT THIS EXACT MOMENT....
...BY SOMEONE WHO BELIEVES THEY CAN COMPEL US TO SERVE SOME UNKNOWN PURPOSE.
I'D AT LEAST LIKE TO KNOW WHO HAS THE MOXIE TO ATTEMPT SUCH A THING BEFORE YOU AND I TRY TO KILL ONE ANOTHER.
AGREED.

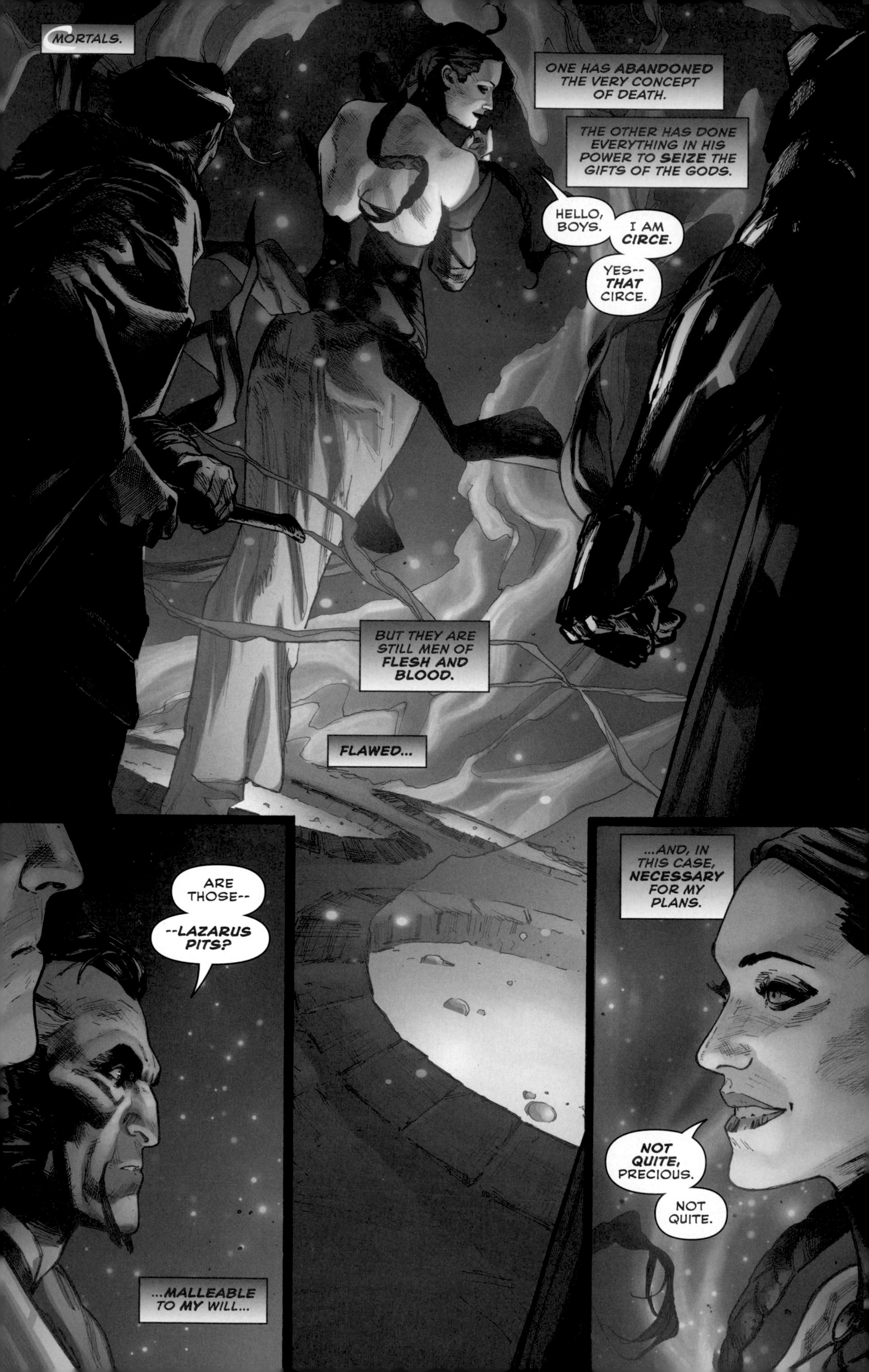
MORTALS.
ONE HAS ABANDONED THE VERY CONCEPT OF DEATH.
THE OTHER HAS DONE EVERYTHING IN HIS POWER TO SEIZE THE GIFTS OF THE GODS.
HELLO, BOYS.
I AM CIRCE.
YES-- THAT CIRCE.
BUT THEY ARE STILL MEN OF FLESH AND BLOOD.
FLAWED...
ARE THOSE--
--LAZARUS PITS?
...MALLEABLE TO MY WILL...
...AND, IN THIS CASE, NECESSARY FOR MY PLANS.
NOT QUITE, PRECIOUS.
NOT QUITE.

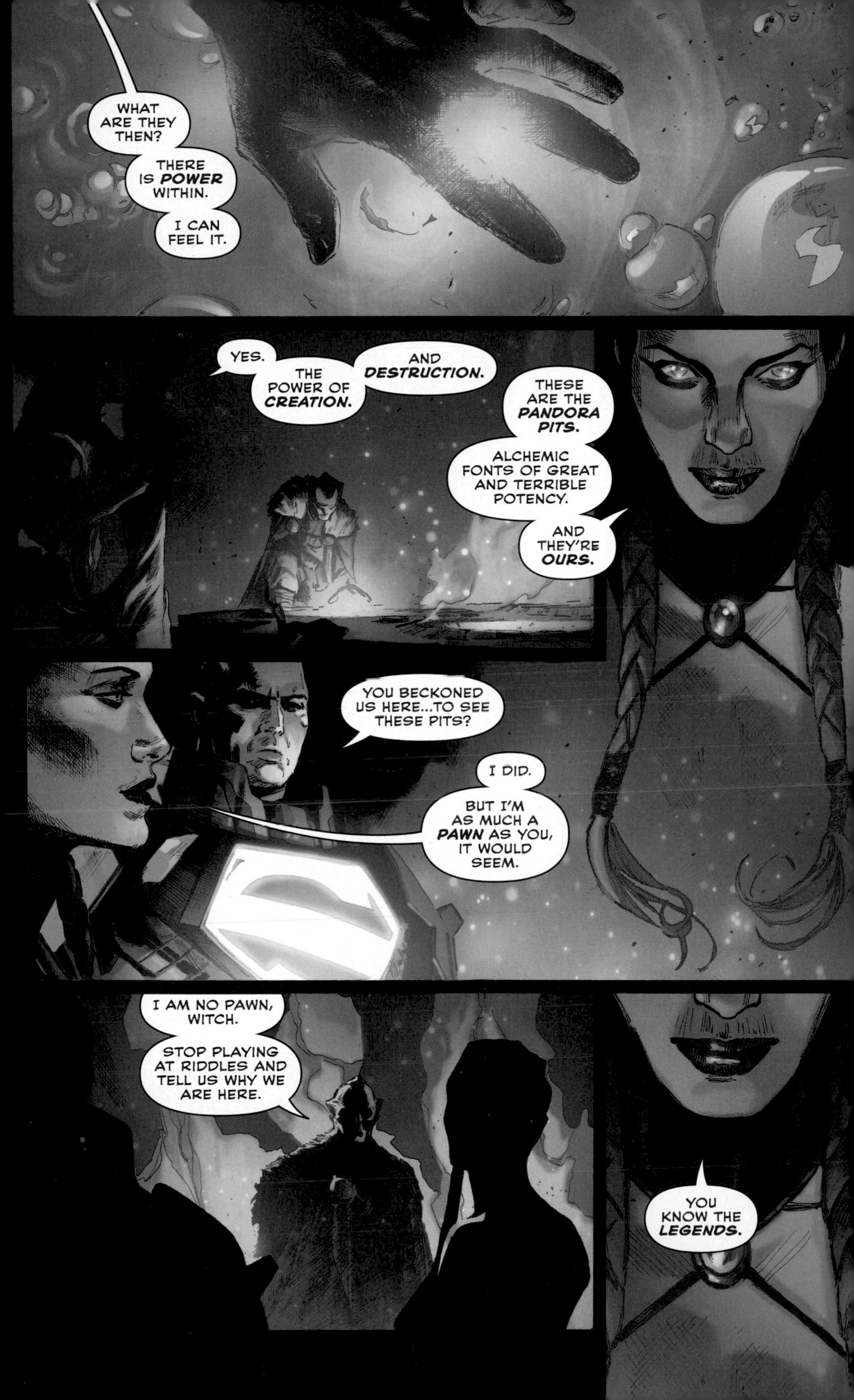
WHAT ARE THEY THEN?
THERE IS **POWER** WITHIN.
I CAN FEEL IT.
YES.
THE POWER OF **CREATION.**
AND **DESTRUCTION.**
THESE ARE THE **PANDORA PITS.**
ALCHEMIC FONTS OF GREAT AND TERRIBLE POTENCY.
AND THEY'RE **OURS.**
YOU BECKONED US HERE...TO SEE THESE PITS?
I DID.
BUT I'M AS MUCH A **PAWN** AS YOU, IT WOULD SEEM.
I AM NO PAWN, WITCH.
STOP PLAYING AT RIDDLES AND TELL US WHY WE ARE HERE.
YOU KNOW THE **LEGENDS.**

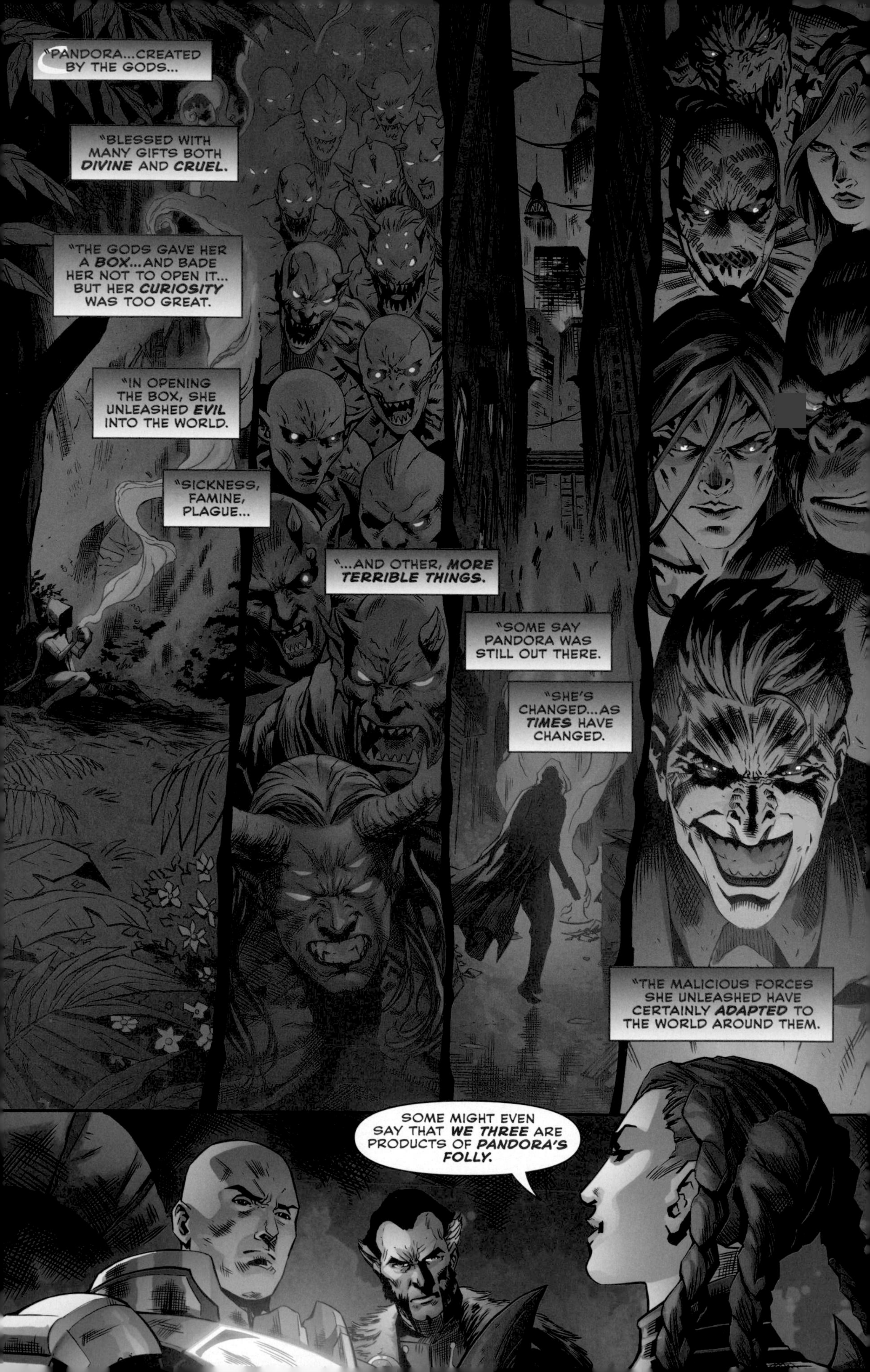
"PANDORA...CREATED BY THE GODS...
"BLESSED WITH MANY GIFTS BOTH DIVINE AND CRUEL.
"THE GODS GAVE HER A BOX...AND BADE HER NOT TO OPEN IT... BUT HER CURIOSITY WAS TOO GREAT.
"IN OPENING THE BOX, SHE UNLEASHED EVIL INTO THE WORLD.
"SICKNESS, FAMINE, PLAGUE...
"...AND OTHER, MORE TERRIBLE THINGS.
"SOME SAY PANDORA WAS STILL OUT THERE.
"SHE'S CHANGED...AS TIMES HAVE CHANGED.
"THE MALICIOUS FORCES SHE UNLEASHED HAVE CERTAINLY ADAPTED TO THE WORLD AROUND THEM.
SOME MIGHT EVEN SAY THAT WE THREE ARE PRODUCTS OF PANDORA'S FOLLY.

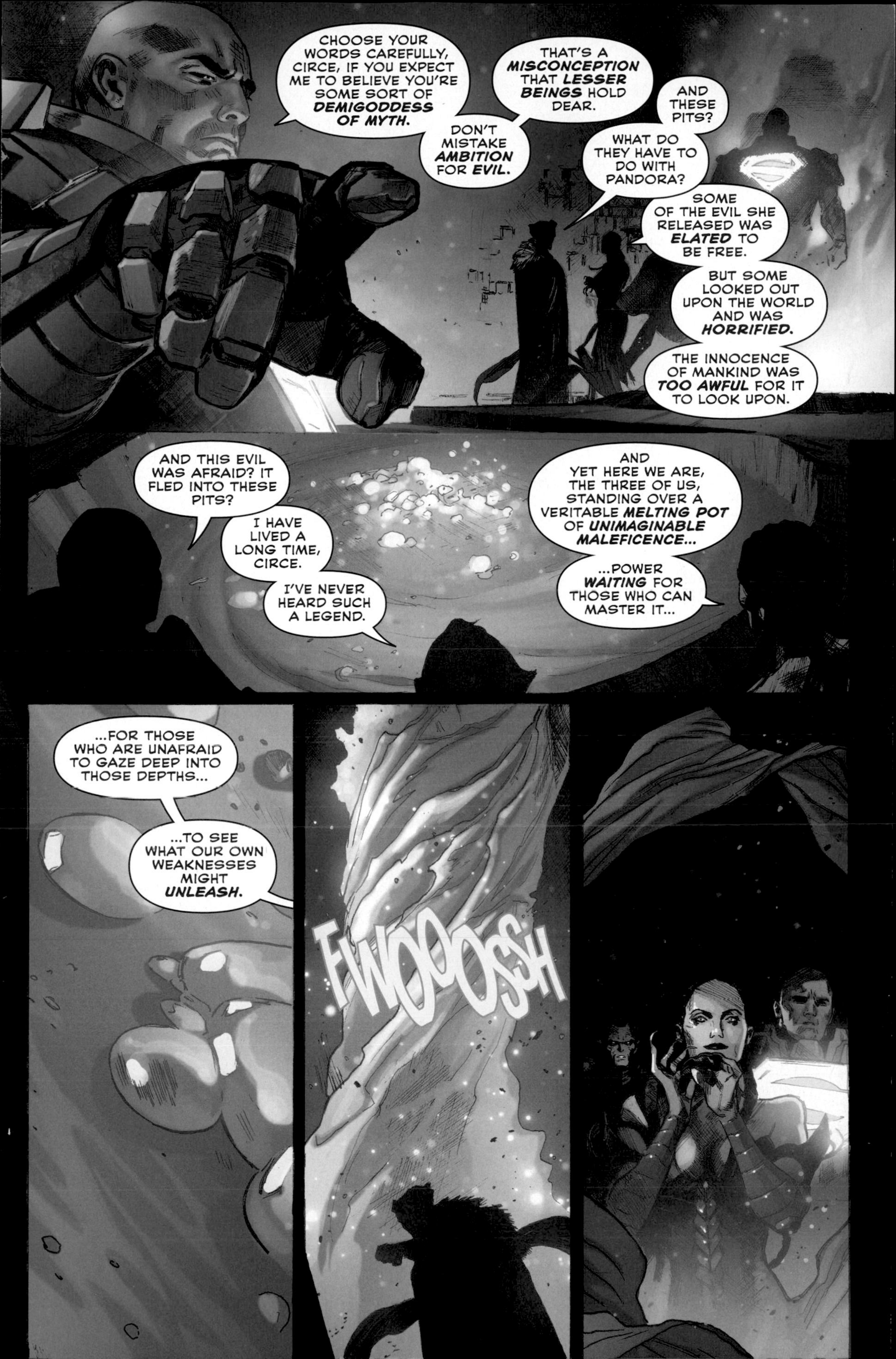
CHOOSE YOUR WORDS CAREFULLY, CIRCE, IF YOU EXPECT ME TO BELIEVE YOU'RE SOME SORT OF **DEMIGODDESS OF MYTH.**
THAT'S A **MISCONCEPTION** THAT **LESSER BEINGS** HOLD DEAR.
DON'T MISTAKE **AMBITION** FOR **EVIL.**
AND THESE PITS?
WHAT DO THEY HAVE TO DO WITH PANDORA?
SOME OF THE EVIL SHE RELEASED WAS **ELATED** TO BE FREE.
BUT SOME LOOKED OUT UPON THE WORLD AND WAS **HORRIFIED.**
THE INNOCENCE OF MANKIND WAS **TOO AWFUL** FOR IT TO LOOK UPON.
AND THIS EVIL WAS AFRAID? IT FLED INTO THESE PITS?
I HAVE LIVED A LONG TIME, CIRCE.
I'VE NEVER HEARD SUCH A LEGEND.
AND YET HERE WE ARE, THE THREE OF US, STANDING OVER A VERITABLE **MELTING POT** OF **UNIMAGINABLE MALEFICENCE...**
...POWER **WAITING** FOR THOSE WHO CAN MASTER IT...
...FOR THOSE WHO ARE UNAFRAID TO GAZE DEEP INTO THOSE DEPTHS...
...TO SEE WHAT OUR OWN WEAKNESSES MIGHT **UNLEASH.**
FWOOOSH

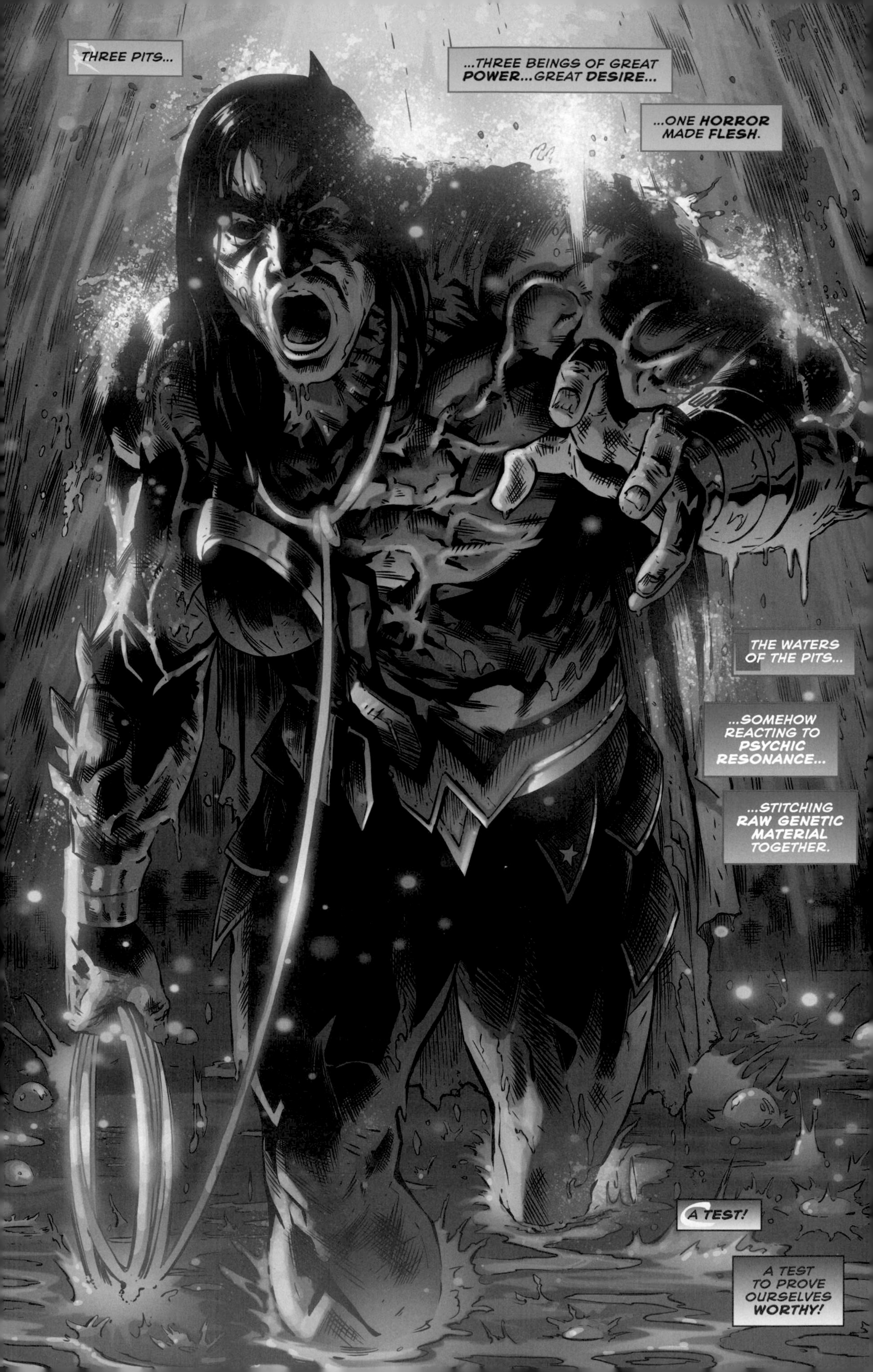
THREE PITS...
...THREE BEINGS OF GREAT POWER...GREAT DESIRE...
...ONE HORROR MADE FLESH.
THE WATERS OF THE PITS...
...SOMEHOW REACTING TO PSYCHIC RESONANCE...
...STITCHING RAW GENETIC MATERIAL TOGETHER.
A TEST!
A TEST TO PROVE OURSELVES WORTHY!

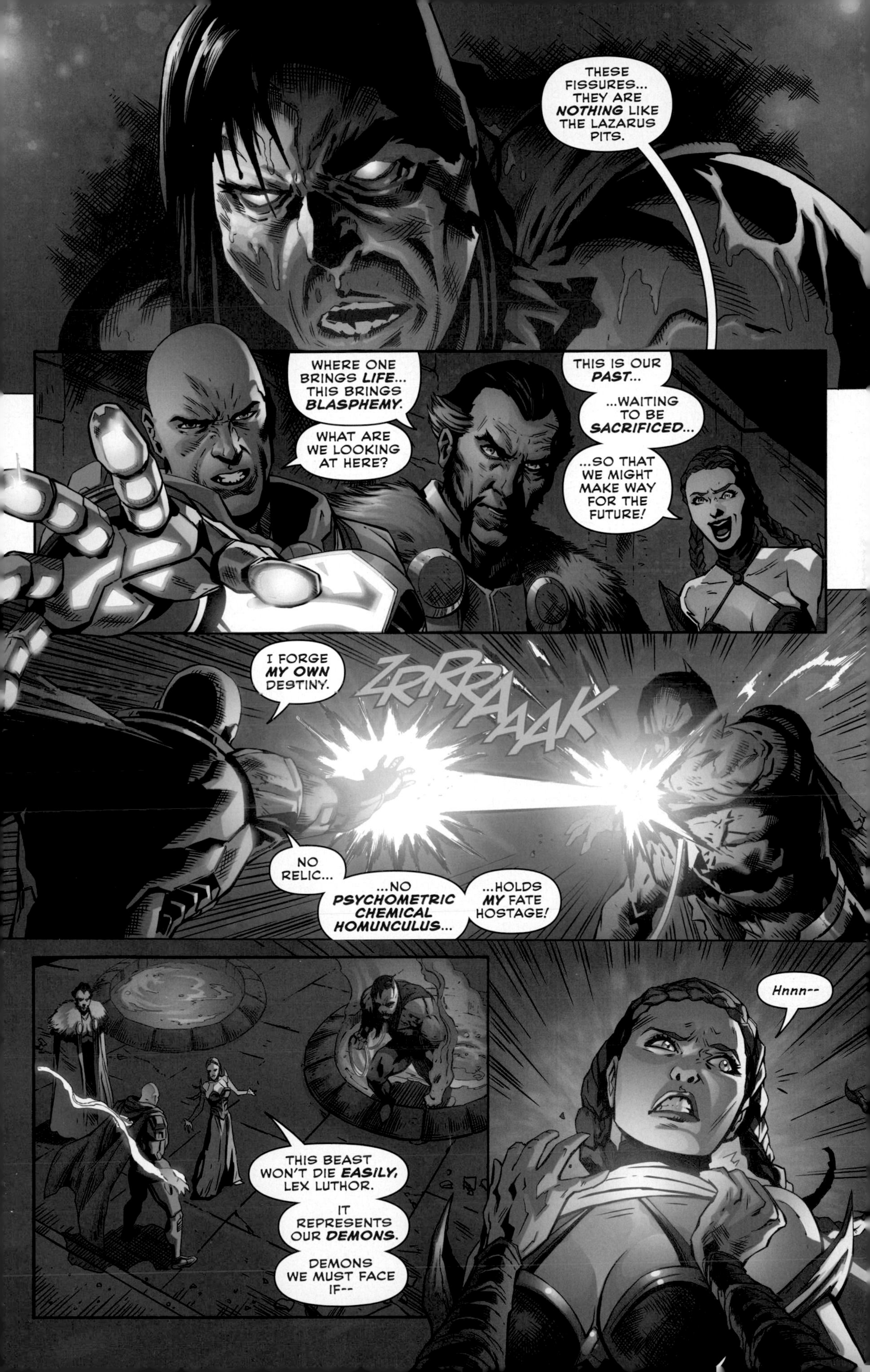
THESE FISSURES... THEY ARE NOTHING LIKE THE LAZARUS PITS.
WHERE ONE BRINGS LIFE... THIS BRINGS BLASPHEMY.
WHAT ARE WE LOOKING AT HERE?
THIS IS OUR PAST...
...WAITING TO BE SACRIFICED...
...SO THAT WE MIGHT MAKE WAY FOR THE FUTURE!
I FORGE MY OWN DESTINY.
ZRRRAAAK
NO RELIC...
...NO PSYCHOMETRIC CHEMICAL HOMUNCULUS...
...HOLDS MY FATE HOSTAGE!
THIS BEAST WON'T DIE EASILY, LEX LUTHOR.
IT REPRESENTS OUR DEMONS.
DEMONS WE MUST FACE IF--
Hnnn--

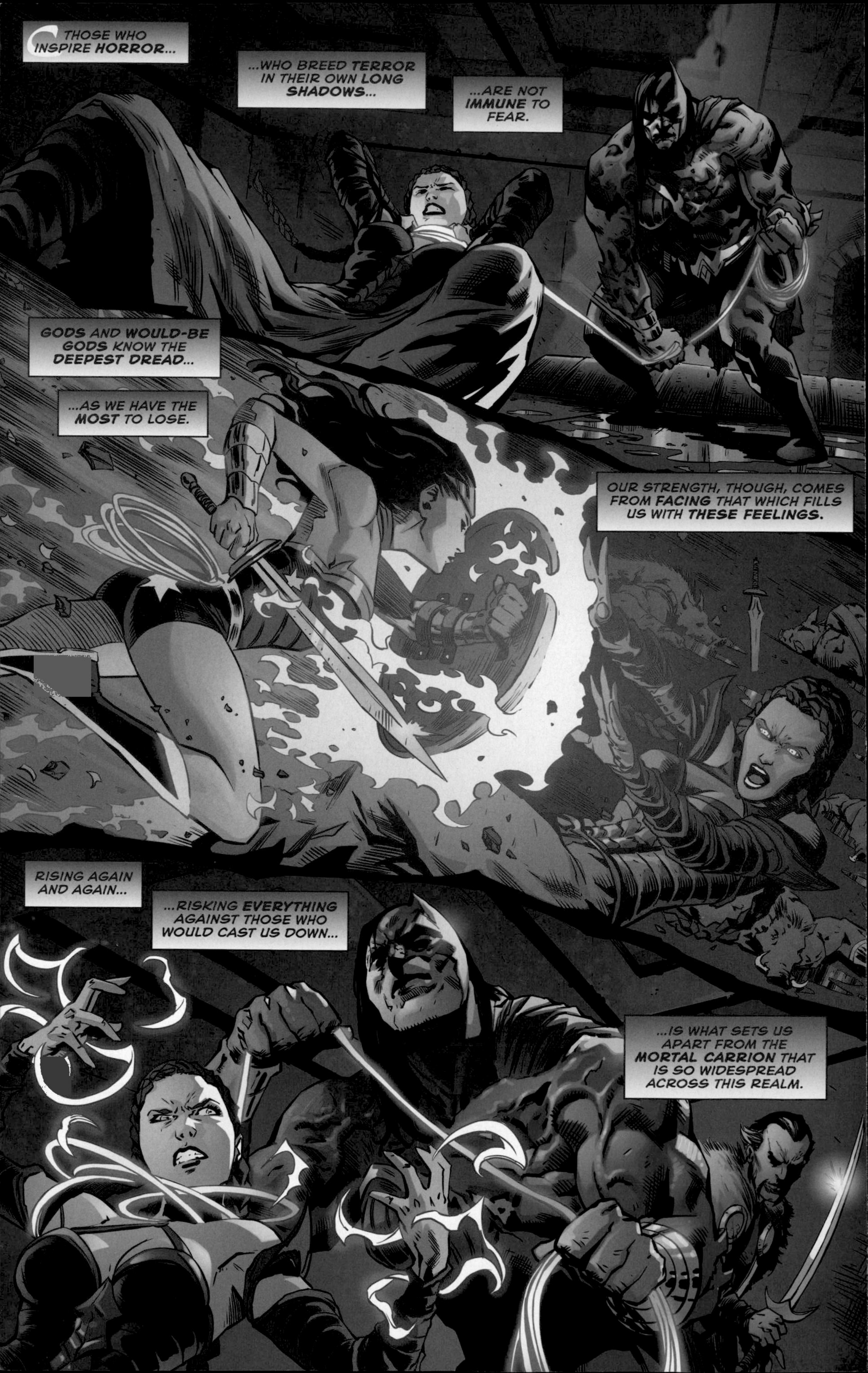
THOSE WHO INSPIRE HORROR...
...WHO BREED TERROR IN THEIR OWN LONG SHADOWS...
...ARE NOT IMMUNE TO FEAR.
GODS AND WOULD-BE GODS KNOW THE DEEPEST DREAD...
...AS WE HAVE THE MOST TO LOSE.
OUR STRENGTH, THOUGH, COMES FROM FACING THAT WHICH FILLS US WITH THESE FEELINGS.
RISING AGAIN AND AGAIN...
...RISKING EVERYTHING AGAINST THOSE WHO WOULD CAST US DOWN...
...IS WHAT SETS US APART FROM THE MORTAL CARRION THAT IS SO WIDESPREAD ACROSS THIS REALM.

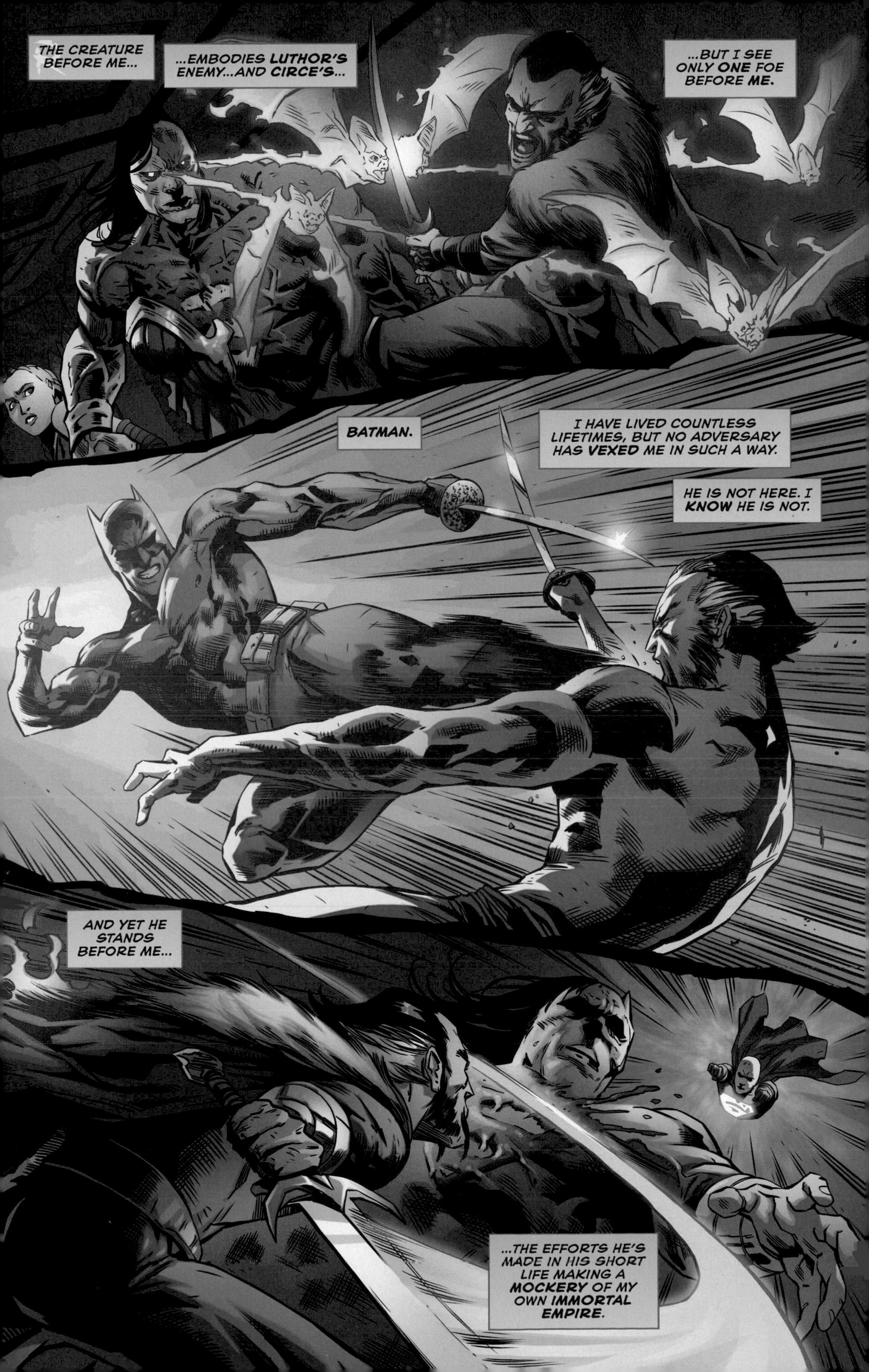
THE CREATURE BEFORE ME...
...EMBODIES LUTHOR'S ENEMY...AND CIRCE'S...
...BUT I SEE ONLY ONE FOE BEFORE ME.
BATMAN.
I HAVE LIVED COUNTLESS LIFETIMES, BUT NO ADVERSARY HAS VEXED ME IN SUCH A WAY.
HE IS NOT HERE. I KNOW HE IS NOT.
AND YET HE STANDS BEFORE ME...
...THE EFFORTS HE'S MADE IN HIS SHORT LIFE MAKING A MOCKERY OF MY OWN IMMORTAL EMPIRE.

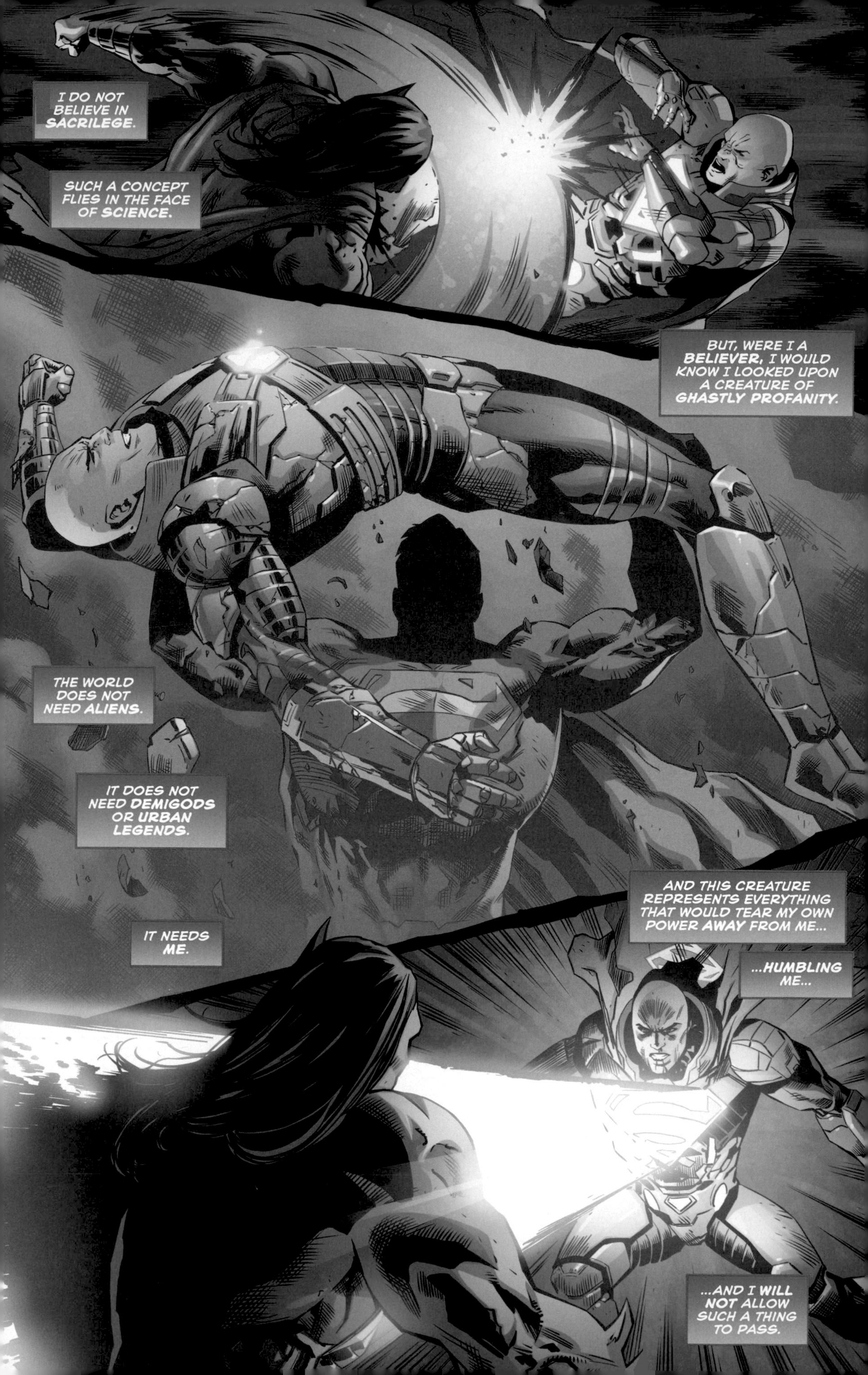
I DO NOT BELIEVE IN SACRILEGE.
SUCH A CONCEPT FLIES IN THE FACE OF SCIENCE.
BUT, WERE I A BELIEVER, I WOULD KNOW I LOOKED UPON A CREATURE OF GHASTLY PROFANITY.
THE WORLD DOES NOT NEED ALIENS.
IT DOES NOT NEED DEMIGODS OR URBAN LEGENDS.
IT NEEDS ME.
AND THIS CREATURE REPRESENTS EVERYTHING THAT WOULD TEAR MY OWN POWER AWAY FROM ME...
...HUMBLING ME...
...AND I WILL NOT ALLOW SUCH A THING TO PASS.

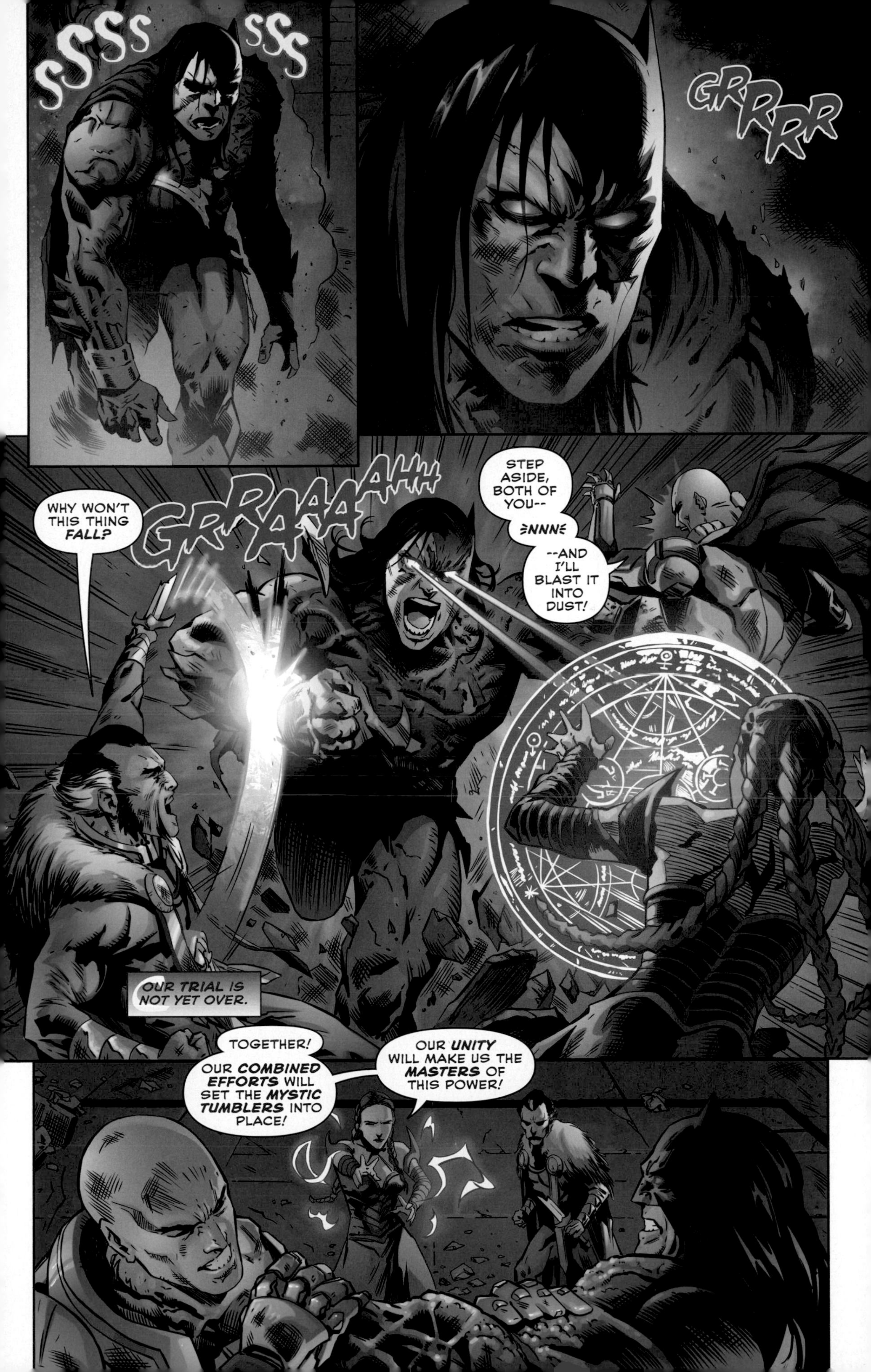
sSSSs SSS
GRRRR
WHY WON'T THIS THING FALL?
GRRAAAAHH
STEP ASIDE, BOTH OF YOU--
NNN
--AND I'LL BLAST IT INTO DUST!
OUR TRIAL IS NOT YET OVER.
TOGETHER!
OUR COMBINED EFFORTS WILL SET THE MYSTIC TUMBLERS INTO PLACE!
OUR UNITY WILL MAKE US THE MASTERS OF THIS POWER!

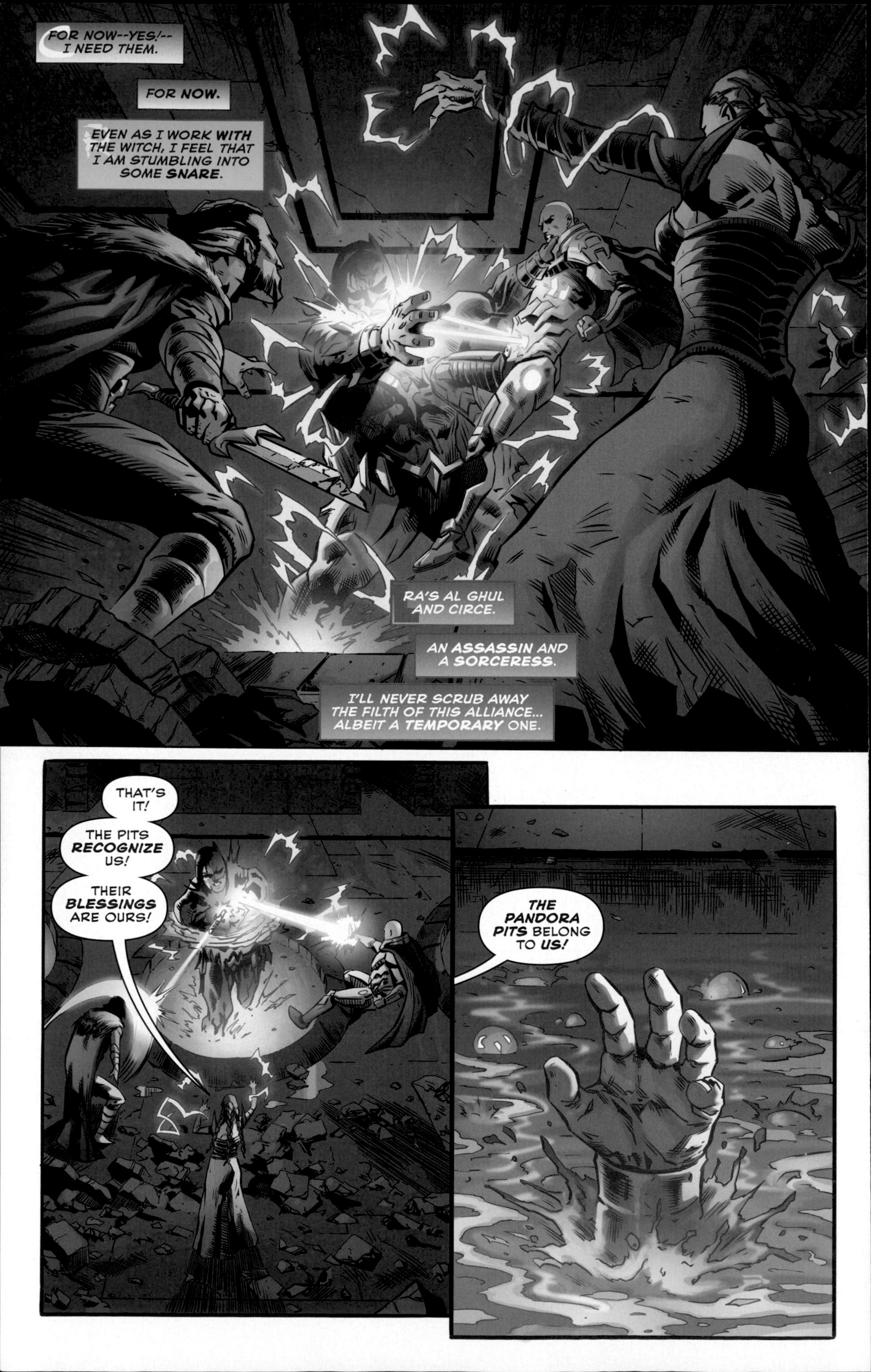
FOR NOW--YES!-- I NEED THEM.
FOR NOW.
EVEN AS I WORK WITH THE WITCH, I FEEL THAT I AM STUMBLING INTO SOME SNARE.
RA'S AL GHUL AND CIRCE.
AN ASSASSIN AND A SORCERESS.
I'LL NEVER SCRUB AWAY THE FILTH OF THIS ALLIANCE... ALBEIT A TEMPORARY ONE.
THAT'S IT!
THE PITS RECOGNIZE US!
THEIR BLESSINGS ARE OURS!
THE PANDORA PITS BELONG TO US!

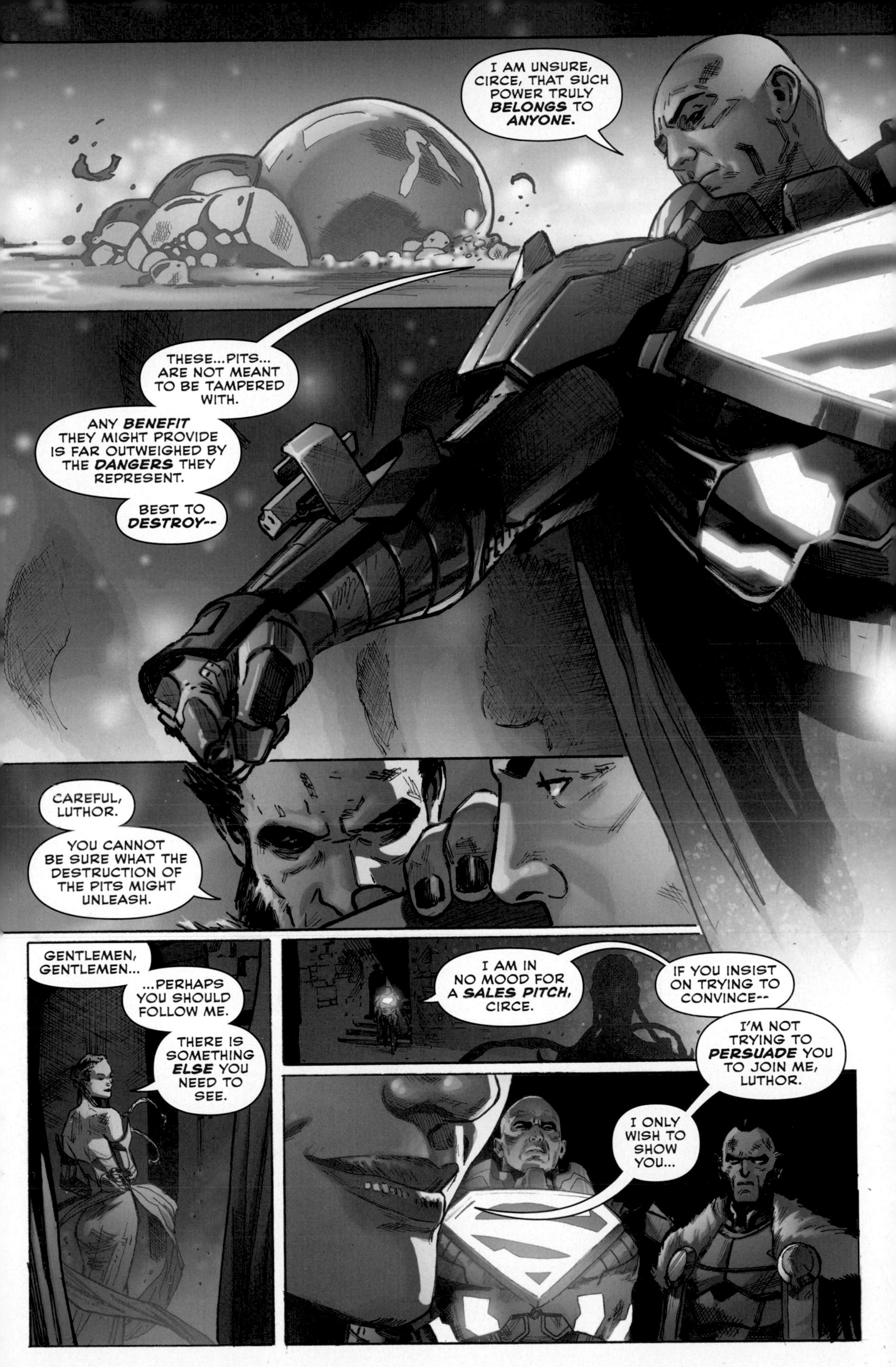
I AM UNSURE, CIRCE, THAT SUCH POWER TRULY BELONGS TO ANYONE.
THESE...PITS... ARE NOT MEANT TO BE TAMPERED WITH.
ANY BENEFIT THEY MIGHT PROVIDE IS FAR OUTWEIGHED BY THE DANGERS THEY REPRESENT.
BEST TO DESTROY--
CAREFUL, LUTHOR.
YOU CANNOT BE SURE WHAT THE DESTRUCTION OF THE PITS MIGHT UNLEASH.
GENTLEMEN, GENTLEMEN...
...PERHAPS YOU SHOULD FOLLOW ME.
THERE IS SOMETHING ELSE YOU NEED TO SEE.
I AM IN NO MOOD FOR A SALES PITCH, CIRCE.
IF YOU INSIST ON TRYING TO CONVINCE--
I'M NOT TRYING TO PERSUADE YOU TO JOIN ME, LUTHOR.
I ONLY WISH TO SHOW YOU...

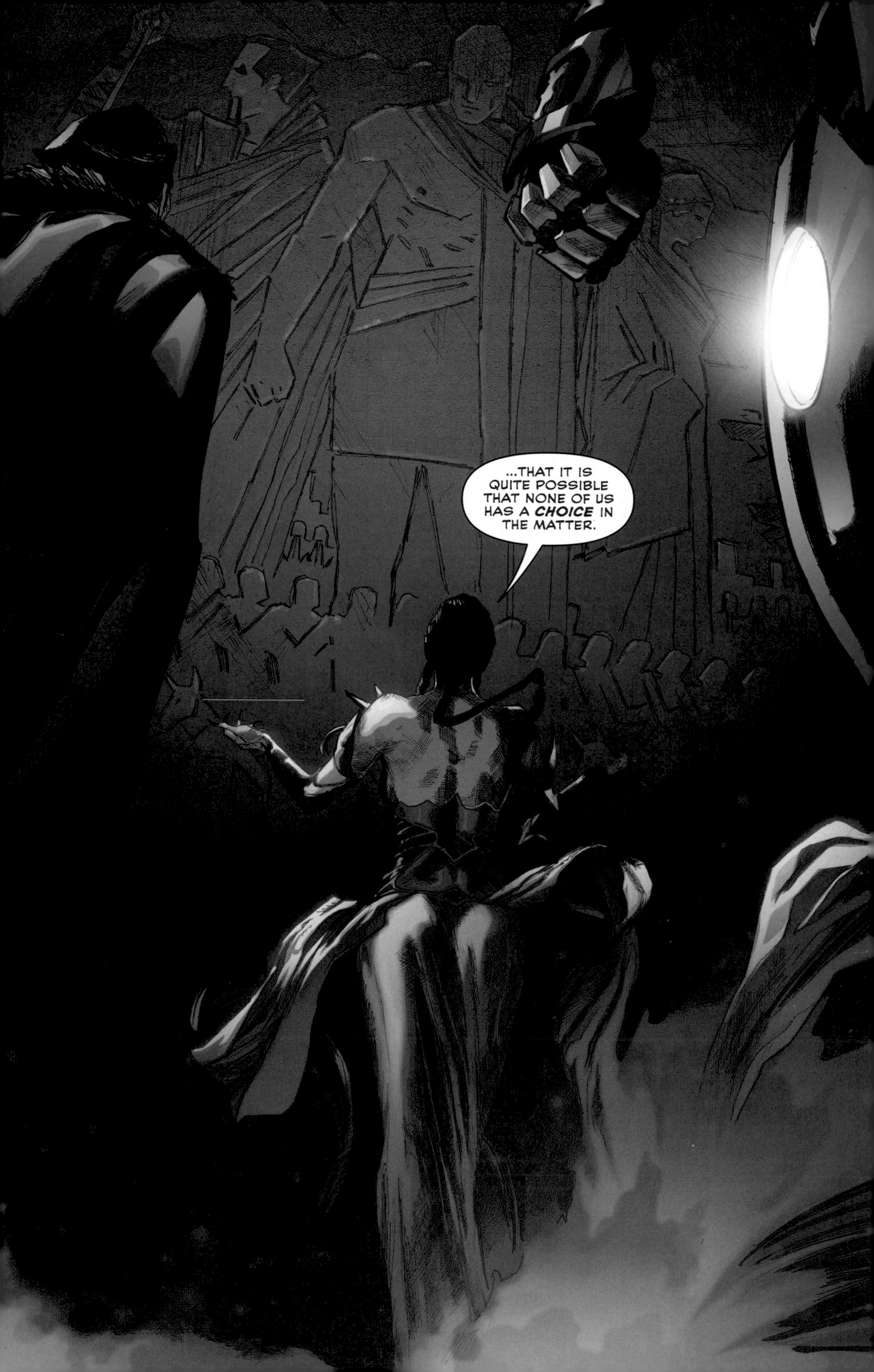
...THAT IT IS QUITE POSSIBLE THAT NONE OF US HAS A *CHOICE* IN THE MATTER.

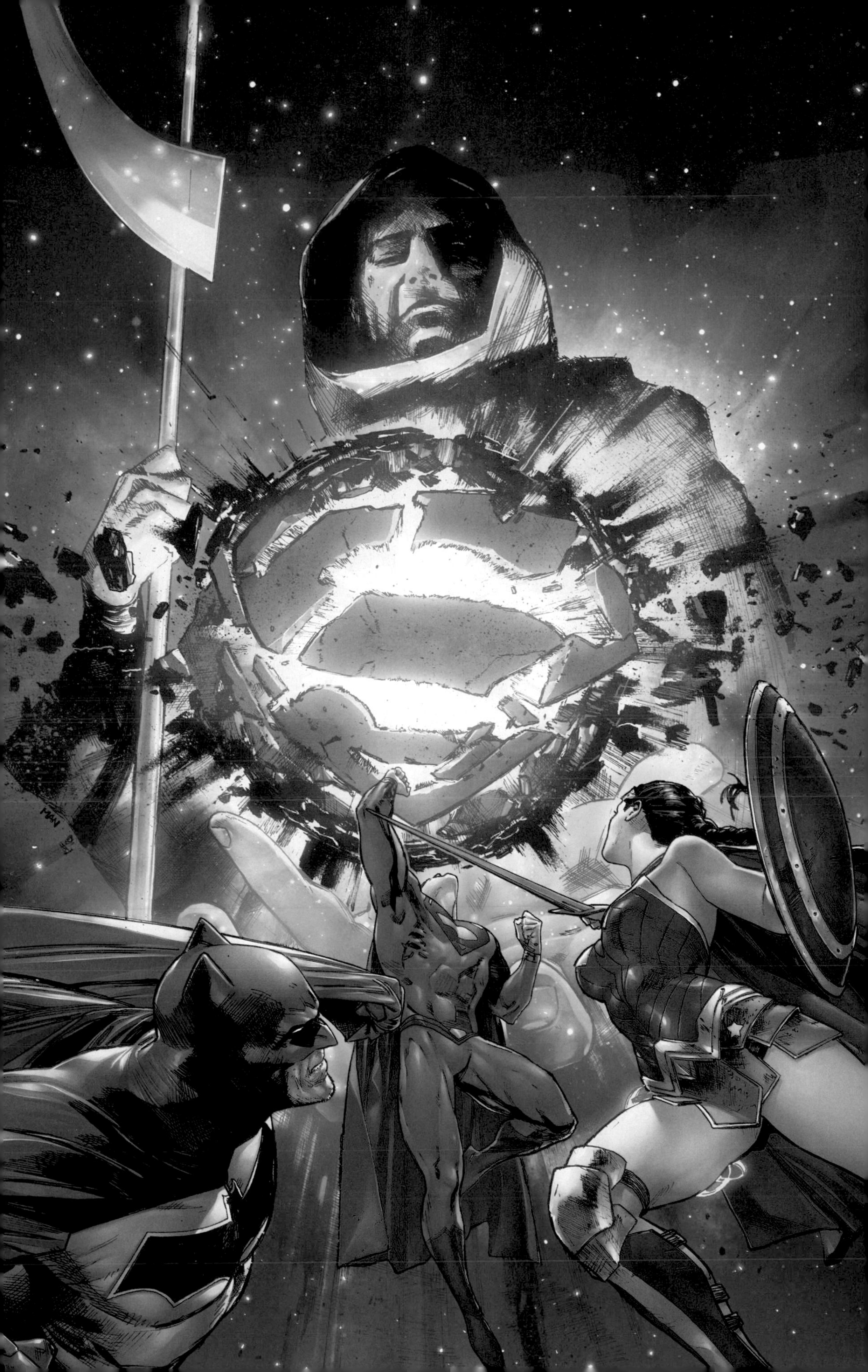

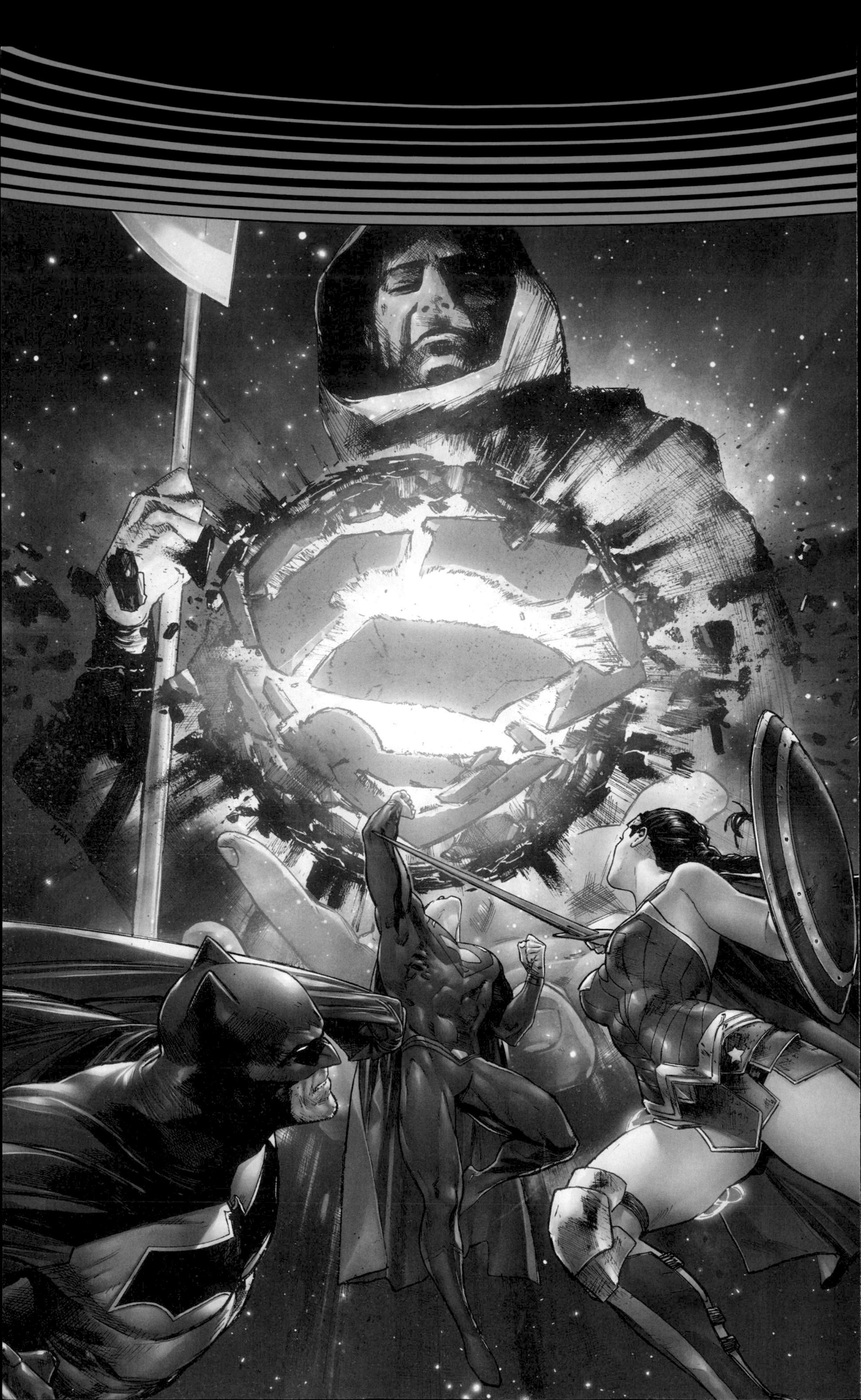

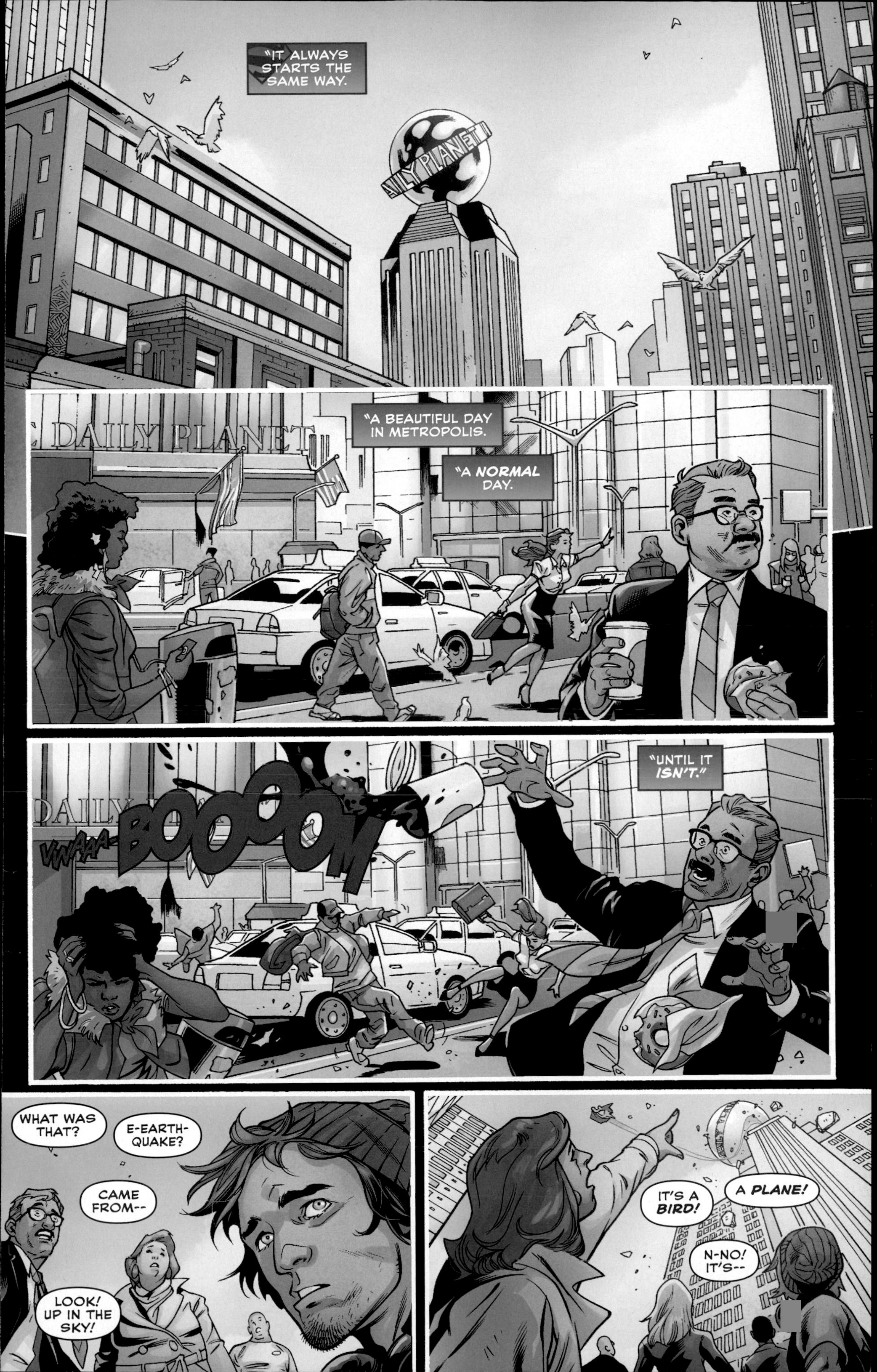

"IT ALWAYS STARTS THE SAME WAY.
DAILY PLANET
DAILY PLANET
"A BEAUTIFUL DAY IN METROPOLIS.
"A NORMAL DAY.
"UNTIL IT ISN'T."
VWAAA-BOOOOM
WHAT WAS THAT?
E-EARTH-QUAKE?
CAME FROM--
LOOK! UP IN THE SKY!
IT'S A BIRD!
A PLANE!
N-NO! IT'S--

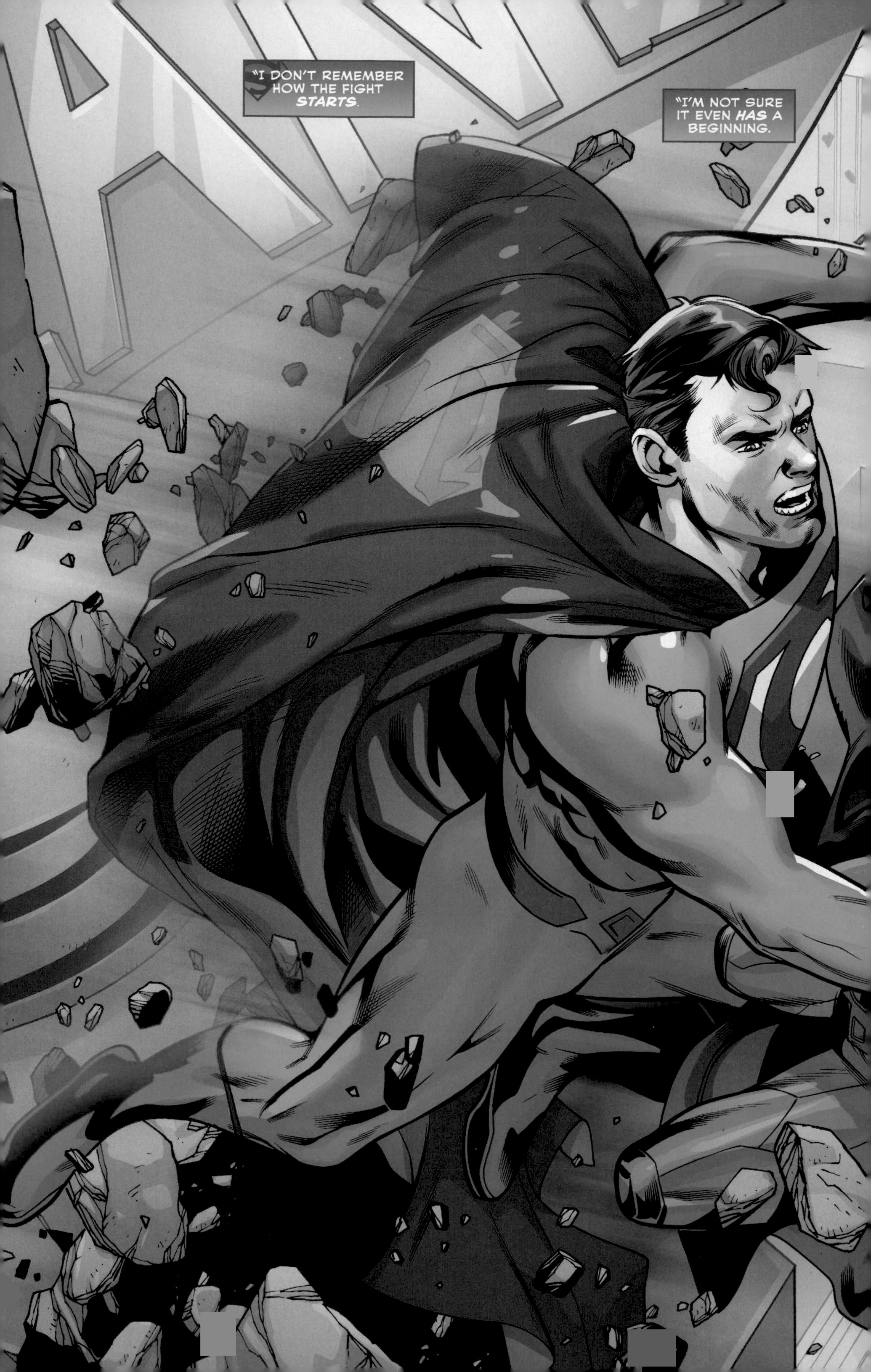
"I DON'T REMEMBER HOW THE FIGHT STARTS.
"I'M NOT SURE IT EVEN HAS A BEGINNING.

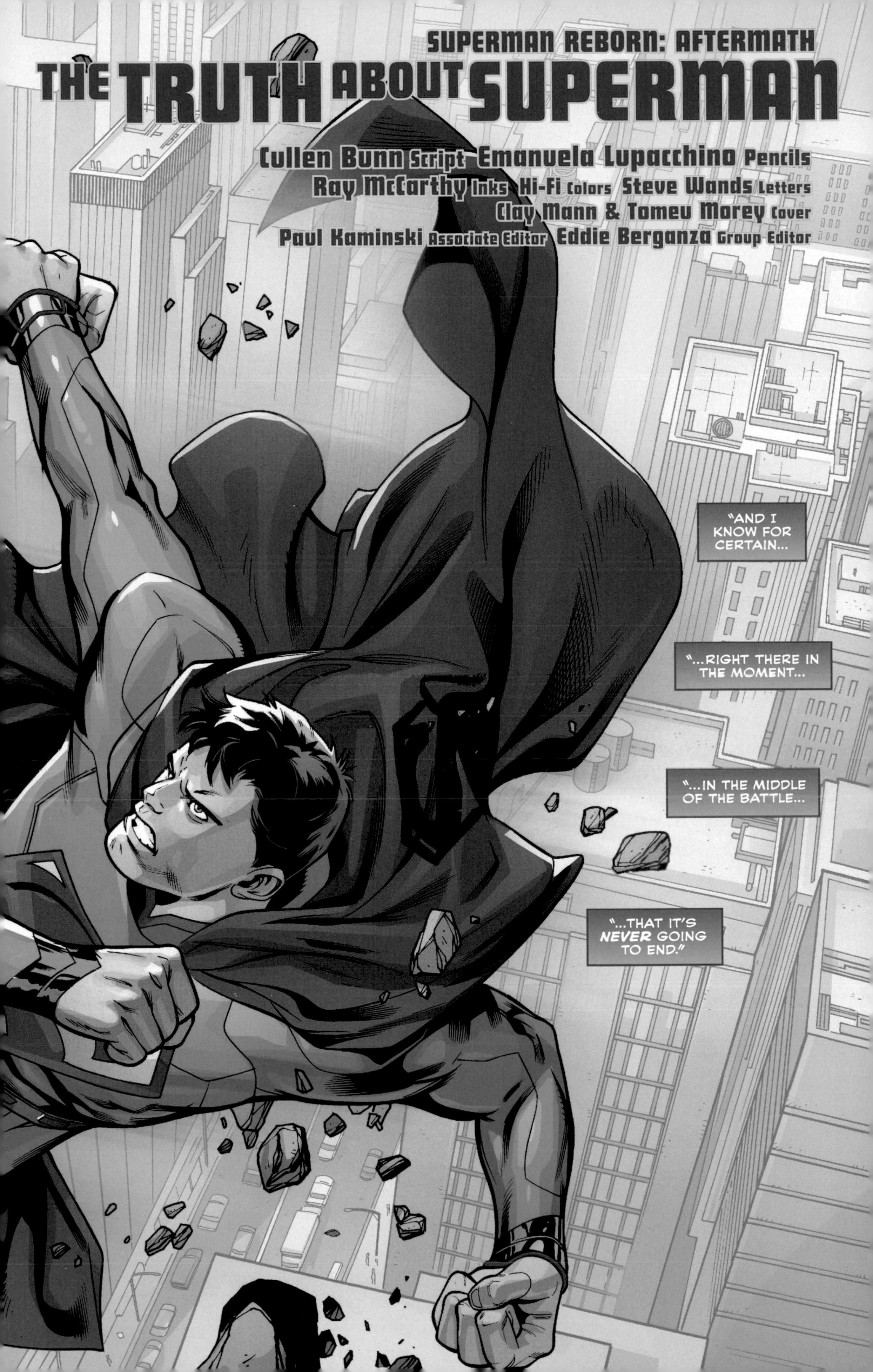
SUPERMAN REBORN: AFTERMATH
THE TRUTH ABOUT SUPERMAN
Cullen Bunn Script Emanuela Lupacchino Pencils
Ray McCarthy Inks Hi-Fi Colors Steve Wands Letters
Clay Mann & Tomeu Morey Cover
Paul Kaminski Associate Editor Eddie Berganza Group Editor
"AND I KNOW FOR CERTAIN...
"...RIGHT THERE IN THE MOMENT...
"...IN THE MIDDLE OF THE BATTLE...
"...THAT IT'S *NEVER* GOING TO END."

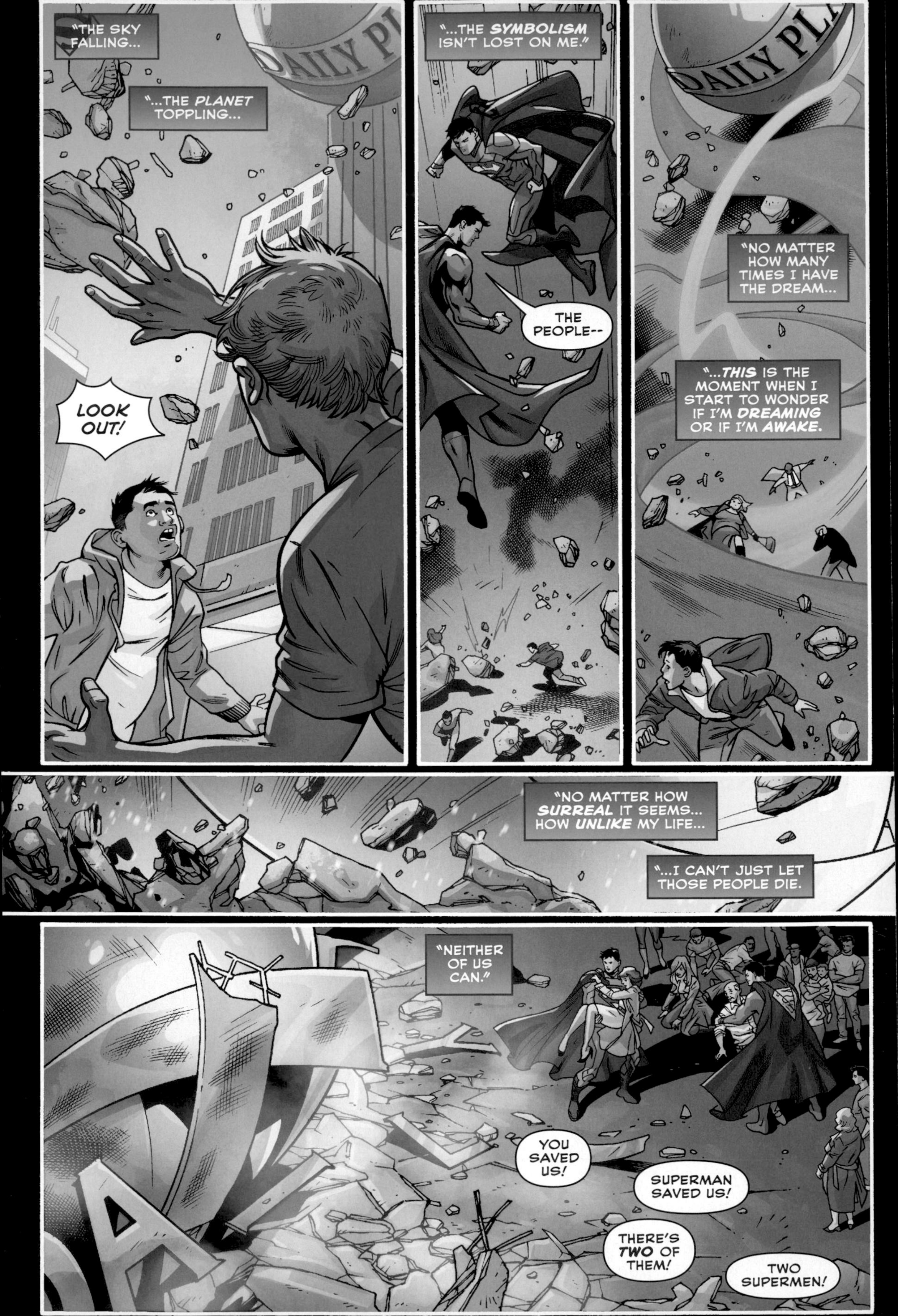
"THE SKY FALLING...
"...THE PLANET TOPPLING...
LOOK OUT!
"...THE SYMBOLISM ISN'T LOST ON ME."
THE PEOPLE--
"NO MATTER HOW MANY TIMES I HAVE THE DREAM...
"...THIS IS THE MOMENT WHEN I START TO WONDER IF I'M DREAMING OR IF I'M AWAKE.
"NO MATTER HOW SURREAL IT SEEMS... HOW UNLIKE MY LIFE...
"...I CAN'T JUST LET THOSE PEOPLE DIE.
"NEITHER OF US CAN."
YOU SAVED US!
SUPERMAN SAVED US!
THERE'S TWO OF THEM!
TWO SUPERMEN!

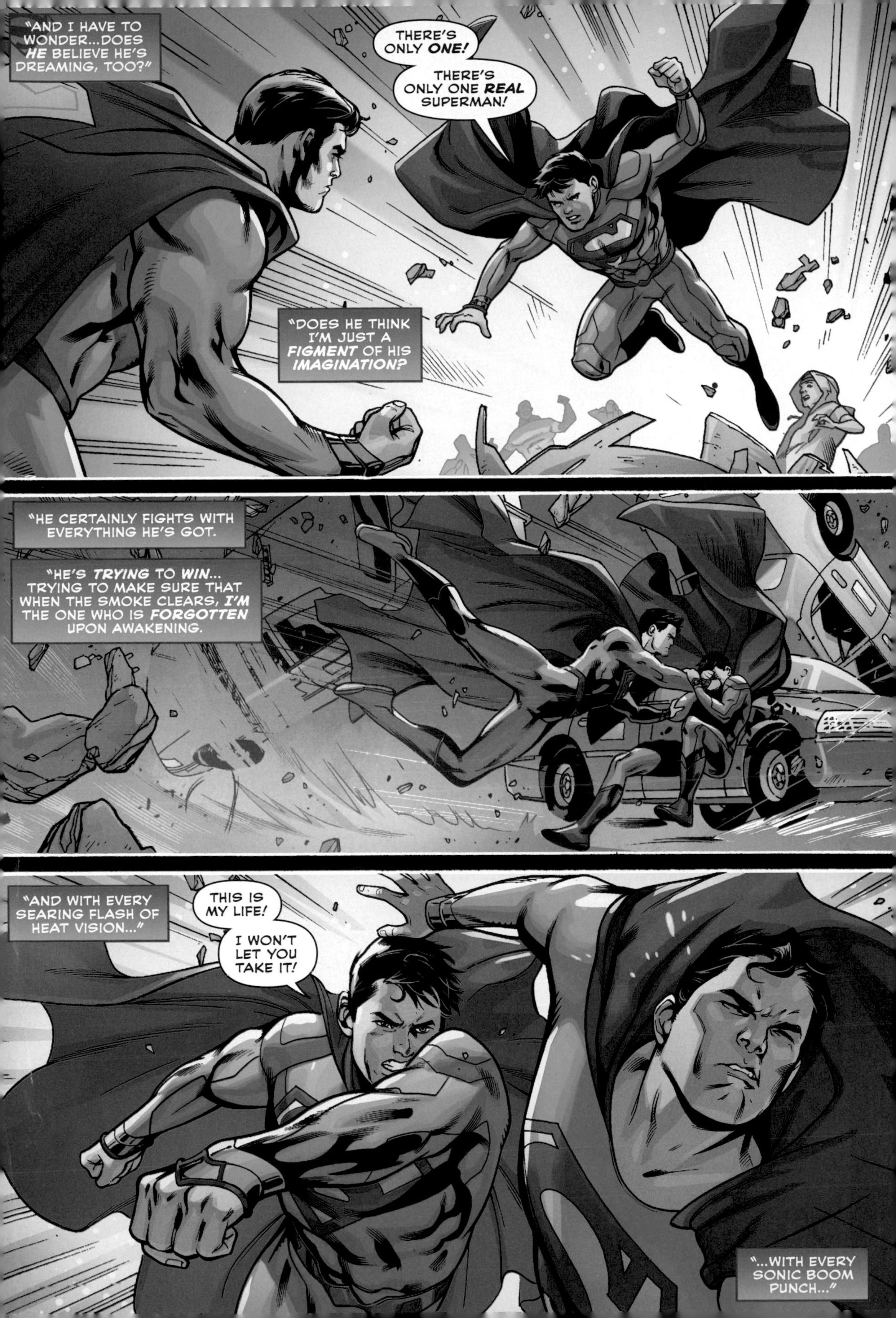
"AND I HAVE TO WONDER...DOES HE BELIEVE HE'S DREAMING, TOO?"
THERE'S ONLY ONE!
THERE'S ONLY ONE REAL SUPERMAN!
"DOES HE THINK I'M JUST A FIGMENT OF HIS IMAGINATION?
"HE CERTAINLY FIGHTS WITH EVERYTHING HE'S GOT.
"HE'S TRYING TO WIN... TRYING TO MAKE SURE THAT WHEN THE SMOKE CLEARS, I'M THE ONE WHO IS FORGOTTEN UPON AWAKENING.
"AND WITH EVERY SEARING FLASH OF HEAT VISION..."
THIS IS MY LIFE!
I WON'T LET YOU TAKE IT!
"...WITH EVERY SONIC BOOM PUNCH..."

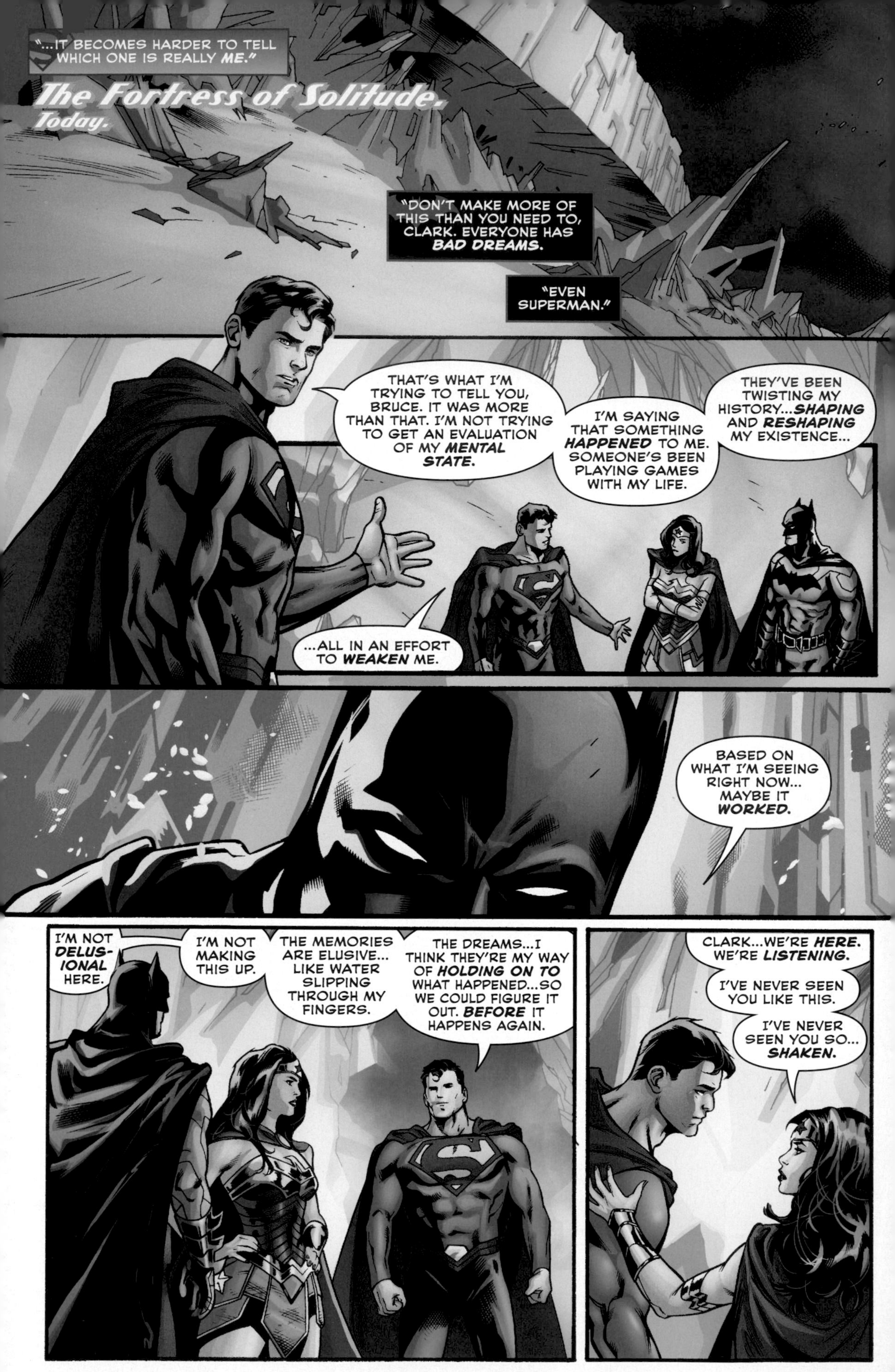
"...IT BECOMES HARDER TO TELL WHICH ONE IS REALLY ME."
The Fortress of Solitude. Today.
"DON'T MAKE MORE OF THIS THAN YOU NEED TO, CLARK. EVERYONE HAS BAD DREAMS.
"EVEN SUPERMAN."
THAT'S WHAT I'M TRYING TO TELL YOU, BRUCE. IT WAS MORE THAN THAT. I'M NOT TRYING TO GET AN EVALUATION OF MY MENTAL STATE.
I'M SAYING THAT SOMETHING HAPPENED TO ME. SOMEONE'S BEEN PLAYING GAMES WITH MY LIFE.
THEY'VE BEEN TWISTING MY HISTORY...SHAPING AND RESHAPING MY EXISTENCE...
...ALL IN AN EFFORT TO WEAKEN ME.
BASED ON WHAT I'M SEEING RIGHT NOW... MAYBE IT WORKED.
I'M NOT DELUSIONAL HERE.
I'M NOT MAKING THIS UP.
THE MEMORIES ARE ELUSIVE... LIKE WATER SLIPPING THROUGH MY FINGERS.
THE DREAMS...I THINK THEY'RE MY WAY OF HOLDING ON TO WHAT HAPPENED...SO WE COULD FIGURE IT OUT. BEFORE IT HAPPENS AGAIN.
CLARK...WE'RE HERE. WE'RE LISTENING.
I'VE NEVER SEEN YOU LIKE THIS.
I'VE NEVER SEEN YOU SO... SHAKEN.

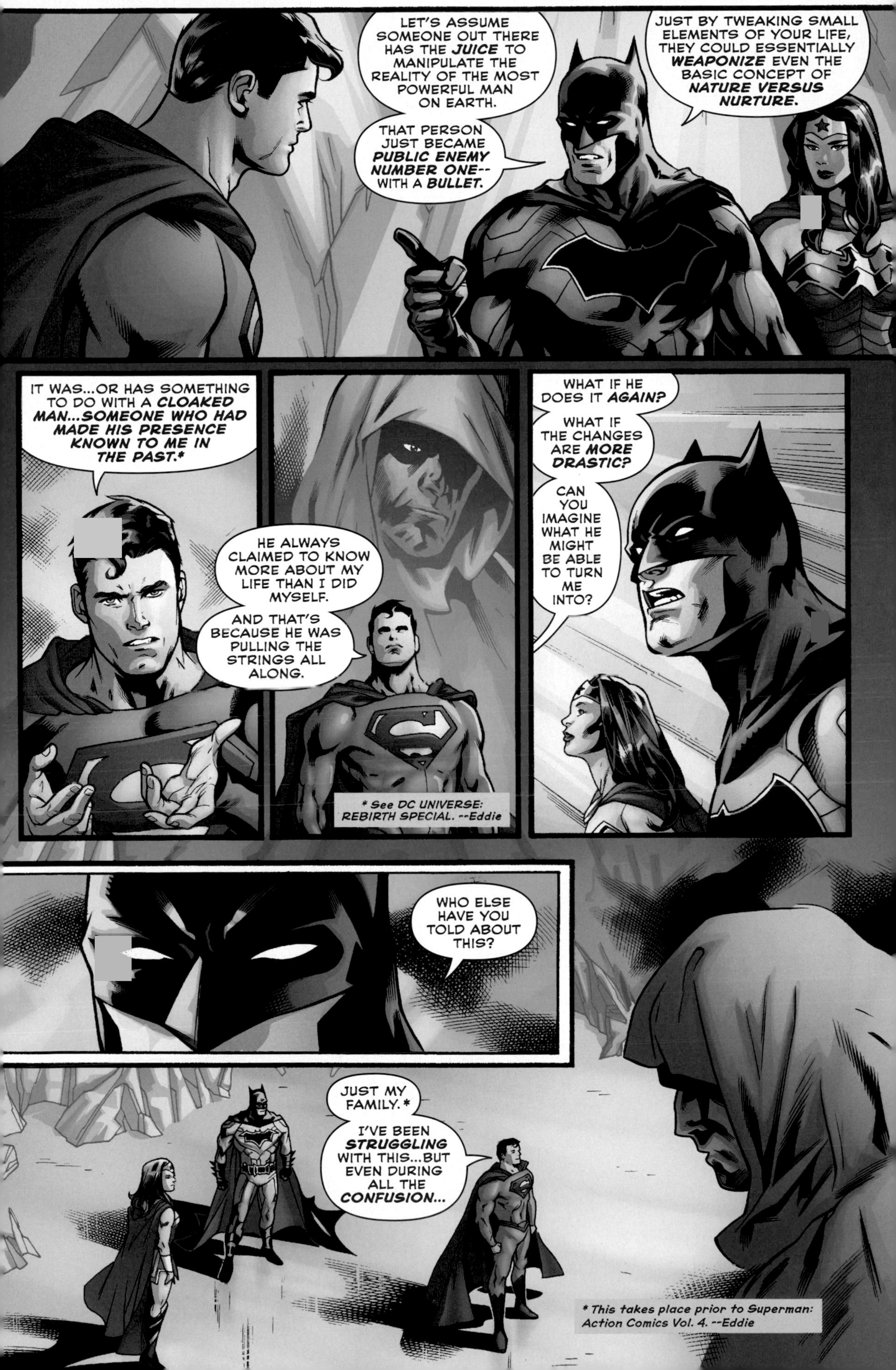
LET'S ASSUME SOMEONE OUT THERE HAS THE JUICE TO MANIPULATE THE REALITY OF THE MOST POWERFUL MAN ON EARTH.
THAT PERSON JUST BECAME PUBLIC ENEMY NUMBER ONE-- WITH A BULLET.
JUST BY TWEAKING SMALL ELEMENTS OF YOUR LIFE, THEY COULD ESSENTIALLY WEAPONIZE EVEN THE BASIC CONCEPT OF NATURE VERSUS NURTURE.
IT WAS...OR HAS SOMETHING TO DO WITH A CLOAKED MAN...SOMEONE WHO HAD MADE HIS PRESENCE KNOWN TO ME IN THE PAST.*
HE ALWAYS CLAIMED TO KNOW MORE ABOUT MY LIFE THAN I DID MYSELF.
AND THAT'S BECAUSE HE WAS PULLING THE STRINGS ALL ALONG.
* See DC UNIVERSE: REBIRTH SPECIAL. --Eddie
WHAT IF HE DOES IT AGAIN?
WHAT IF THE CHANGES ARE MORE DRASTIC?
CAN YOU IMAGINE WHAT HE MIGHT BE ABLE TO TURN ME INTO?
WHO ELSE HAVE YOU TOLD ABOUT THIS?
JUST MY FAMILY.*
I'VE BEEN STRUGGLING WITH THIS...BUT EVEN DURING ALL THE CONFUSION...
* This takes place prior to Superman: Action Comics Vol. 4. --Eddie

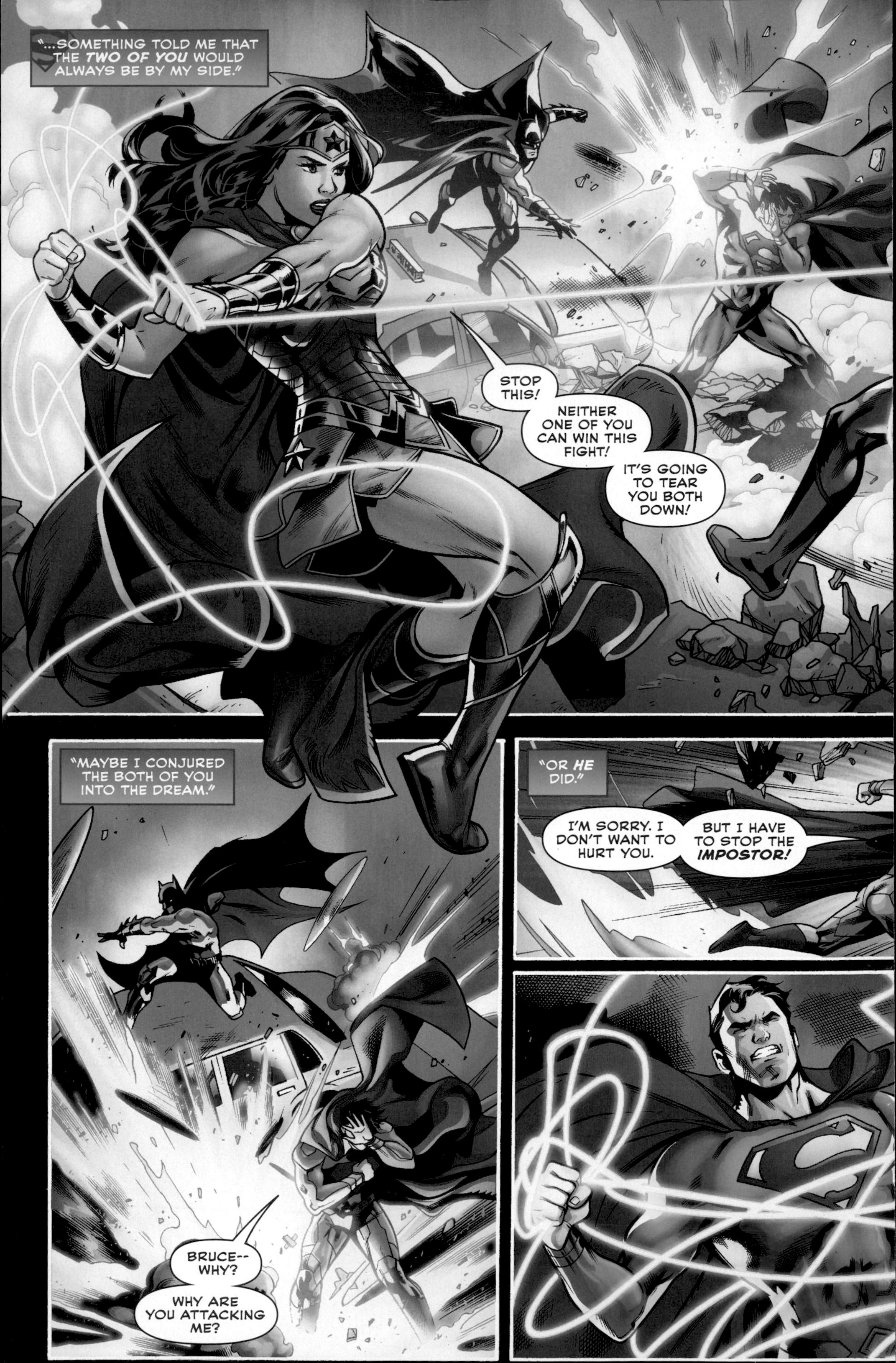
"...SOMETHING TOLD ME THAT THE *TWO OF YOU* WOULD ALWAYS BE BY MY SIDE."
STOP THIS!
NEITHER ONE OF YOU CAN WIN THIS FIGHT!
IT'S GOING TO TEAR YOU BOTH DOWN!
"MAYBE I CONJURED THE BOTH OF YOU INTO THE DREAM."
BRUCE-- WHY?
WHY ARE YOU ATTACKING ME?
"OR *HE* DID."
I'M SORRY. I DON'T WANT TO HURT YOU.
BUT I HAVE TO STOP THE *IMPOSTOR!*

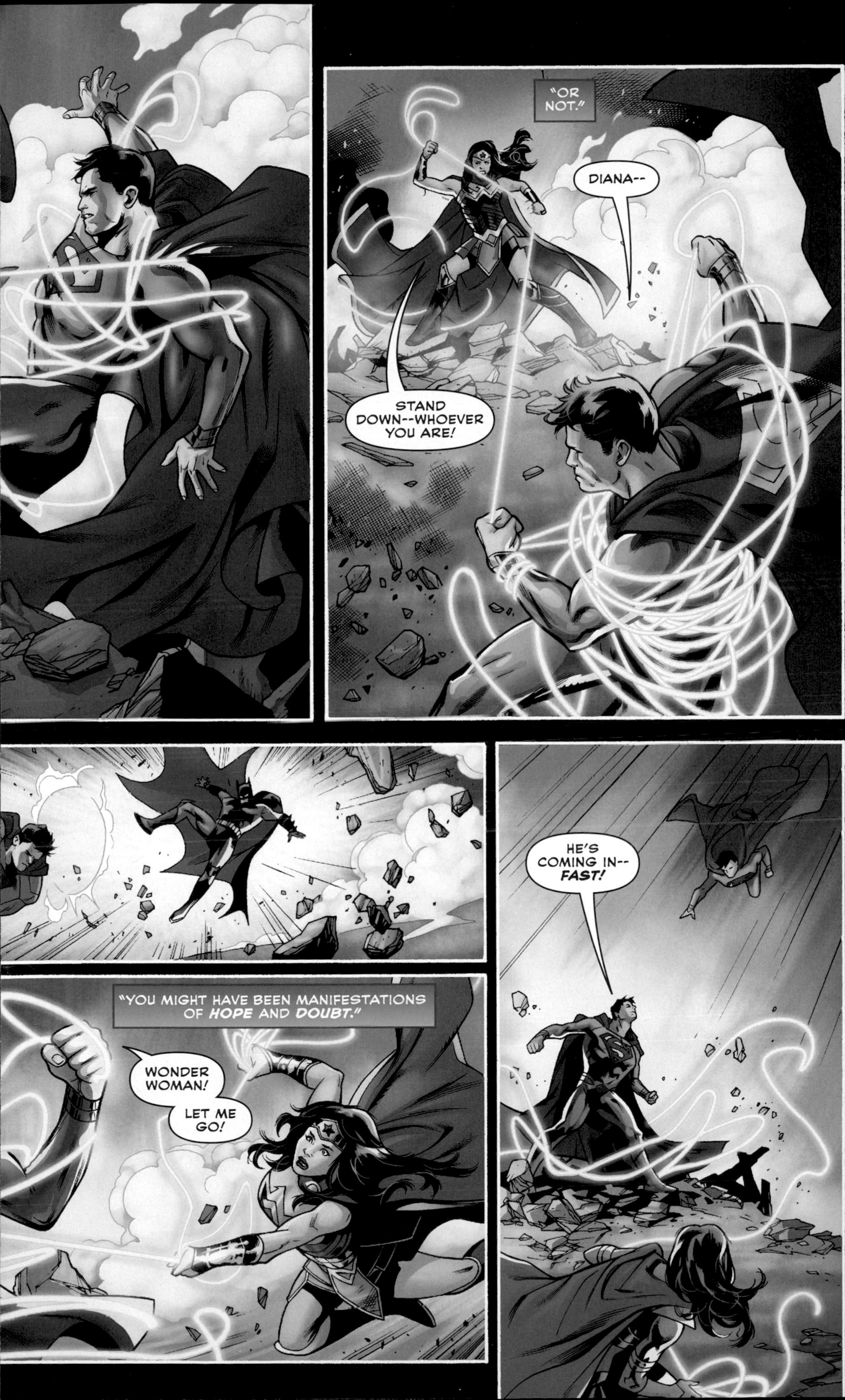
"OR NOT."
DIANA--
STAND DOWN--WHOEVER YOU ARE!
HE'S COMING IN-- *FAST!*
"YOU MIGHT HAVE BEEN MANIFESTATIONS OF *HOPE* AND *DOUBT*."
WONDER WOMAN!
LET ME GO!

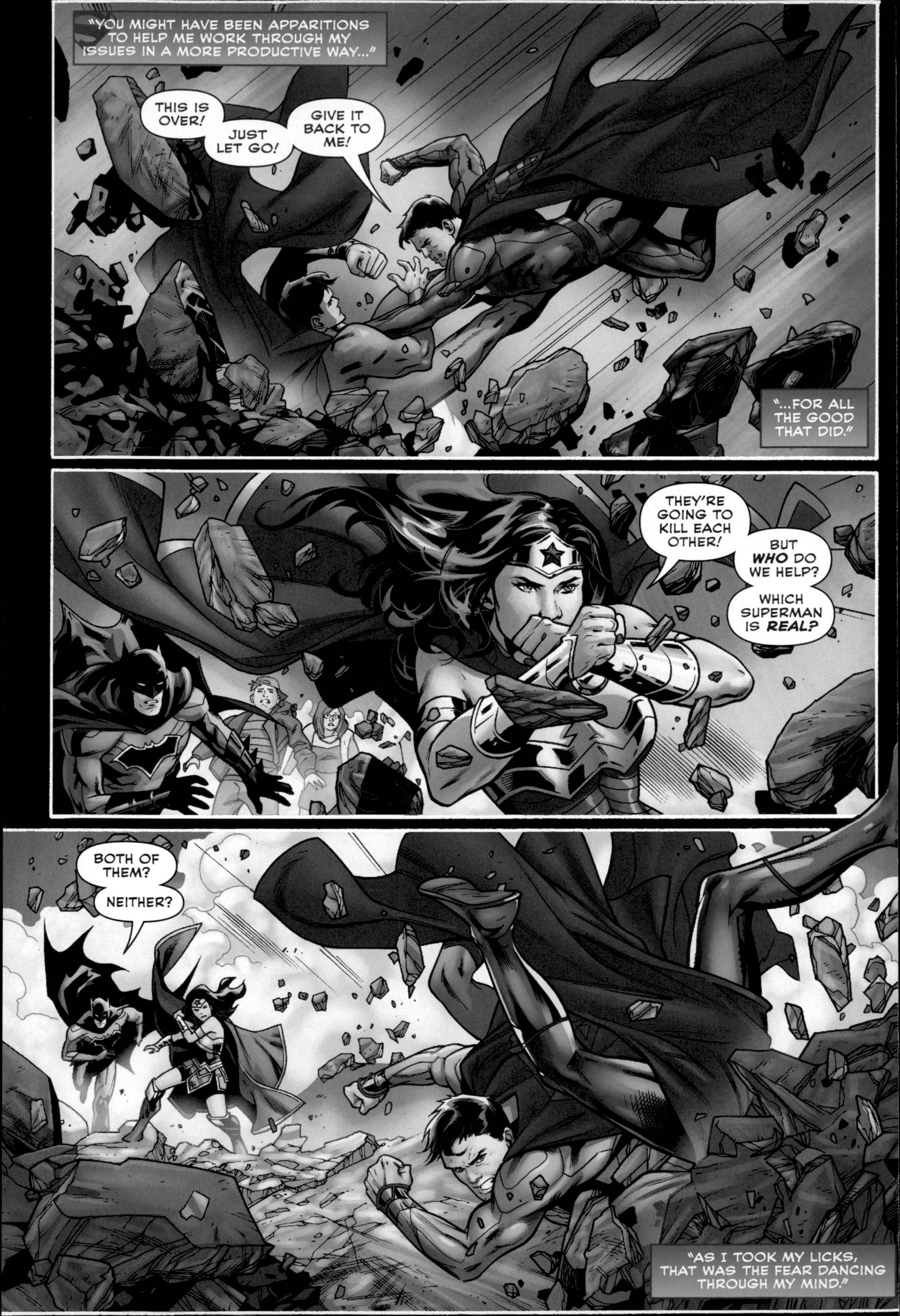
"YOU MIGHT HAVE BEEN APPARITIONS TO HELP ME WORK THROUGH MY ISSUES IN A MORE PRODUCTIVE WAY..."
THIS IS OVER!
JUST LET GO!
GIVE IT BACK TO ME!
"...FOR ALL THE GOOD THAT DID."
THEY'RE GOING TO KILL EACH OTHER!
BUT WHO DO WE HELP?
WHICH SUPERMAN IS REAL?
BOTH OF THEM?
NEITHER?
"AS I TOOK MY LICKS, THAT WAS THE FEAR DANCING THROUGH MY MIND."

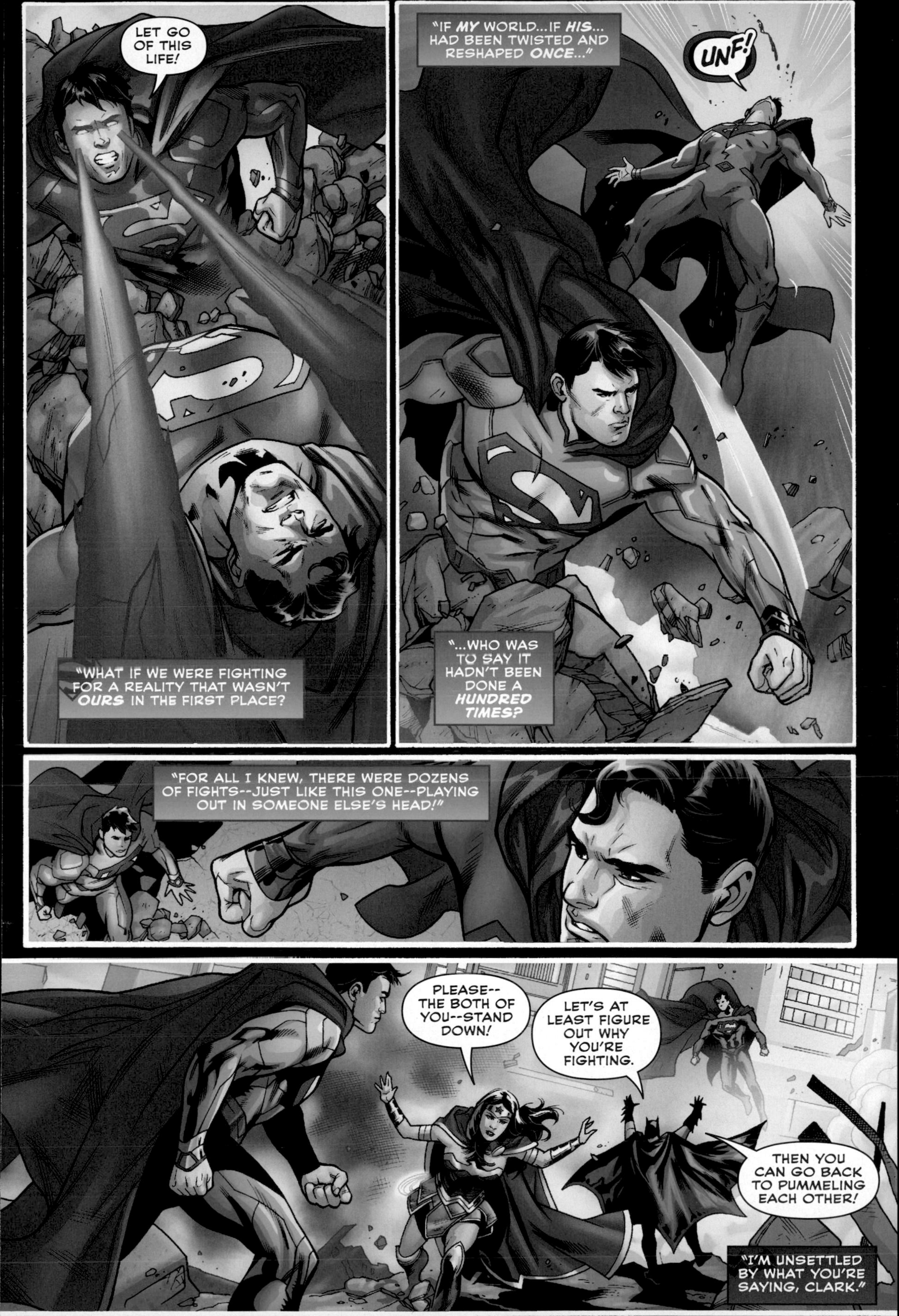
LET GO OF THIS LIFE!
"WHAT IF WE WERE FIGHTING FOR A REALITY THAT WASN'T OURS IN THE FIRST PLACE?
"IF MY WORLD...IF HIS... HAD BEEN TWISTED AND RESHAPED ONCE..."
UNF!
"...WHO WAS TO SAY IT HADN'T BEEN DONE A HUNDRED TIMES?
"FOR ALL I KNEW, THERE WERE DOZENS OF FIGHTS--JUST LIKE THIS ONE--PLAYING OUT IN SOMEONE ELSE'S HEAD!"
PLEASE-- THE BOTH OF YOU--STAND DOWN!
LET'S AT LEAST FIGURE OUT WHY YOU'RE FIGHTING.
THEN YOU CAN GO BACK TO PUMMELING EACH OTHER!
"I'M UNSETTLED BY WHAT YOU'RE SAYING, CLARK."

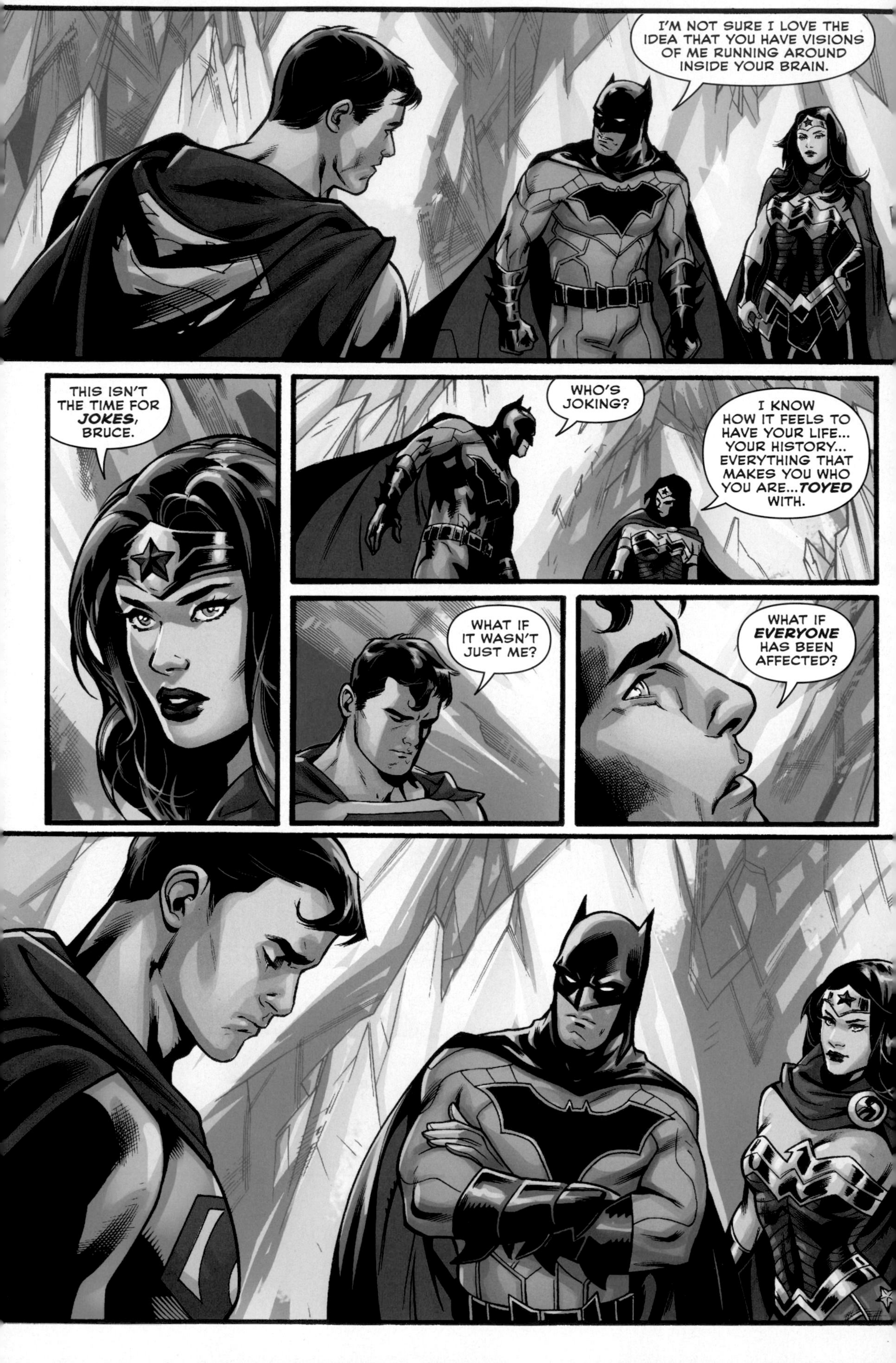
I'M NOT SURE I LOVE THE IDEA THAT YOU HAVE VISIONS OF ME RUNNING AROUND INSIDE YOUR BRAIN.
THIS ISN'T THE TIME FOR *JOKES*, BRUCE.
WHO'S JOKING?
I KNOW HOW IT FEELS TO HAVE YOUR LIFE... YOUR HISTORY... EVERYTHING THAT MAKES YOU WHO YOU ARE...*TOYED* WITH.
WHAT IF IT WASN'T JUST ME?
WHAT IF *EVERYONE* HAS BEEN AFFECTED?

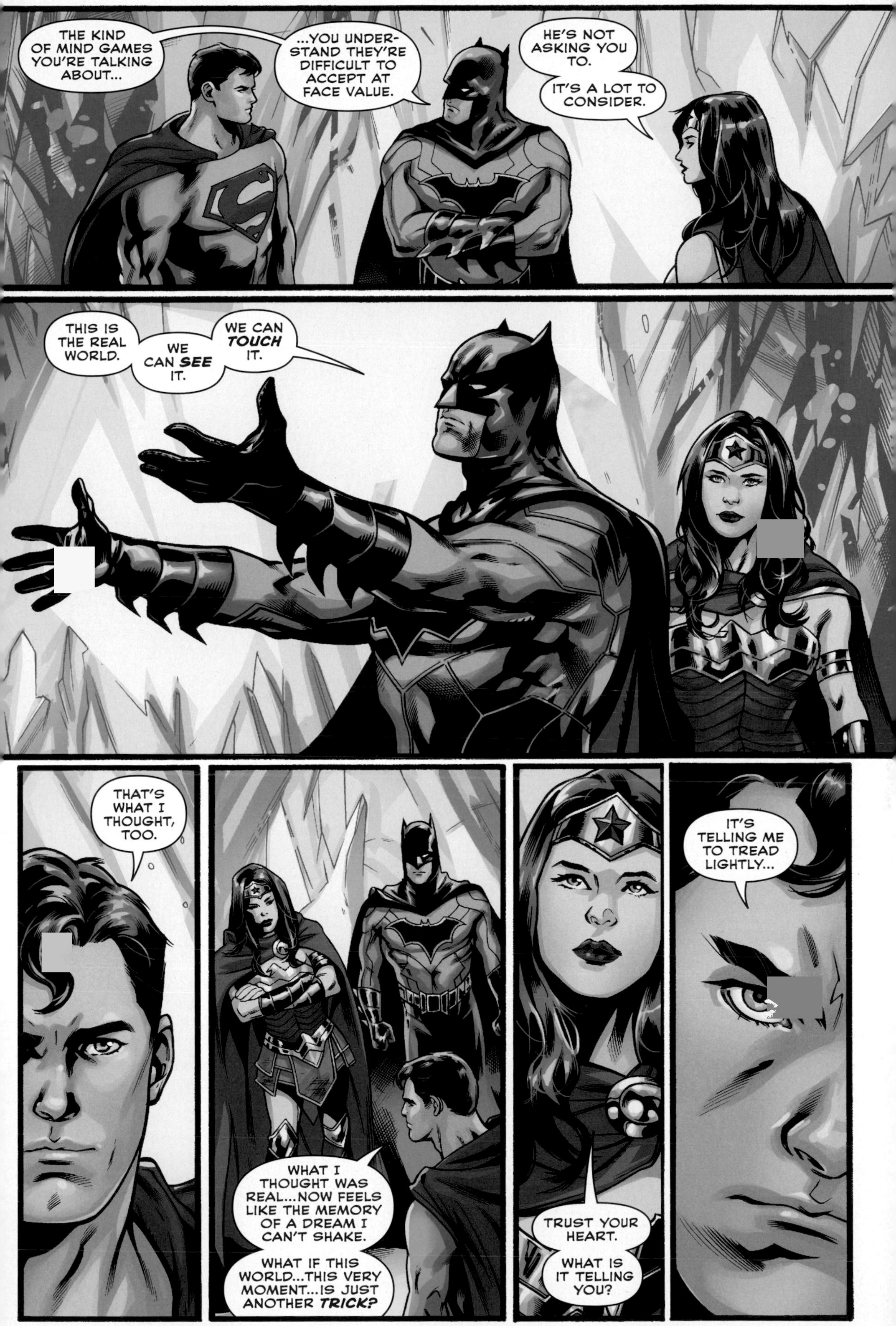
THE KIND OF MIND GAMES YOU'RE TALKING ABOUT...
...YOU UNDER-STAND THEY'RE DIFFICULT TO ACCEPT AT FACE VALUE.
HE'S NOT ASKING YOU TO.
IT'S A LOT TO CONSIDER.
THIS IS THE REAL WORLD.
WE CAN SEE IT.
WE CAN TOUCH IT.
THAT'S WHAT I THOUGHT, TOO.
WHAT I THOUGHT WAS REAL...NOW FEELS LIKE THE MEMORY OF A DREAM I CAN'T SHAKE.
WHAT IF THIS WORLD...THIS VERY MOMENT...IS JUST ANOTHER TRICK?
TRUST YOUR HEART.
WHAT IS IT TELLING YOU?
IT'S TELLING ME TO TREAD LIGHTLY...

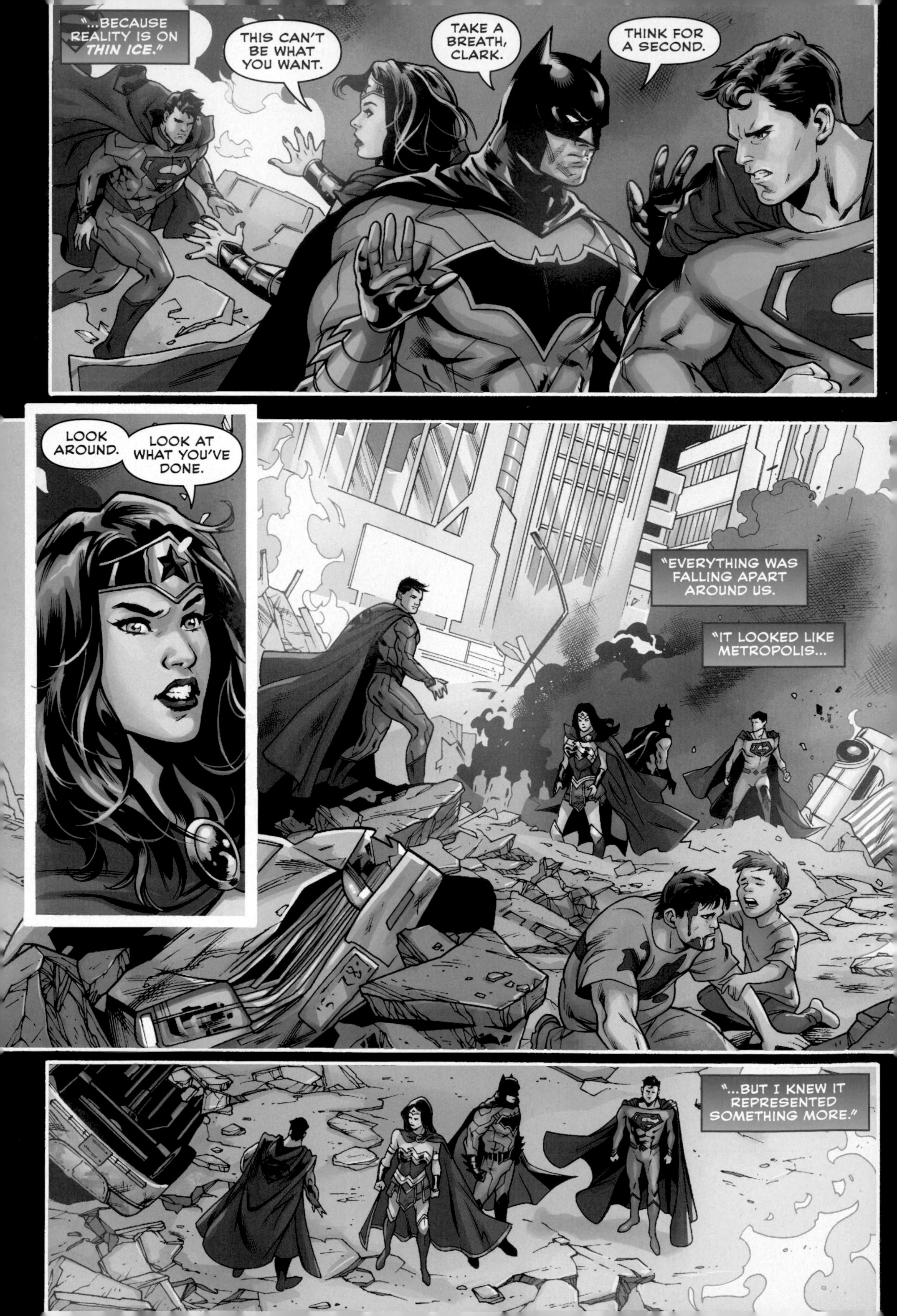
"...BECAUSE REALITY IS ON *THIN ICE.*"
THIS CAN'T BE WHAT YOU WANT.
TAKE A BREATH, CLARK.
THINK FOR A SECOND.
LOOK AROUND.
LOOK AT WHAT YOU'VE DONE.
"EVERYTHING WAS FALLING APART AROUND US.
"IT LOOKED LIKE METROPOLIS...
"...BUT I KNEW IT REPRESENTED SOMETHING MORE."

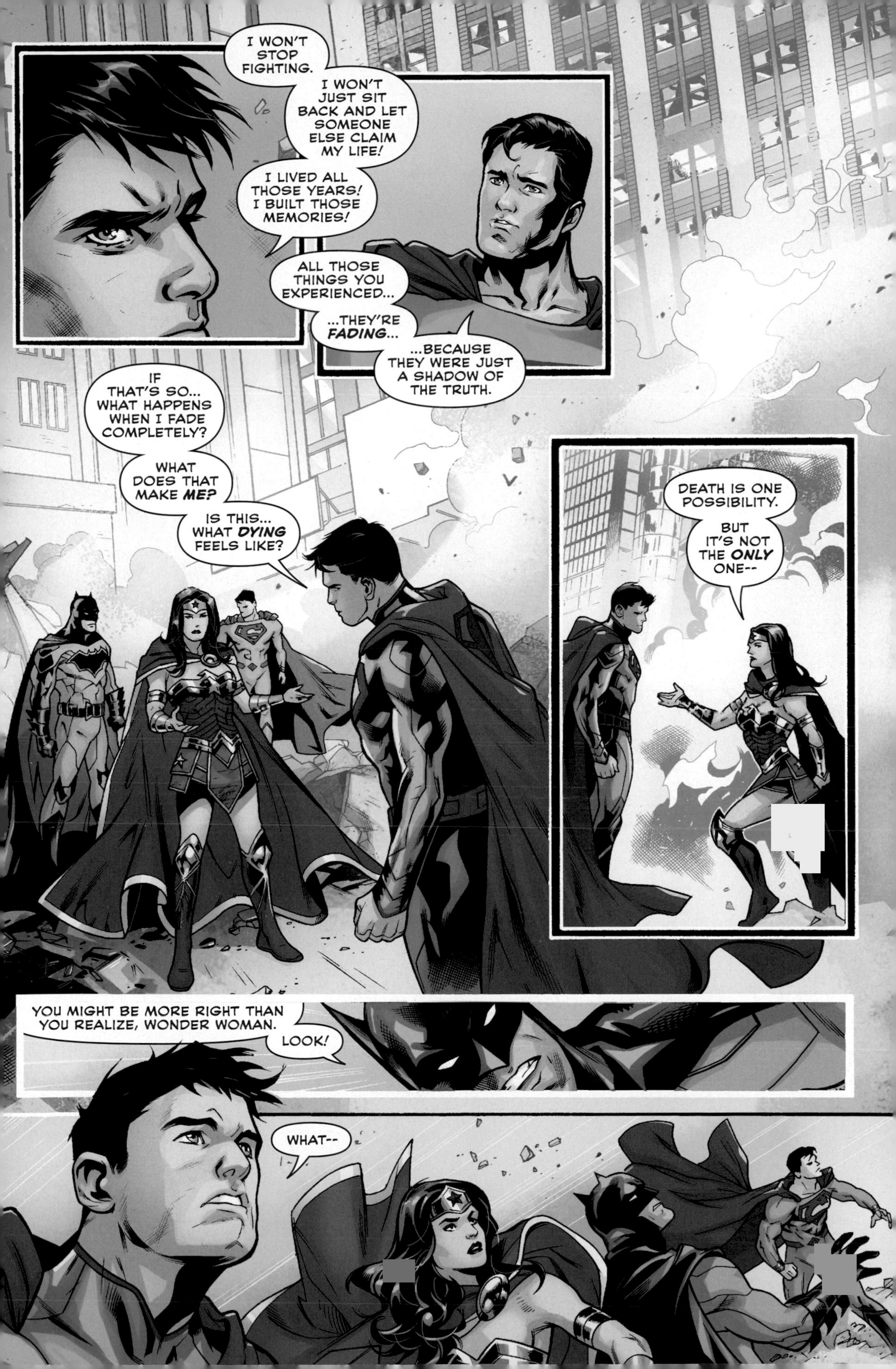
I WON'T STOP FIGHTING.
I WON'T JUST SIT BACK AND LET SOMEONE ELSE CLAIM MY LIFE!
I LIVED ALL THOSE YEARS! I BUILT THOSE MEMORIES!
ALL THOSE THINGS YOU EXPERIENCED...
...THEY'RE *FADING*...
...BECAUSE THEY WERE JUST A SHADOW OF THE TRUTH.
IF THAT'S SO... WHAT HAPPENS WHEN I FADE COMPLETELY?
WHAT DOES THAT MAKE *ME?*
IS THIS... WHAT *DYING* FEELS LIKE?
DEATH IS ONE POSSIBILITY.
BUT IT'S NOT THE *ONLY* ONE--
YOU MIGHT BE MORE RIGHT THAN YOU REALIZE, WONDER WOMAN.
LOOK!
WHAT--

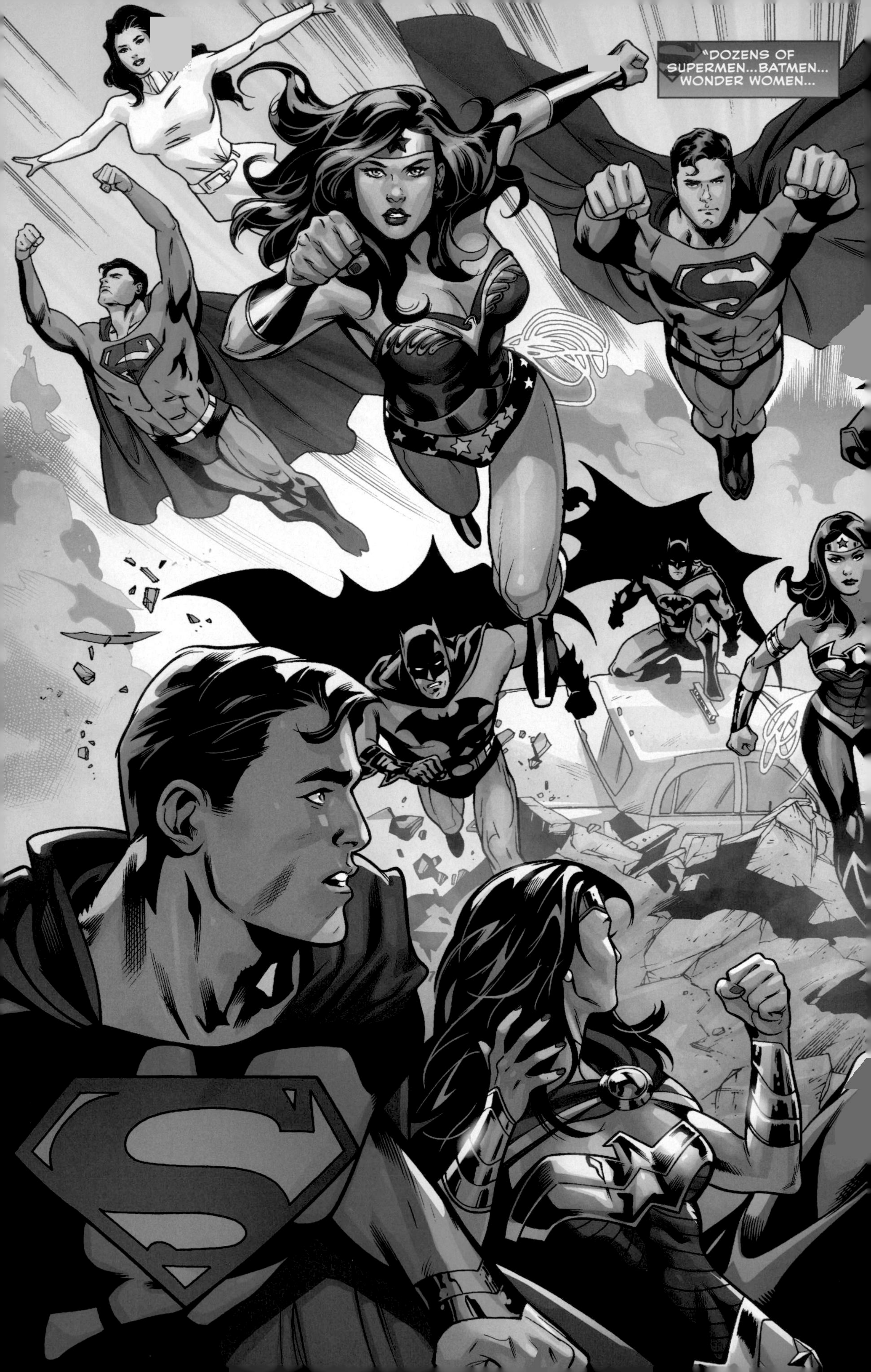
"DOZENS OF SUPERMEN...BATMEN... WONDER WOMEN...

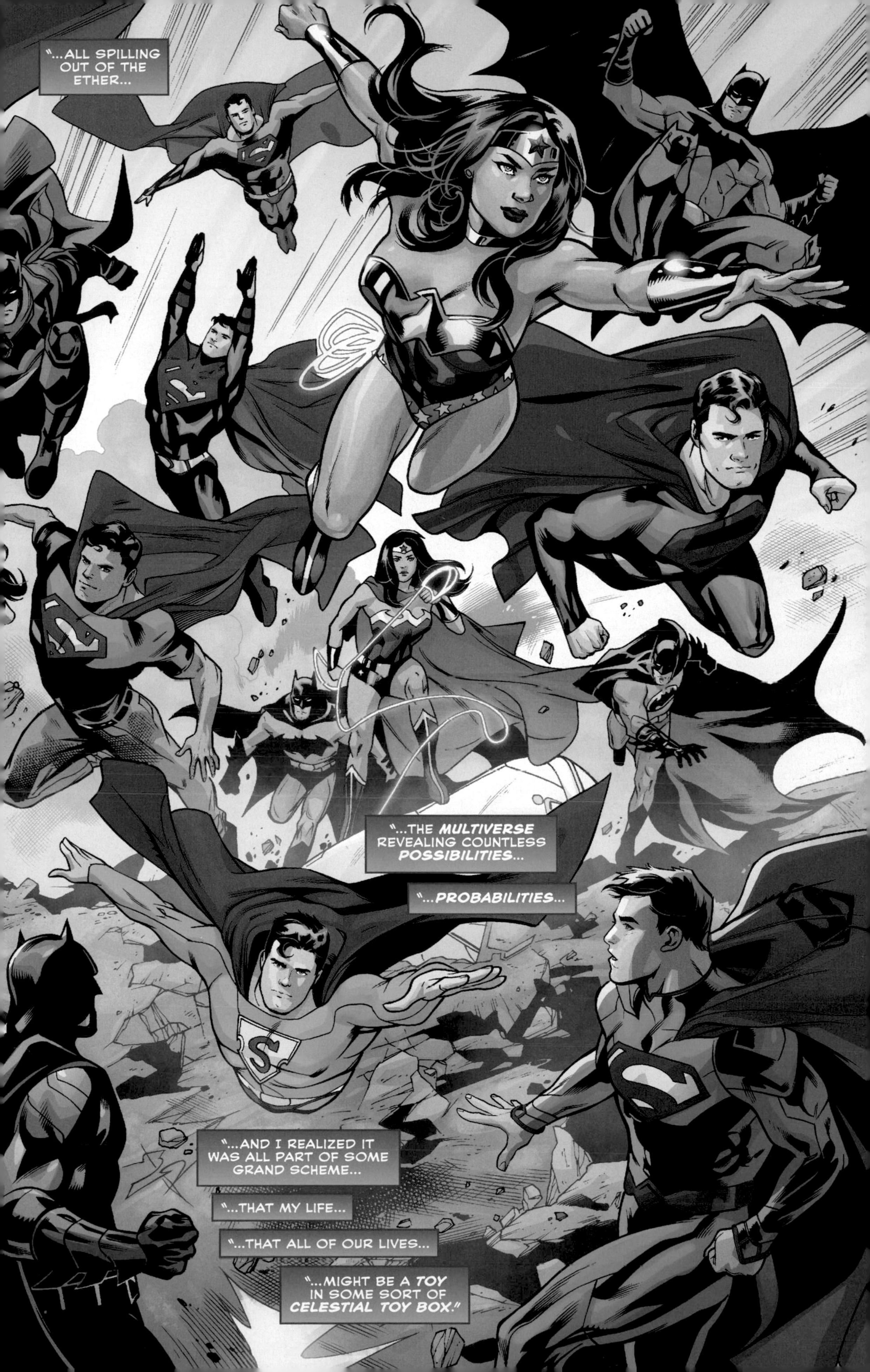
"...ALL SPILLING OUT OF THE ETHER...
"...THE MULTIVERSE REVEALING COUNTLESS POSSIBILITIES...
"...PROBABILITIES...
"...AND I REALIZED IT WAS ALL PART OF SOME GRAND SCHEME...
"...THAT MY LIFE...
"...THAT ALL OF OUR LIVES...
"...MIGHT BE A TOY IN SOME SORT OF CELESTIAL TOY BOX."

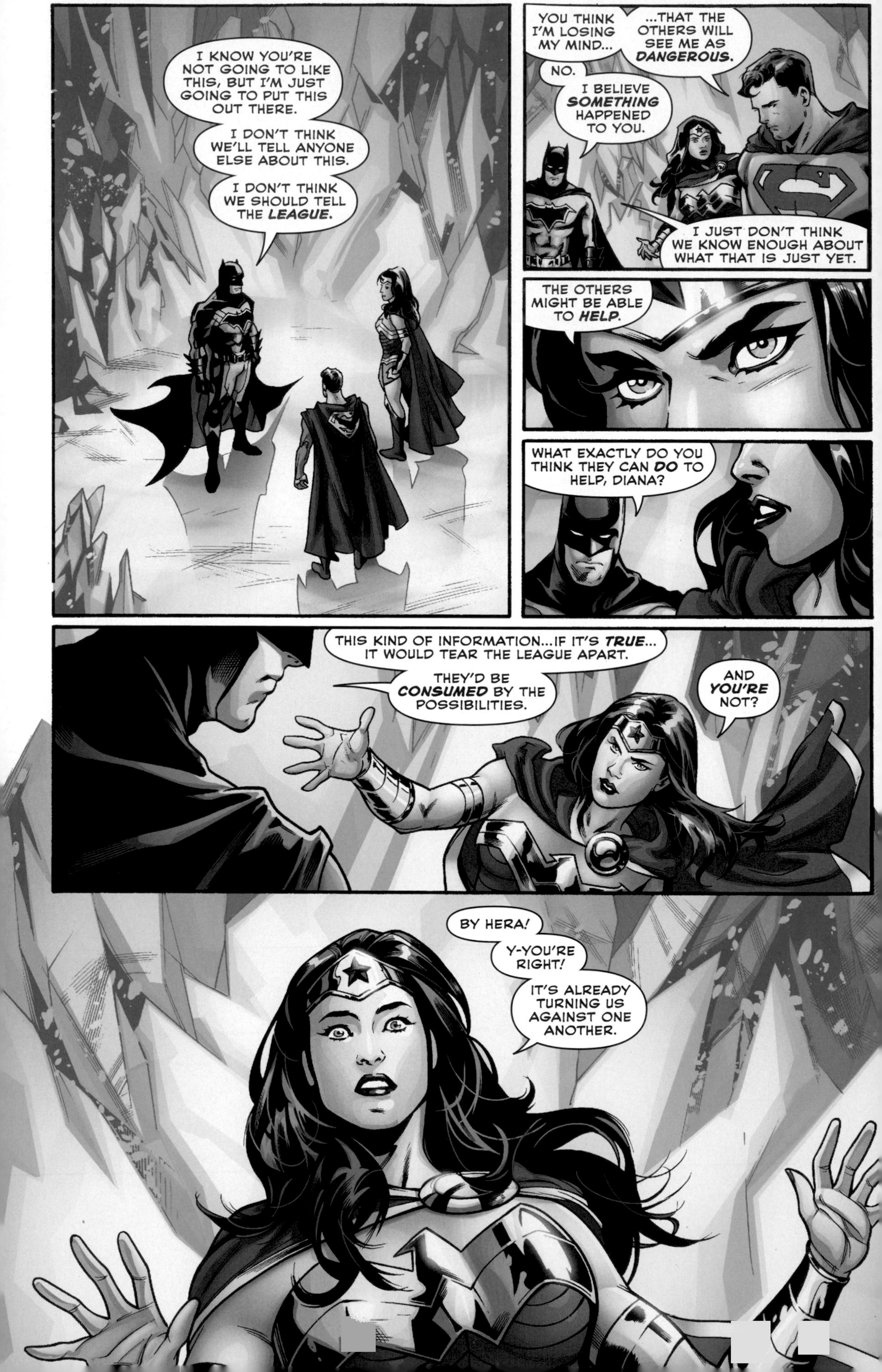
I KNOW YOU'RE NOT GOING TO LIKE THIS, BUT I'M JUST GOING TO PUT THIS OUT THERE.
I DON'T THINK WE'LL TELL ANYONE ELSE ABOUT THIS.
I DON'T THINK WE SHOULD TELL THE *LEAGUE.*
YOU THINK I'M LOSING MY MIND...
...THAT THE OTHERS WILL SEE ME AS *DANGEROUS.*
NO.
I BELIEVE *SOMETHING* HAPPENED TO YOU.
I JUST DON'T THINK WE KNOW ENOUGH ABOUT WHAT THAT IS JUST YET.
THE OTHERS MIGHT BE ABLE TO *HELP.*
WHAT EXACTLY DO YOU THINK THEY CAN *DO* TO HELP, DIANA?
THIS KIND OF INFORMATION...IF IT'S *TRUE*... IT WOULD TEAR THE LEAGUE APART.
THEY'D BE *CONSUMED* BY THE POSSIBILITIES.
AND *YOU'RE* NOT?
BY HERA!
Y-YOU'RE RIGHT!
IT'S ALREADY TURNING US AGAINST ONE ANOTHER.

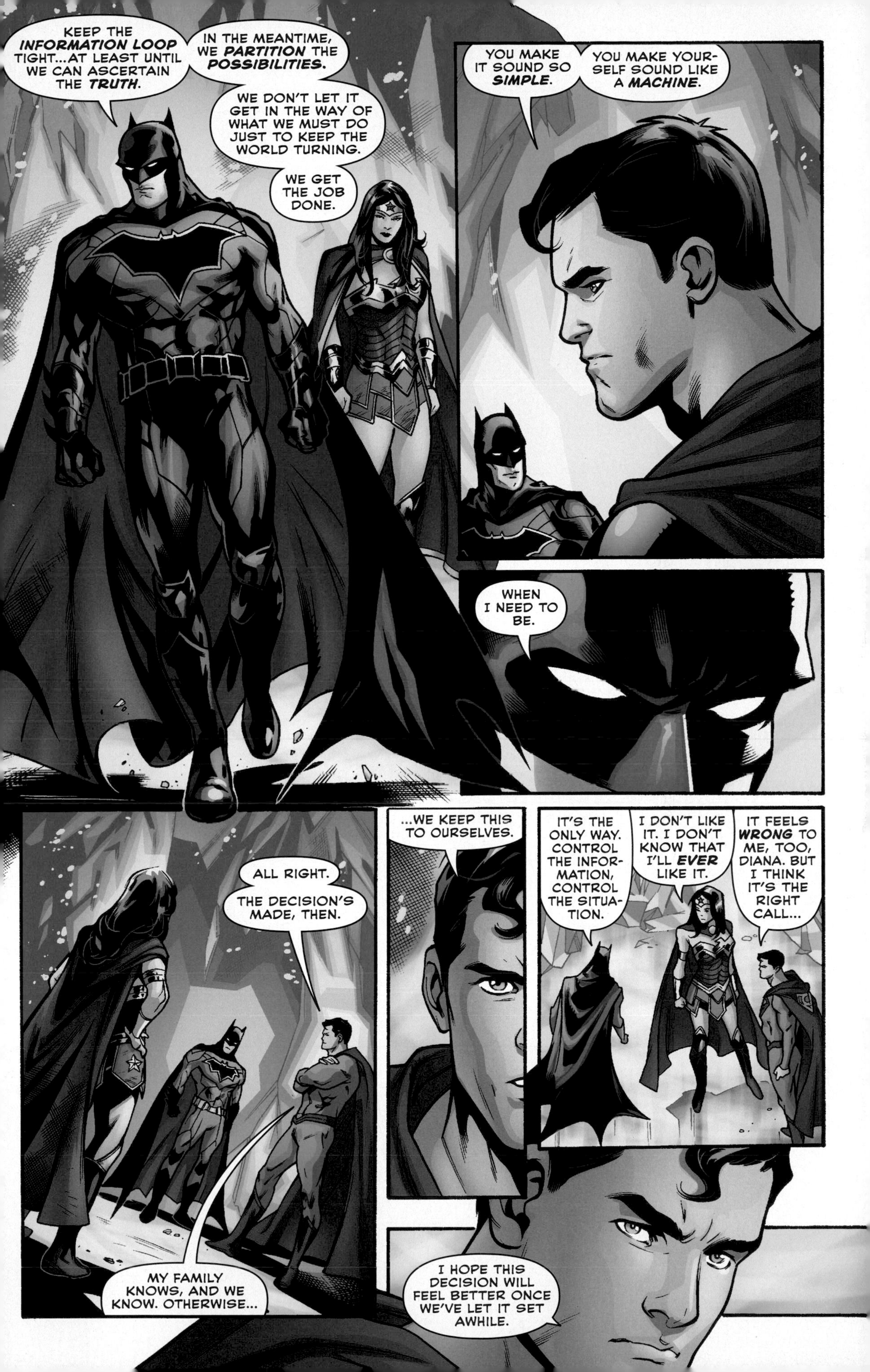

KEEP THE INFORMATION LOOP TIGHT...AT LEAST UNTIL WE CAN ASCERTAIN THE TRUTH.
IN THE MEANTIME, WE PARTITION THE POSSIBILITIES.
WE DON'T LET IT GET IN THE WAY OF WHAT WE MUST DO JUST TO KEEP THE WORLD TURNING.
WE GET THE JOB DONE.
YOU MAKE IT SOUND SO SIMPLE.
YOU MAKE YOURSELF SOUND LIKE A MACHINE.
WHEN I NEED TO BE.
ALL RIGHT.
THE DECISION'S MADE, THEN.
MY FAMILY KNOWS, AND WE KNOW. OTHERWISE...
...WE KEEP THIS TO OURSELVES.
IT'S THE ONLY WAY. CONTROL THE INFORMATION, CONTROL THE SITUATION.
I DON'T LIKE IT. I DON'T KNOW THAT I'LL EVER LIKE IT.
IT FEELS WRONG TO ME, TOO, DIANA. BUT I THINK IT'S THE RIGHT CALL...
I HOPE THIS DECISION WILL FEEL BETTER ONCE WE'VE LET IT SET AWHILE.

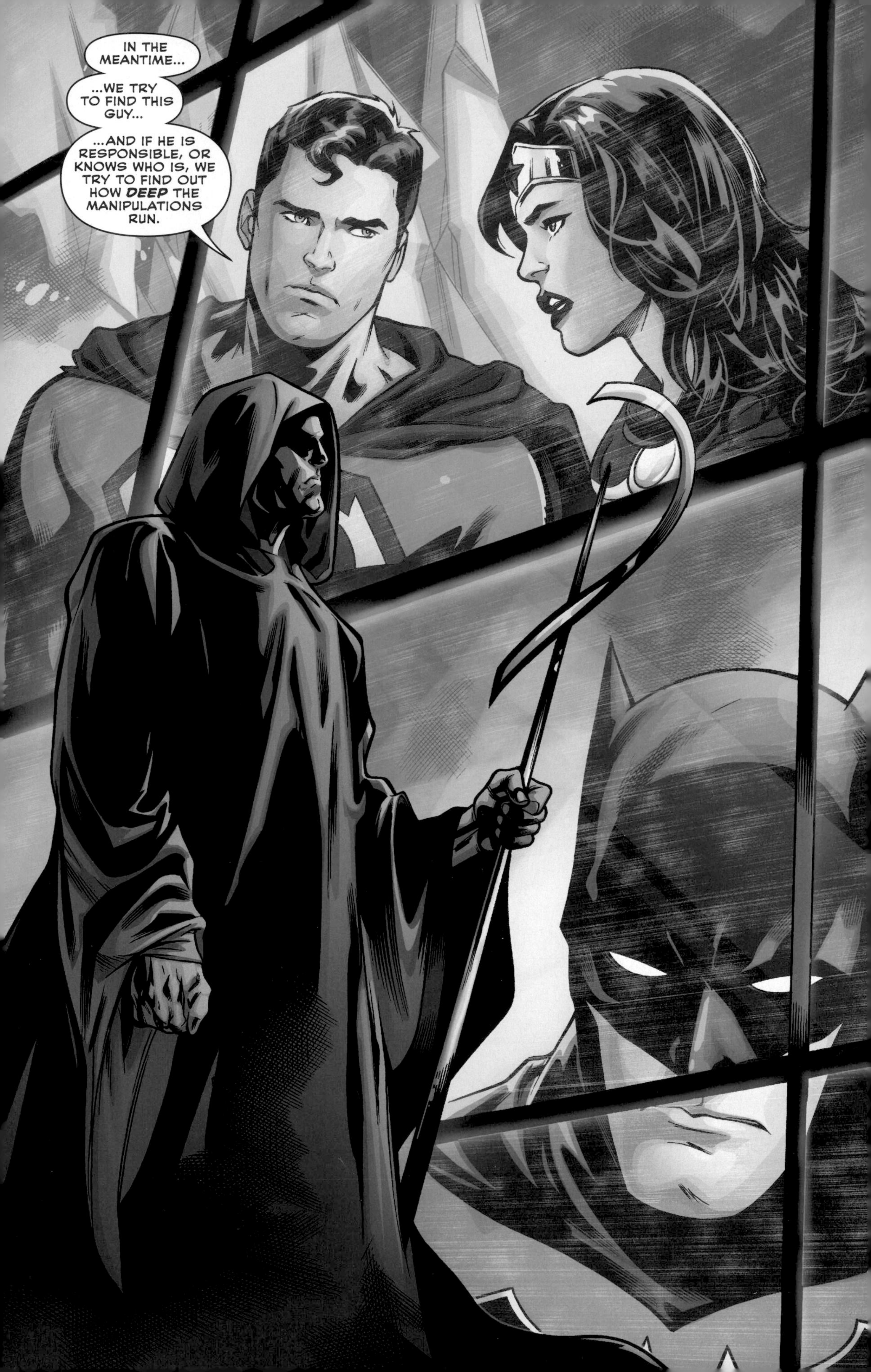
IN THE MEANTIME...
...WE TRY TO FIND THIS GUY...
...AND IF HE IS RESPONSIBLE, OR KNOWS WHO IS, WE TRY TO FIND OUT HOW *DEEP* THE MANIPULATIONS RUN.

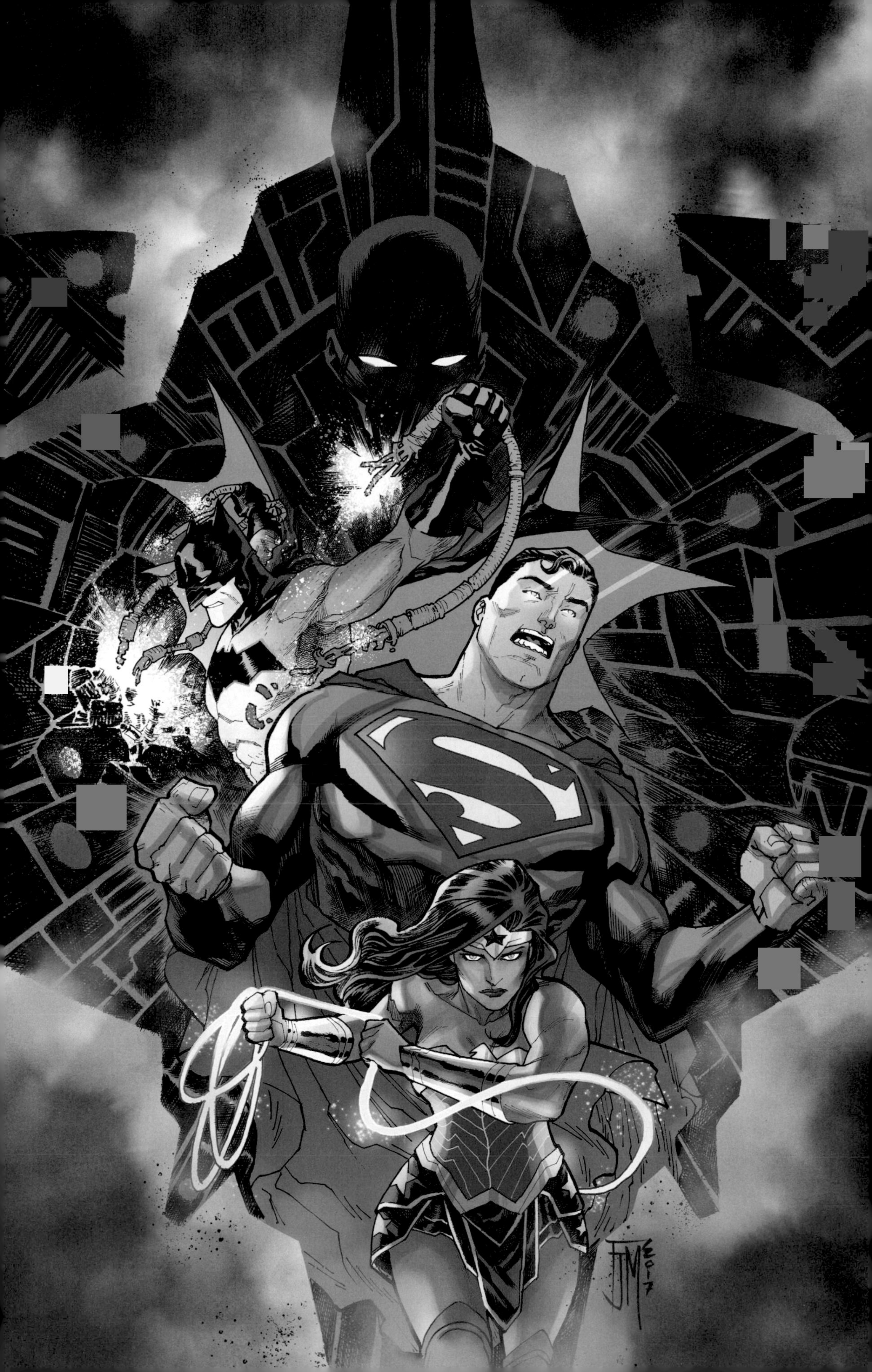

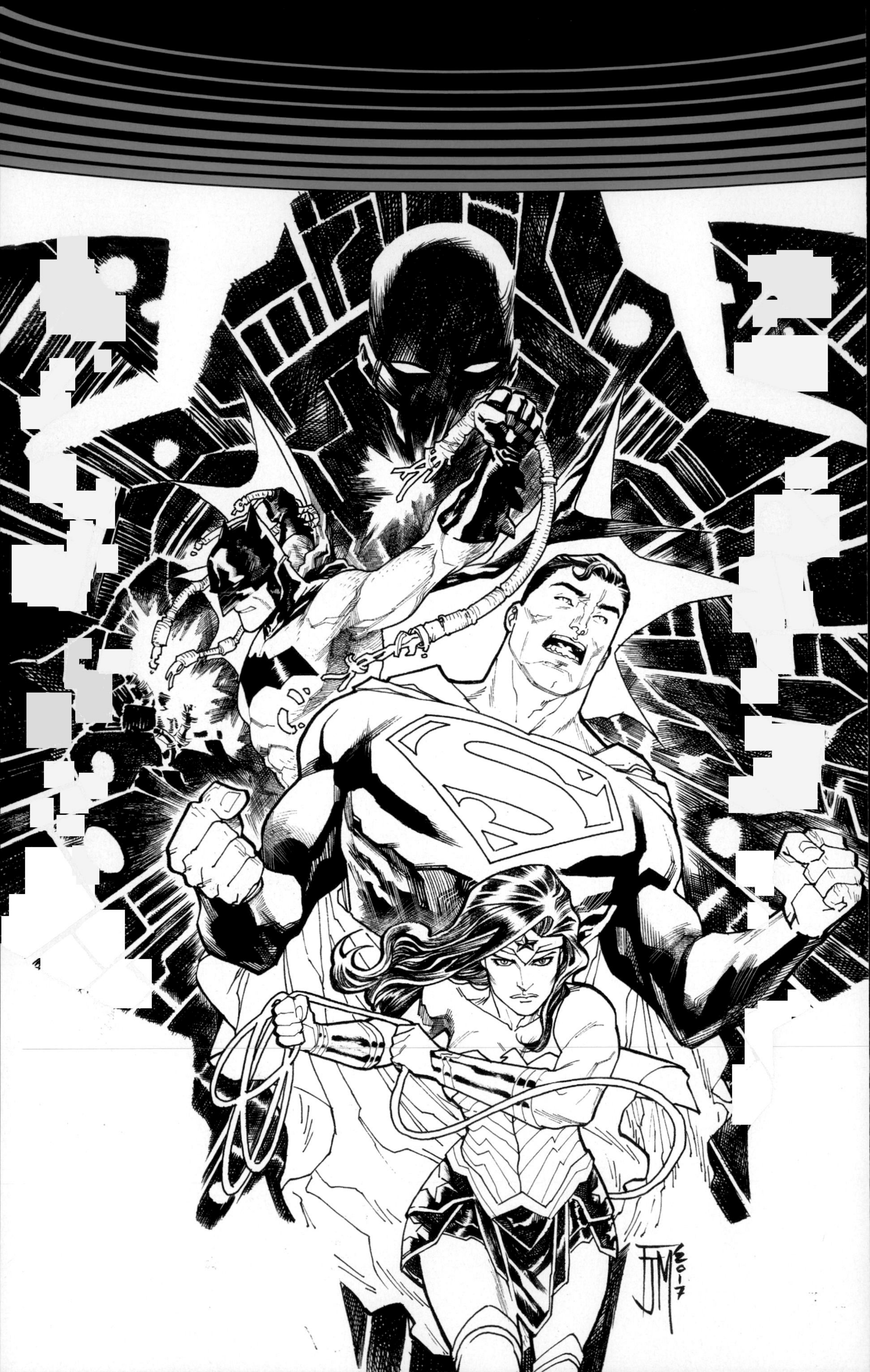

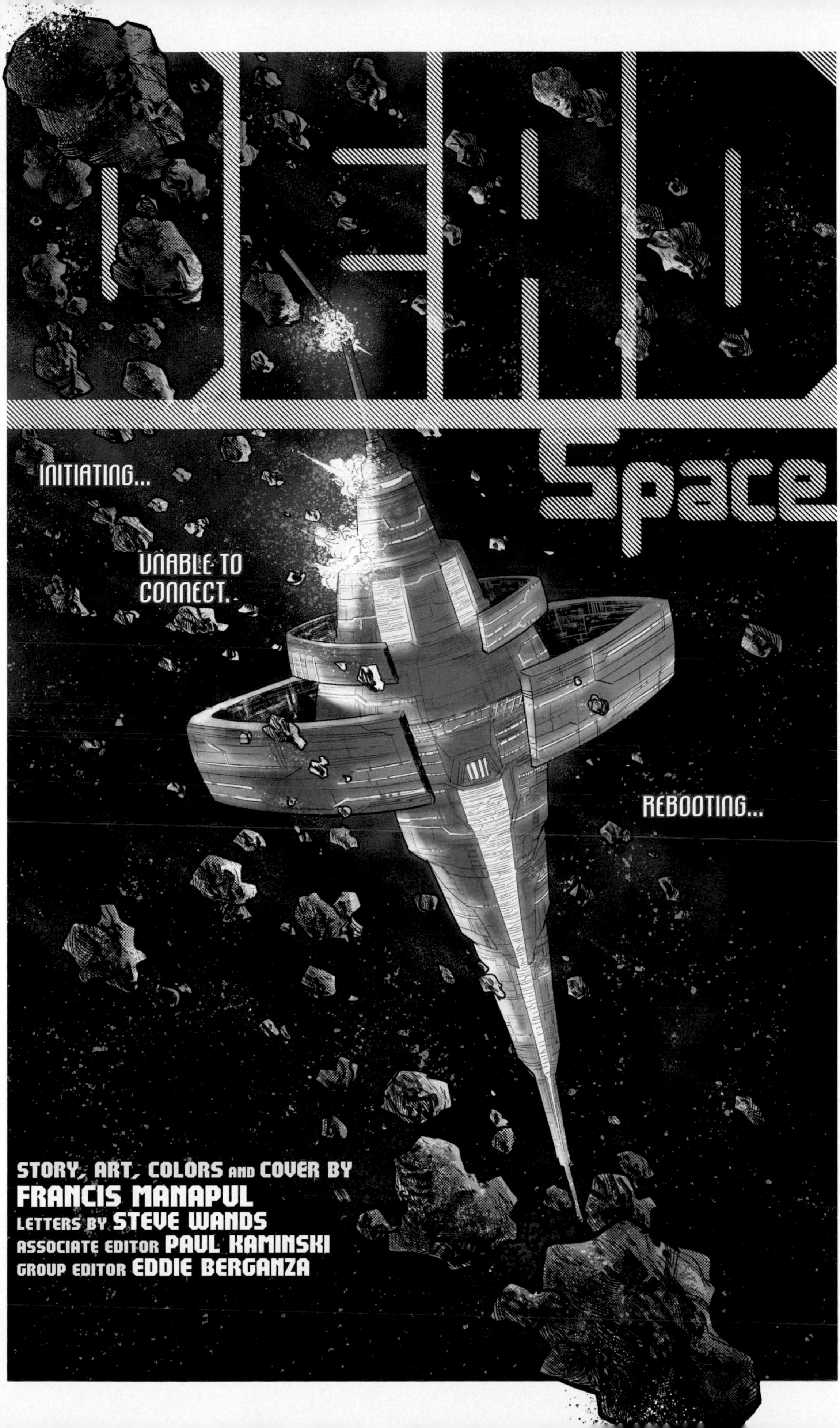

DEAD Space
INITIATING...
UNABLE TO CONNECT.
REBOOTING...
STORY, ART, COLORS AND COVER BY
FRANCIS MANAPUL
LETTERS BY STEVE WANDS
ASSOCIATE EDITOR PAUL KAMINSKI
GROUP EDITOR EDDIE BERGANZA

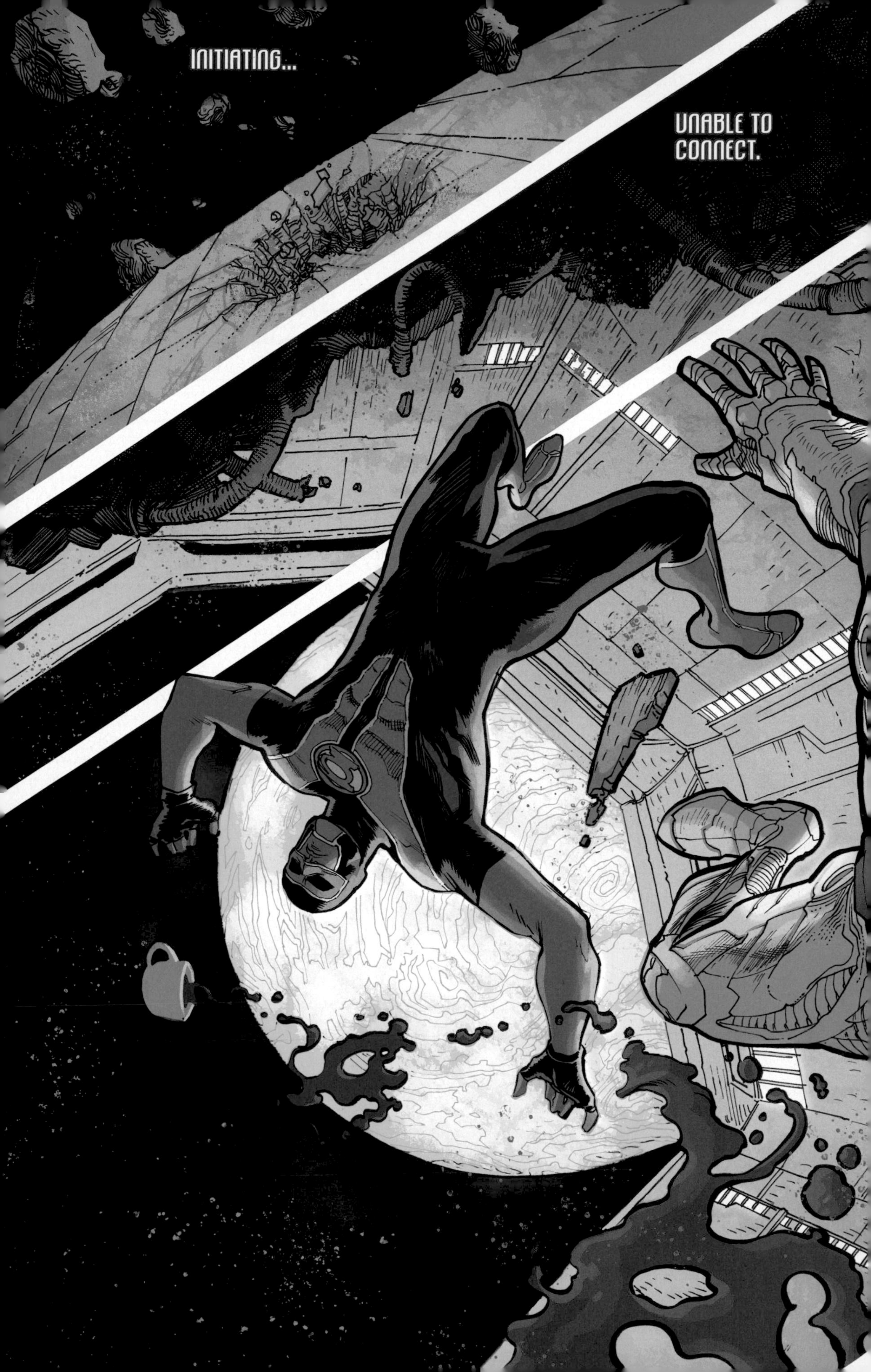
INITIATING...
UNABLE TO CONNECT.

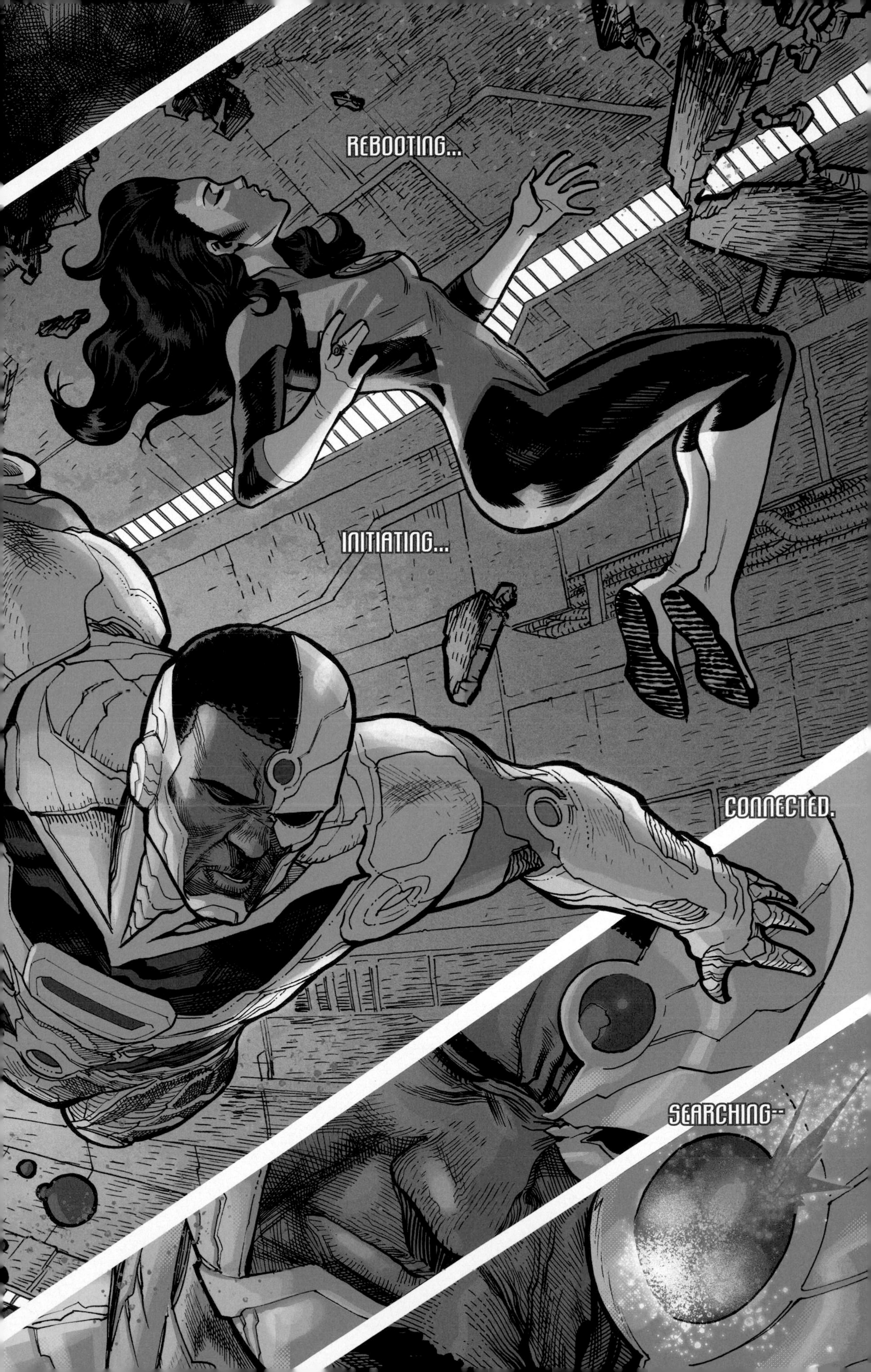
REBOOTING...
INITIATING...
CONNECTED.
SEARCHING--

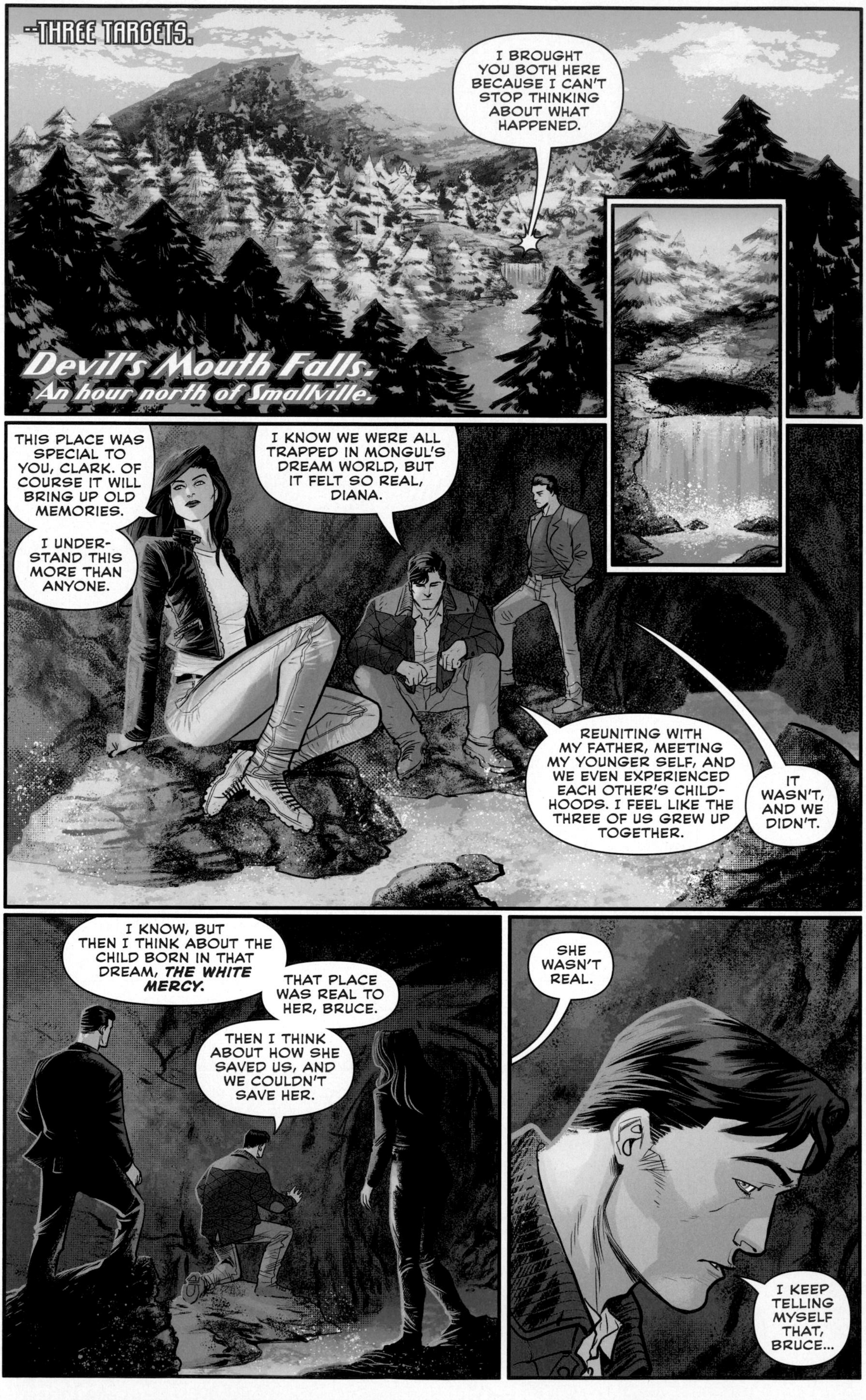
--THREE TARGETS.
I BROUGHT YOU BOTH HERE BECAUSE I CAN'T STOP THINKING ABOUT WHAT HAPPENED.
Devil's Mouth Falls.
An hour north of Smallville.
THIS PLACE WAS SPECIAL TO YOU, CLARK. OF COURSE IT WILL BRING UP OLD MEMORIES.
I UNDER-STAND THIS MORE THAN ANYONE.
I KNOW WE WERE ALL TRAPPED IN MONGUL'S DREAM WORLD, BUT IT FELT SO REAL, DIANA.
REUNITING WITH MY FATHER, MEETING MY YOUNGER SELF, AND WE EVEN EXPERIENCED EACH OTHER'S CHILD-HOODS. I FEEL LIKE THE THREE OF US GREW UP TOGETHER.
IT WASN'T, AND WE DIDN'T.
I KNOW, BUT THEN I THINK ABOUT THE CHILD BORN IN THAT DREAM, ***THE WHITE MERCY.***
THAT PLACE WAS REAL TO HER, BRUCE.
THEN I THINK ABOUT HOW SHE SAVED US, AND WE COULDN'T SAVE HER.
SHE WASN'T REAL.
I KEEP TELLING MYSELF THAT, BRUCE...

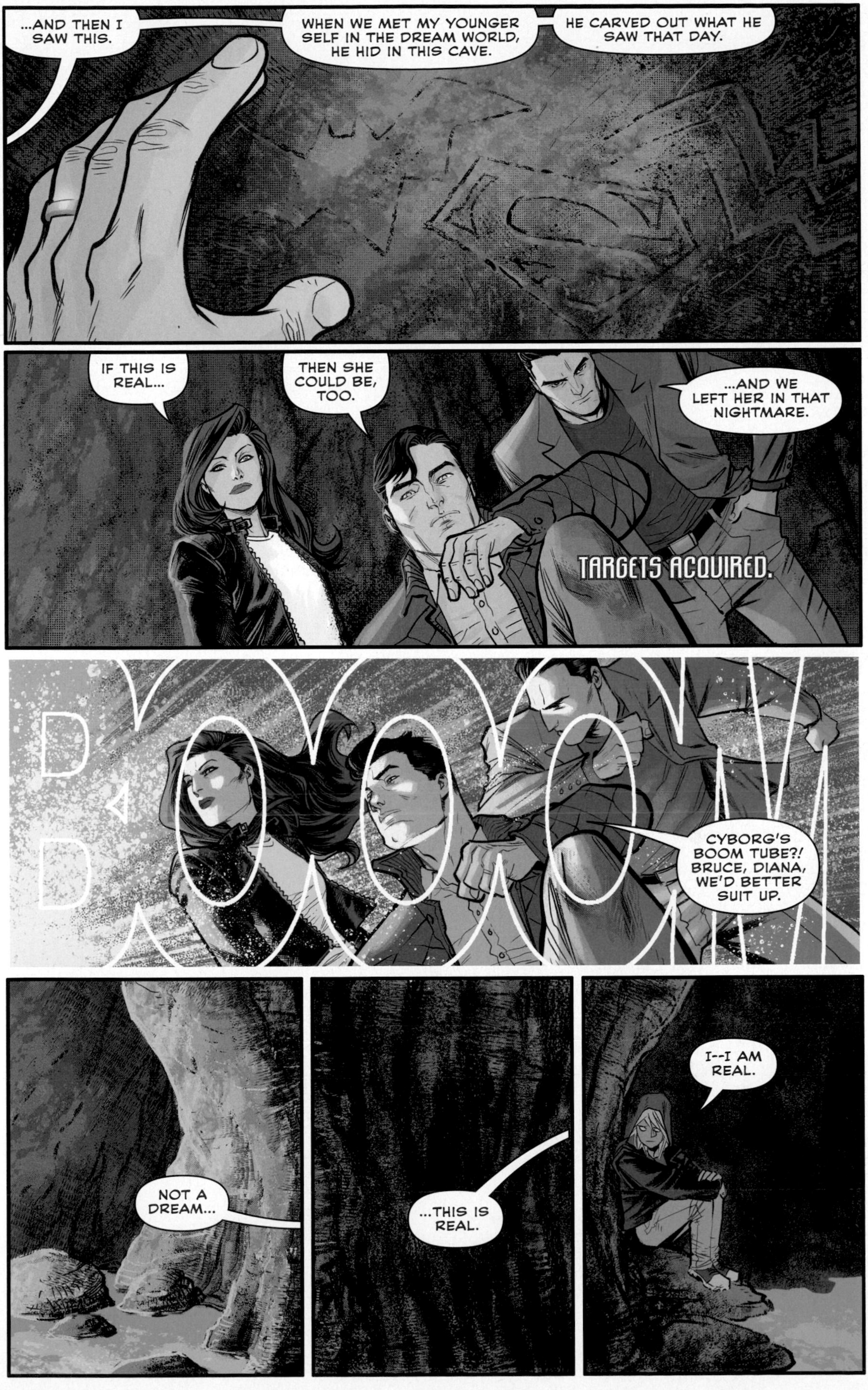
...AND THEN I SAW THIS.
WHEN WE MET MY YOUNGER SELF IN THE DREAM WORLD, HE HID IN THIS CAVE.
HE CARVED OUT WHAT HE SAW THAT DAY.
IF THIS IS REAL...
THEN SHE COULD BE, TOO.
...AND WE LEFT HER IN THAT NIGHTMARE.
TARGETS ACQUIRED.
DOOOOOM
CYBORG'S BOOM TUBE?! BRUCE, DIANA, WE'D BETTER SUIT UP.
NOT A DREAM...
...THIS IS REAL.
I--I AM REAL.

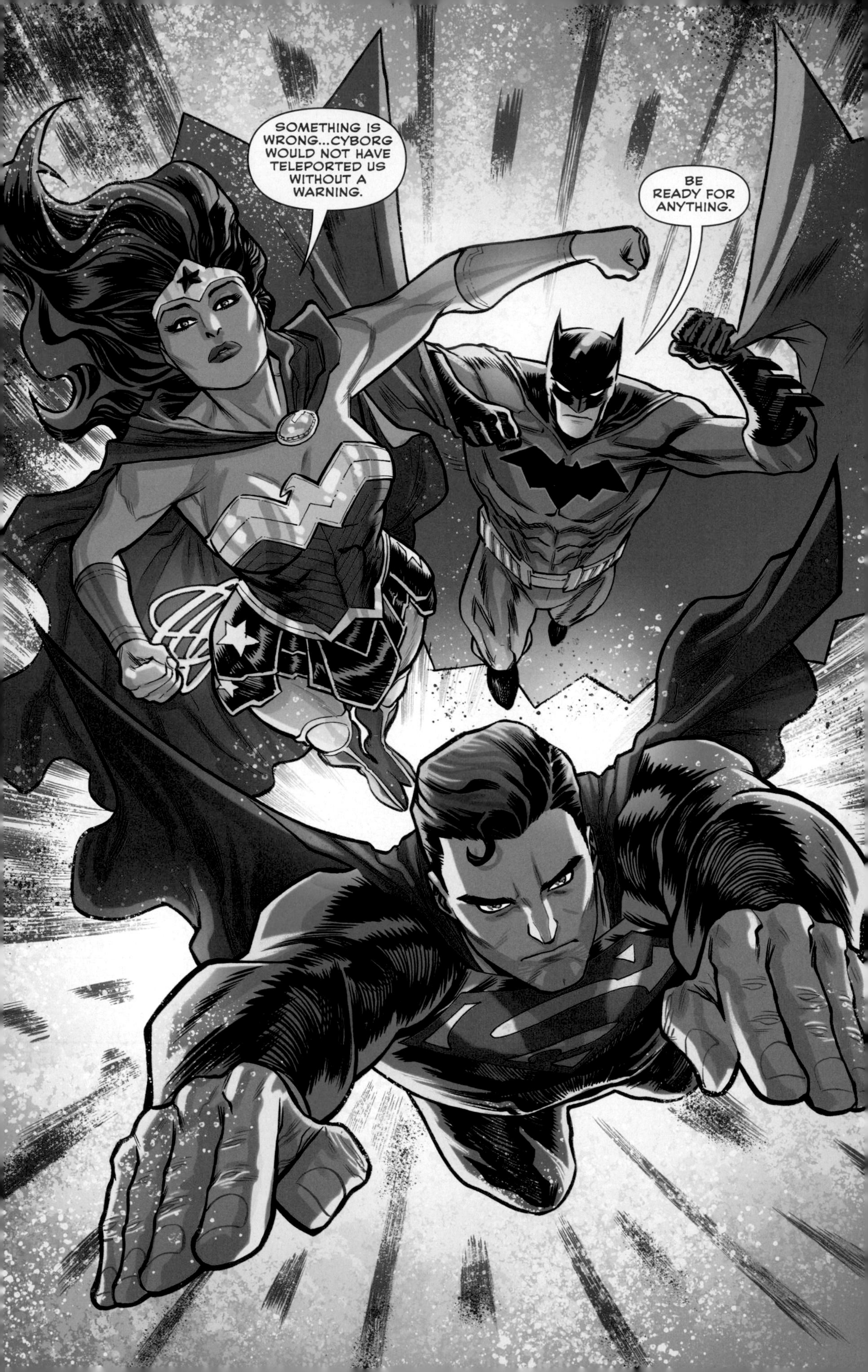
SOMETHING IS WRONG...CYBORG WOULD NOT HAVE TELEPORTED US WITHOUT A WARNING.
BE READY FOR ANYTHING.

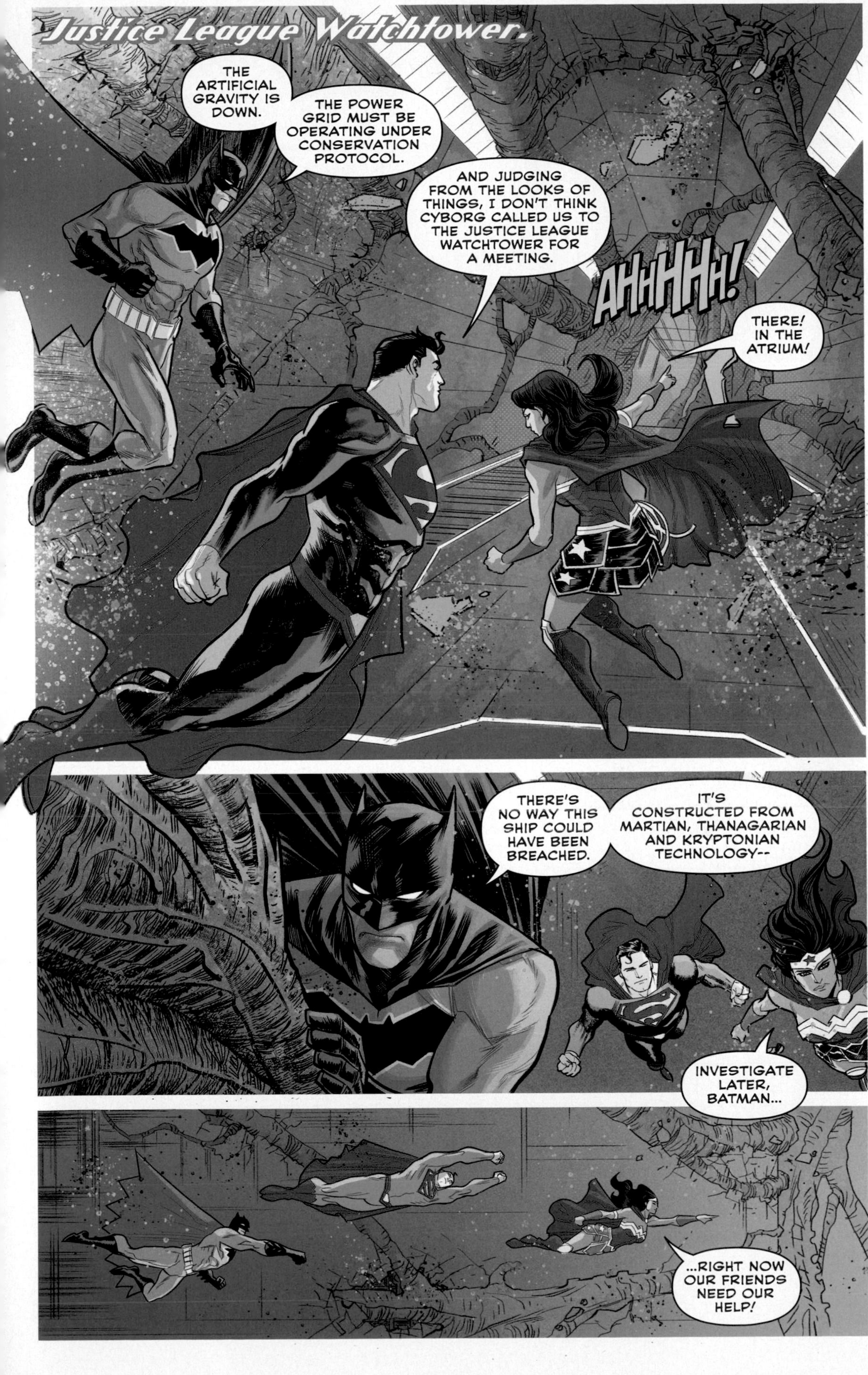
Justice League Watchtower.
THE ARTIFICIAL GRAVITY IS DOWN.
THE POWER GRID MUST BE OPERATING UNDER CONSERVATION PROTOCOL.
AND JUDGING FROM THE LOOKS OF THINGS, I DON'T THINK CYBORG CALLED US TO THE JUSTICE LEAGUE WATCHTOWER FOR A MEETING.
AHHHHH!
THERE! IN THE ATRIUM!
THERE'S NO WAY THIS SHIP COULD HAVE BEEN BREACHED.
IT'S CONSTRUCTED FROM MARTIAN, THANAGARIAN AND KRYPTONIAN TECHNOLOGY--
INVESTIGATE LATER, BATMAN...
...RIGHT NOW OUR FRIENDS NEED OUR HELP!

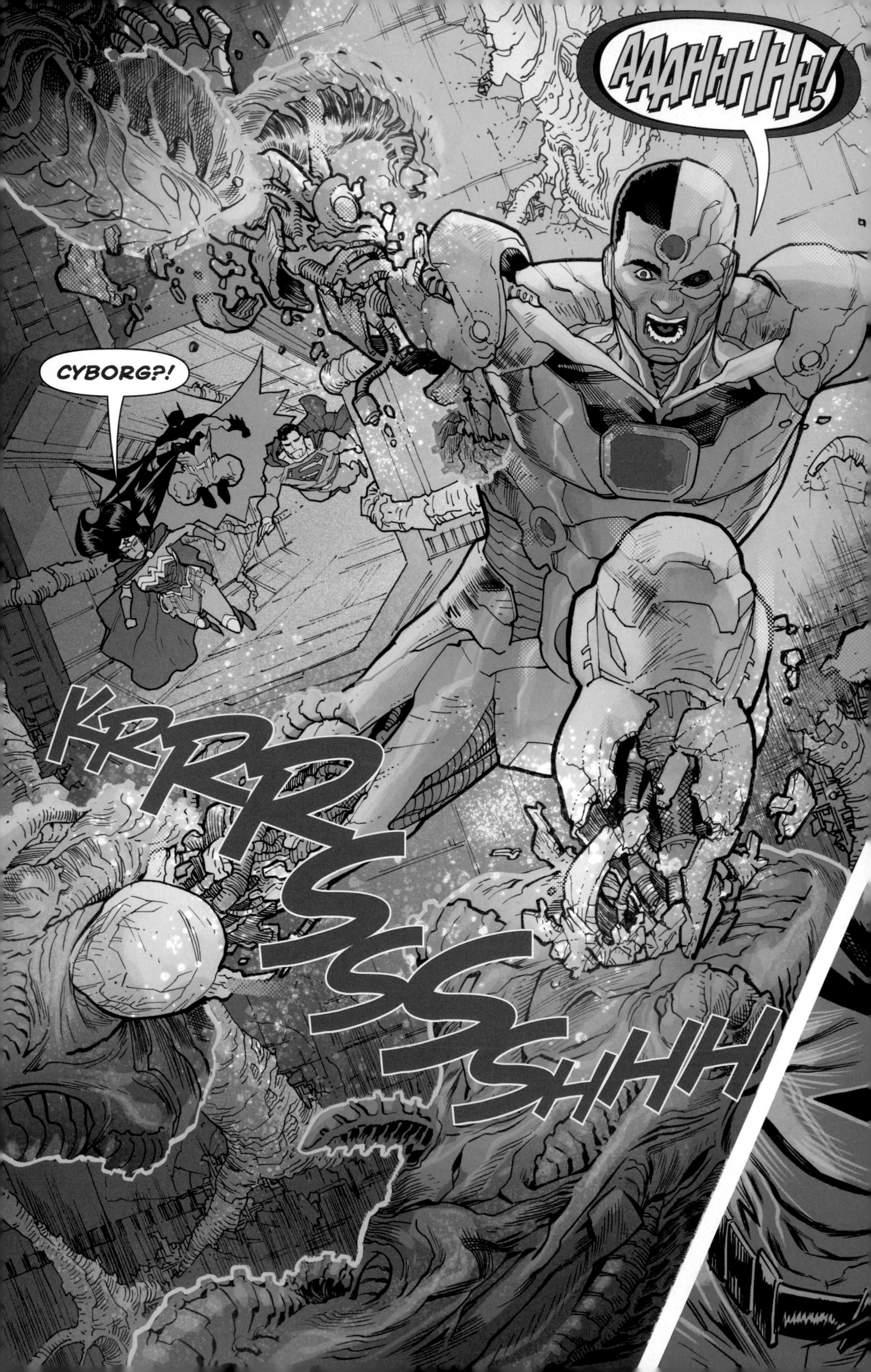
AAAHHHHH!
CYBORG?!
KRRRSSSSHHH

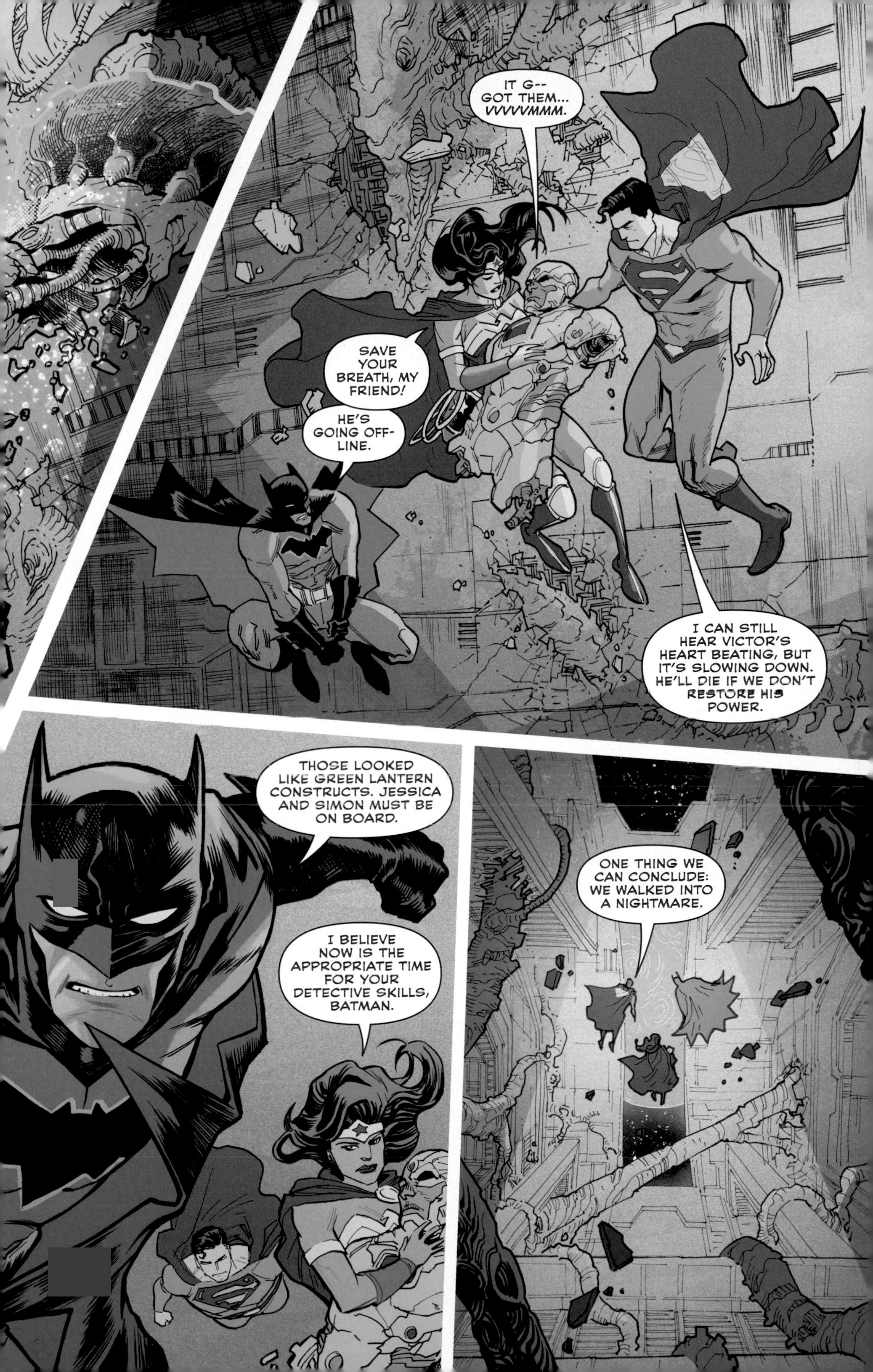
IT G-- GOT THEM... *VVVVVMMM.*
SAVE YOUR BREATH, MY FRIEND!
HE'S GOING OFF-LINE.
I CAN STILL HEAR VICTOR'S HEART BEATING, BUT IT'S SLOWING DOWN. HE'LL DIE IF WE DON'T RESTORE HIS POWER.
THOSE LOOKED LIKE GREEN LANTERN CONSTRUCTS. JESSICA AND SIMON MUST BE ON BOARD.
I BELIEVE NOW IS THE APPROPRIATE TIME FOR YOUR DETECTIVE SKILLS, BATMAN.
ONE THING WE CAN CONCLUDE: WE WALKED INTO A NIGHTMARE.

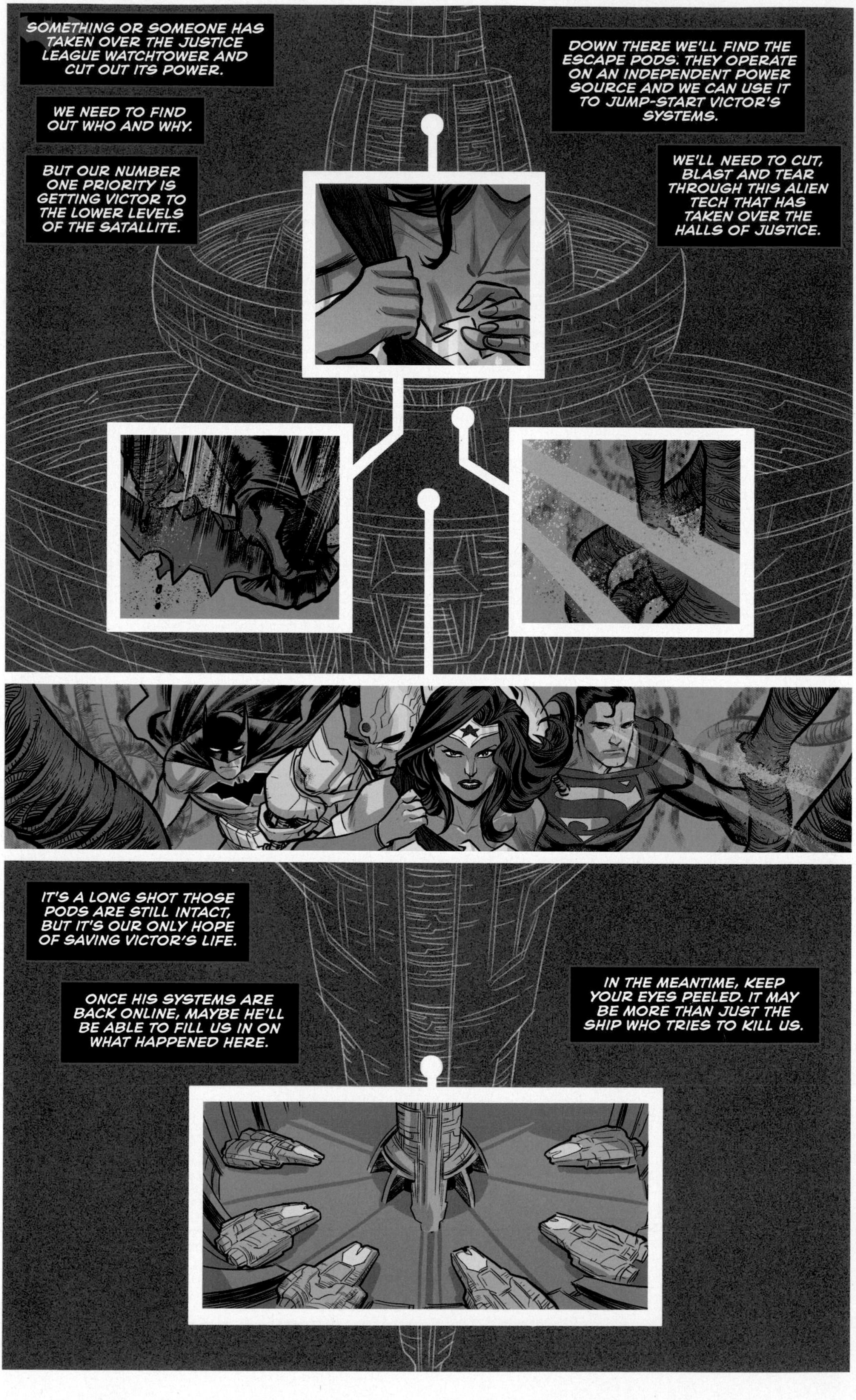
SOMETHING OR SOMEONE HAS TAKEN OVER THE JUSTICE LEAGUE WATCHTOWER AND CUT OUT ITS POWER.
WE NEED TO FIND OUT WHO AND WHY.
BUT OUR NUMBER ONE PRIORITY IS GETTING VICTOR TO THE LOWER LEVELS OF THE SATALLITE.
DOWN THERE WE'LL FIND THE ESCAPE PODS. THEY OPERATE ON AN INDEPENDENT POWER SOURCE AND WE CAN USE IT TO JUMP-START VICTOR'S SYSTEMS.
WE'LL NEED TO CUT, BLAST AND TEAR THROUGH THIS ALIEN TECH THAT HAS TAKEN OVER THE HALLS OF JUSTICE.
IT'S A LONG SHOT THOSE PODS ARE STILL INTACT, BUT IT'S OUR ONLY HOPE OF SAVING VICTOR'S LIFE.
ONCE HIS SYSTEMS ARE BACK ONLINE, MAYBE HE'LL BE ABLE TO FILL US IN ON WHAT HAPPENED HERE.
IN THE MEANTIME, KEEP YOUR EYES PEELED. IT MAY BE MORE THAN JUST THE SHIP WHO TRIES TO KILL US.

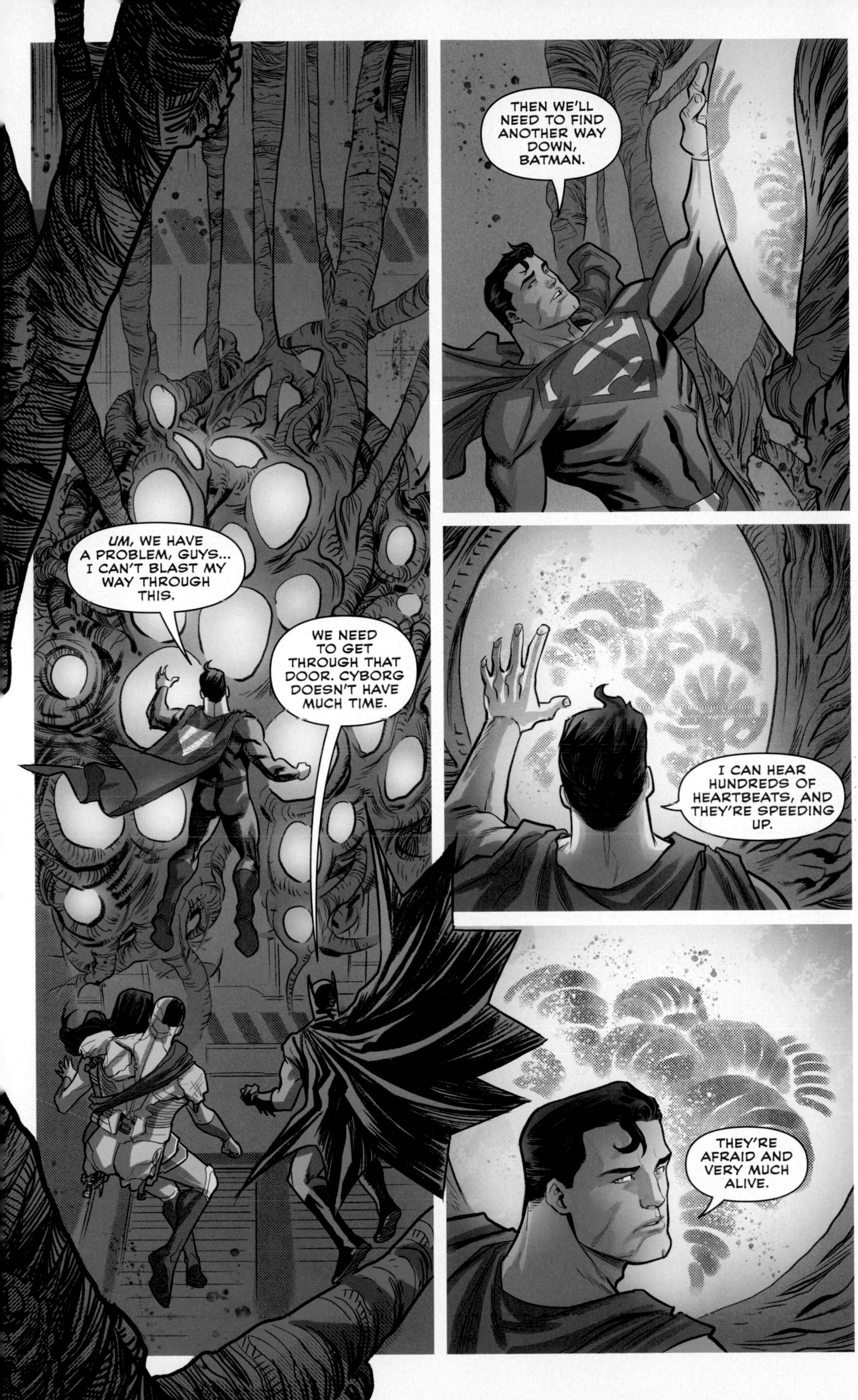
UM, WE HAVE A PROBLEM, GUYS... I CAN'T BLAST MY WAY THROUGH THIS.
WE NEED TO GET THROUGH THAT DOOR. CYBORG DOESN'T HAVE MUCH TIME.
THEN WE'LL NEED TO FIND ANOTHER WAY DOWN, BATMAN.
I CAN HEAR HUNDREDS OF HEARTBEATS, AND THEY'RE SPEEDING UP.
THEY'RE AFRAID AND VERY MUCH ALIVE.

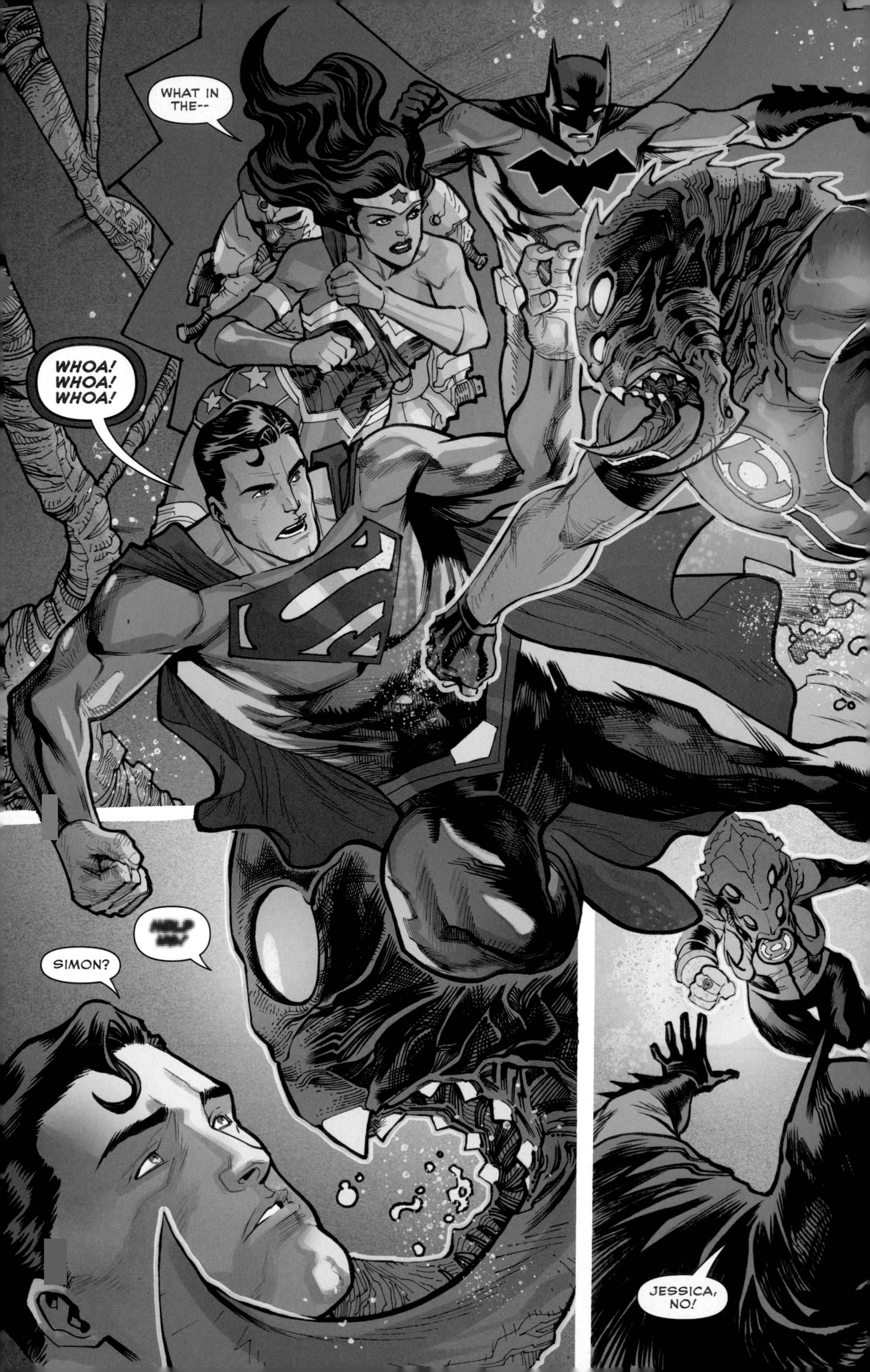
WHAT IN THE--
WHOA! WHOA! WHOA!
SIMON?
JESSICA, NO!

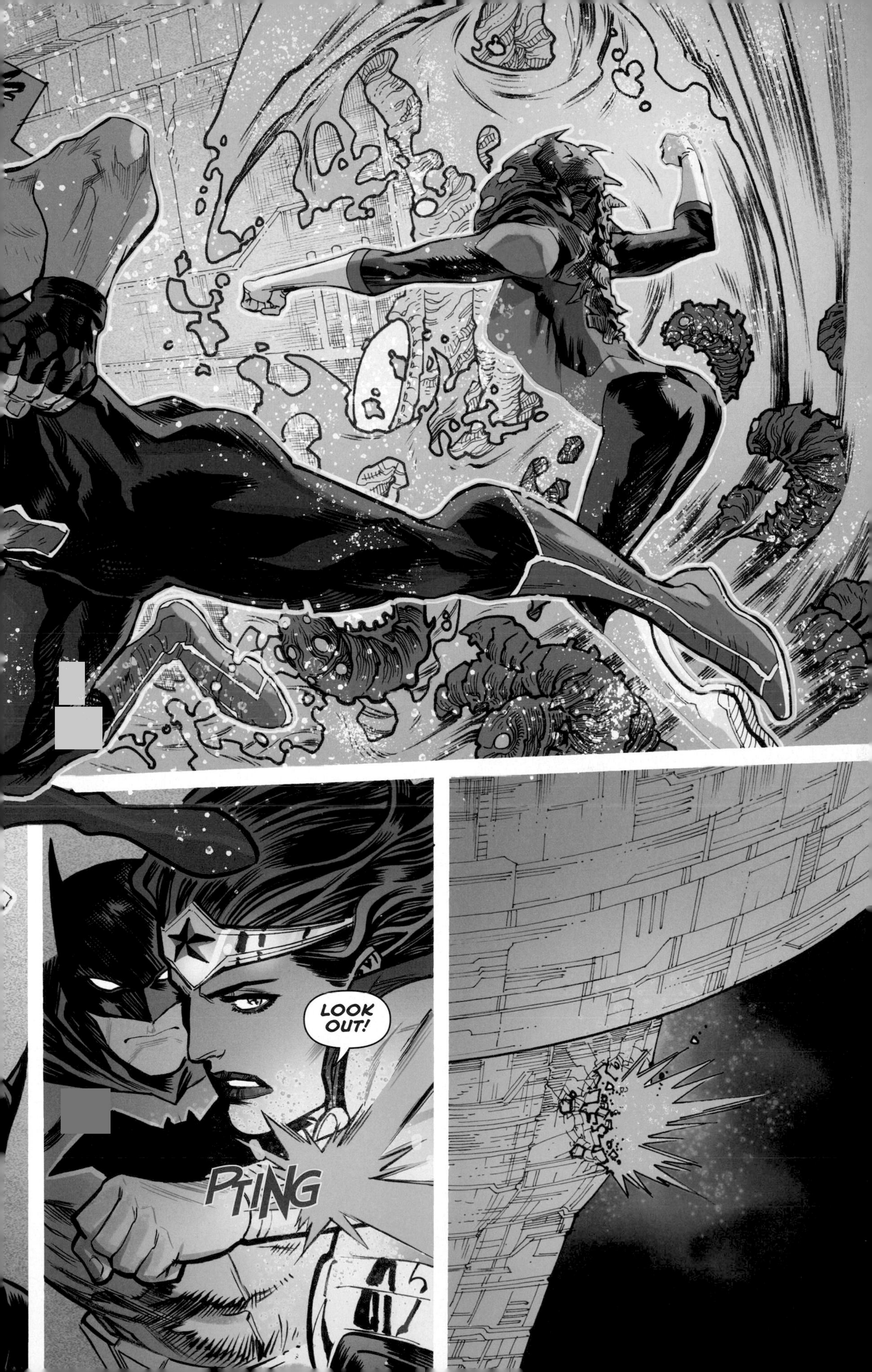
LOOK OUT!
PTING

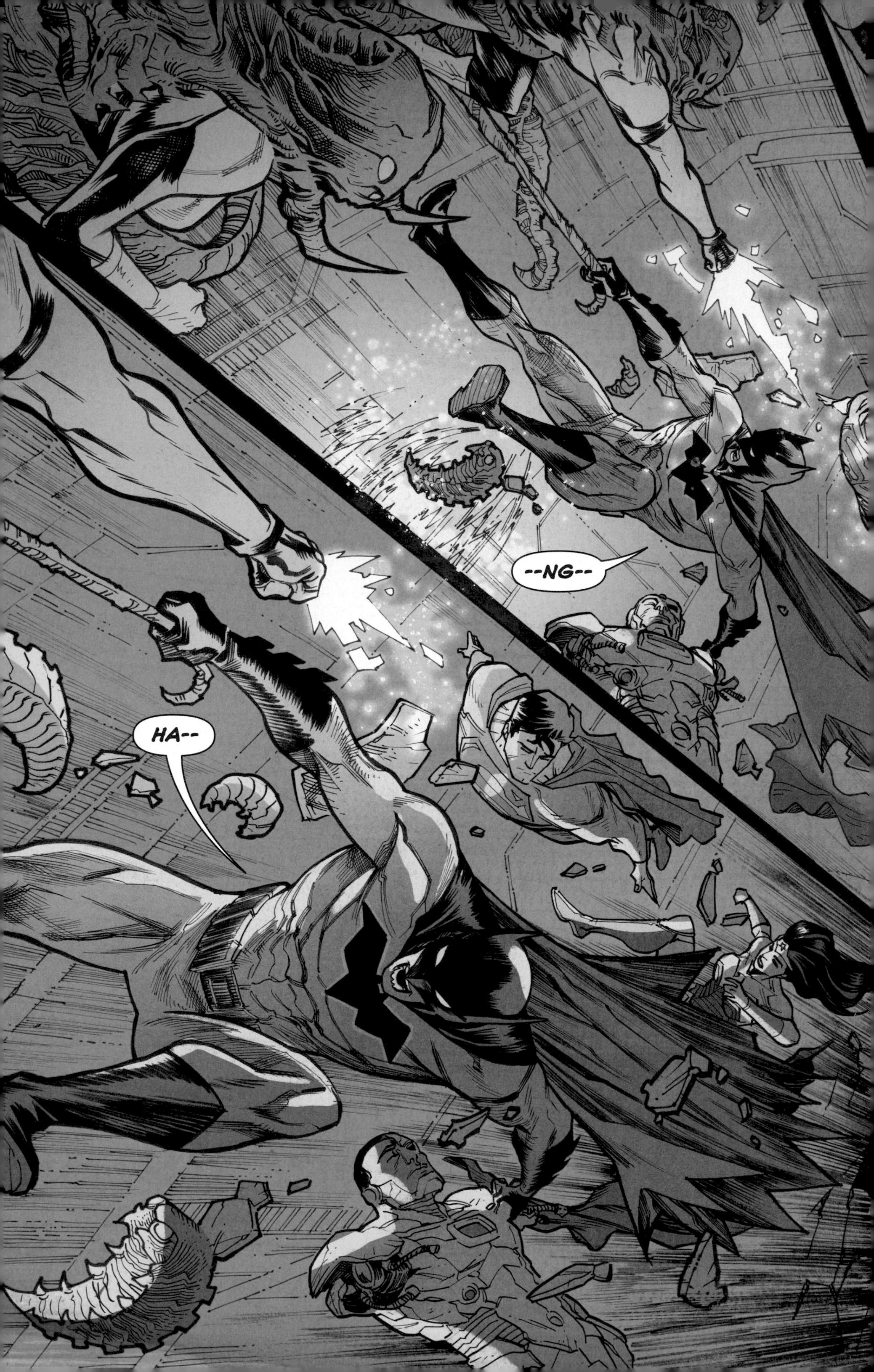
--NG--
HA--

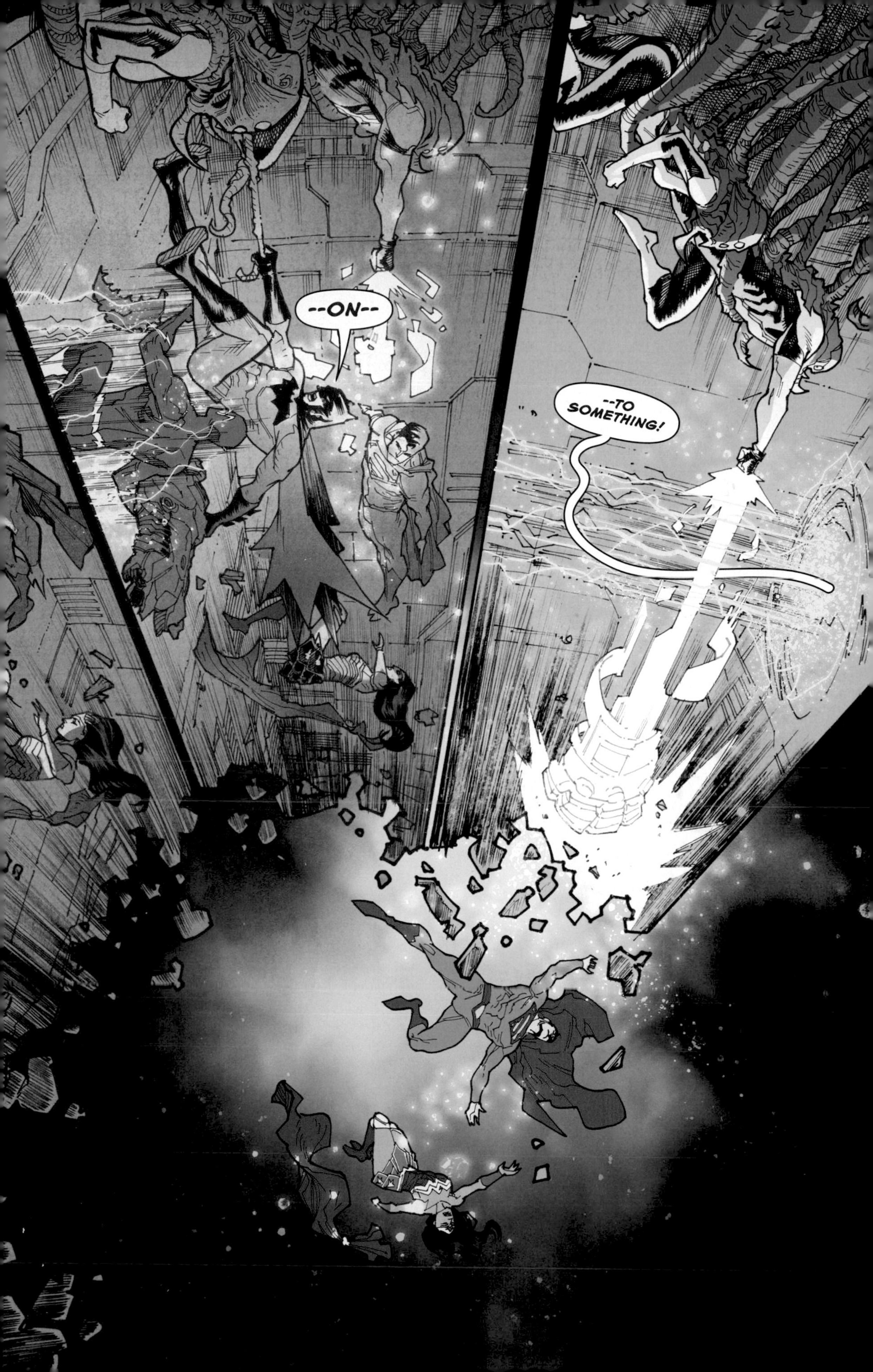
--ON--
--TO SOMETHING!

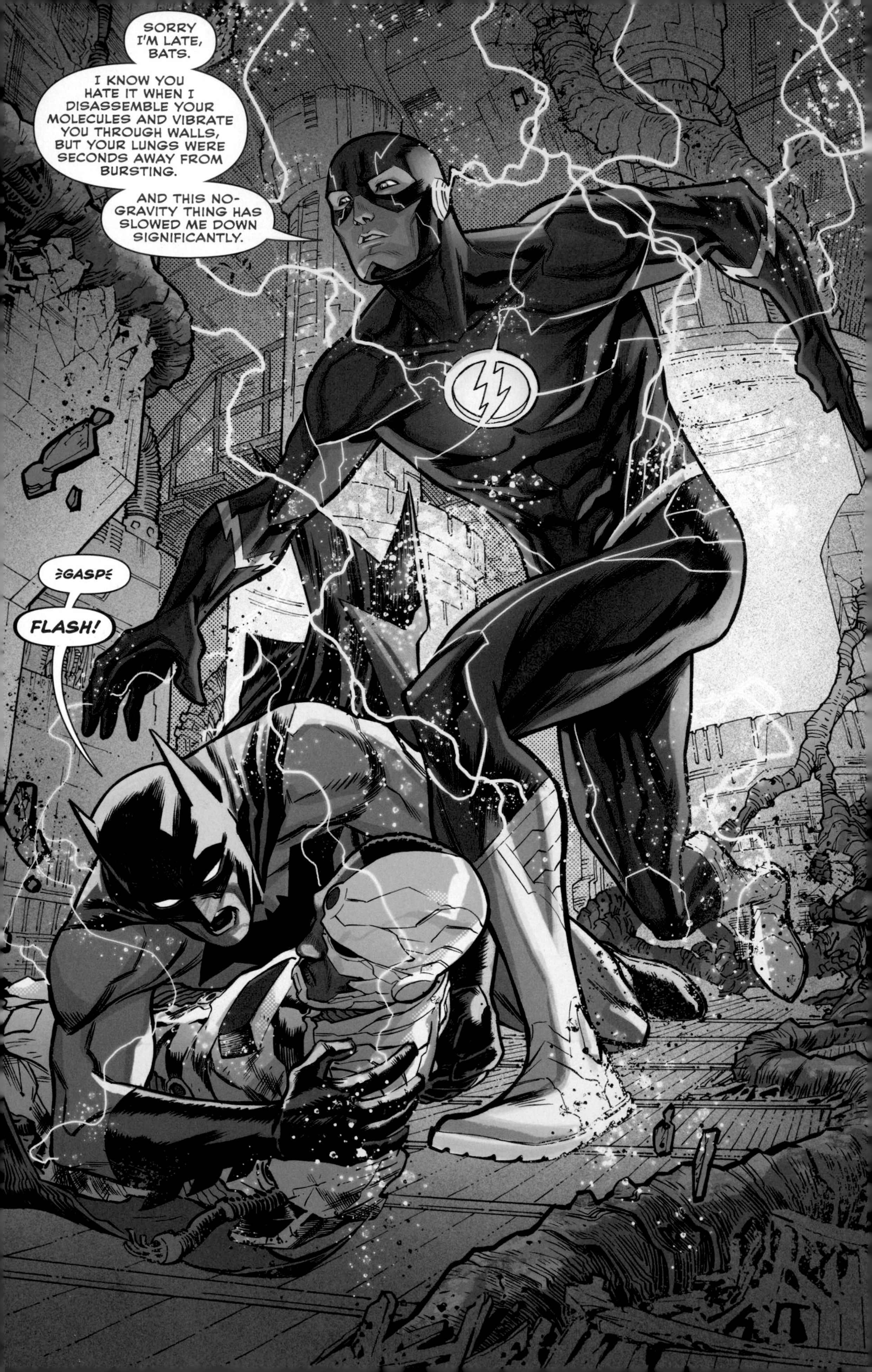
SORRY I'M LATE, BATS.
I KNOW YOU HATE IT WHEN I DISASSEMBLE YOUR MOLECULES AND VIBRATE YOU THROUGH WALLS, BUT YOUR LUNGS WERE SECONDS AWAY FROM BURSTING.
AND THIS NO-GRAVITY THING HAS SLOWED ME DOWN SIGNIFICANTLY.
GASP
FLASH!

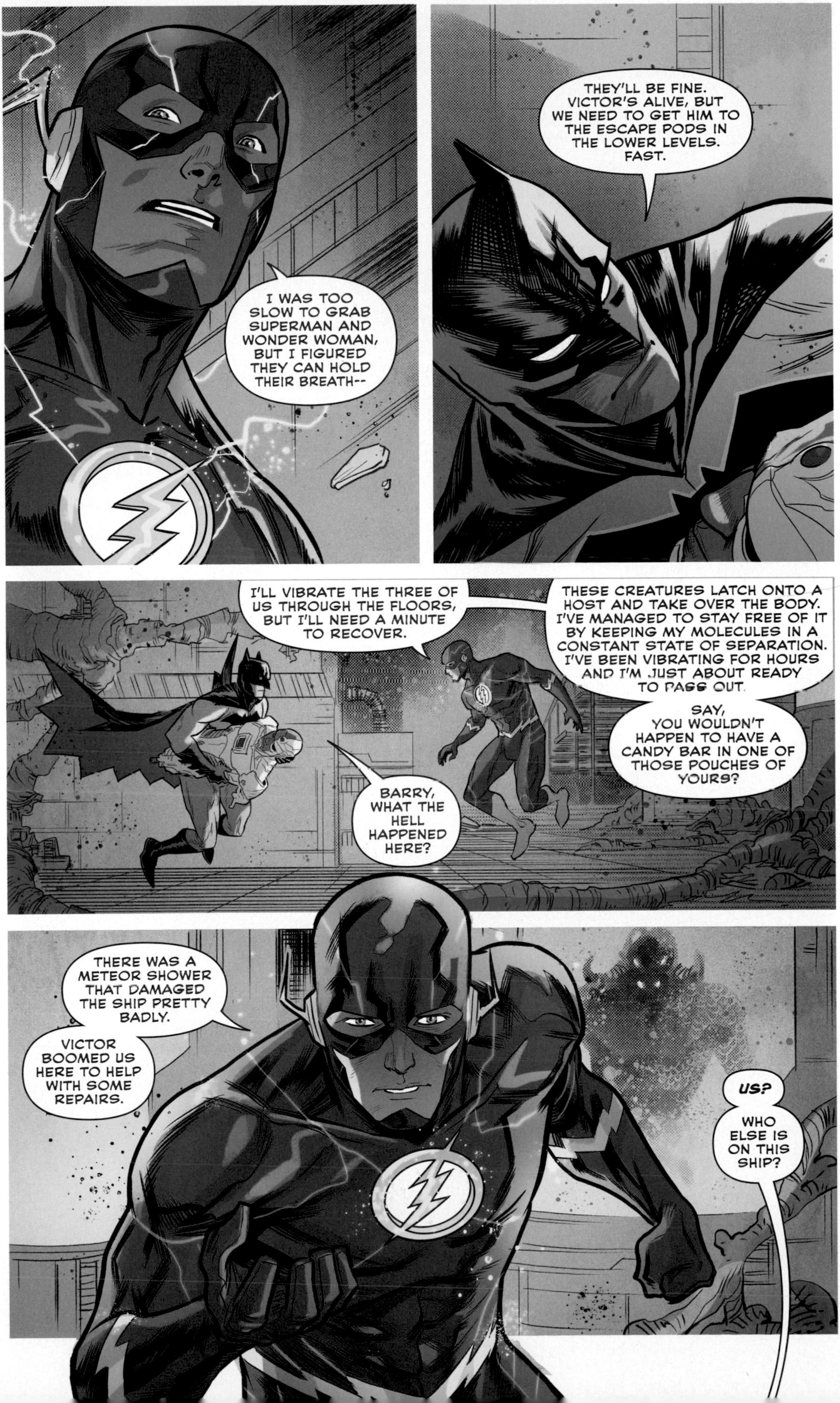
I WAS TOO SLOW TO GRAB SUPERMAN AND WONDER WOMAN, BUT I FIGURED THEY CAN HOLD THEIR BREATH--
THEY'LL BE FINE. VICTOR'S ALIVE, BUT WE NEED TO GET HIM TO THE ESCAPE PODS IN THE LOWER LEVELS. FAST.
I'LL VIBRATE THE THREE OF US THROUGH THE FLOORS, BUT I'LL NEED A MINUTE TO RECOVER.
BARRY, WHAT THE HELL HAPPENED HERE?
THESE CREATURES LATCH ONTO A HOST AND TAKE OVER THE BODY. I'VE MANAGED TO STAY FREE OF IT BY KEEPING MY MOLECULES IN A CONSTANT STATE OF SEPARATION. I'VE BEEN VIBRATING FOR HOURS AND I'M JUST ABOUT READY TO PASS OUT.
SAY, YOU WOULDN'T HAPPEN TO HAVE A CANDY BAR IN ONE OF THOSE POUCHES OF YOURS?
THERE WAS A METEOR SHOWER THAT DAMAGED THE SHIP PRETTY BADLY.
VICTOR BOOMED US HERE TO HELP WITH SOME REPAIRS.
US?
WHO ELSE IS ON THIS SHIP?

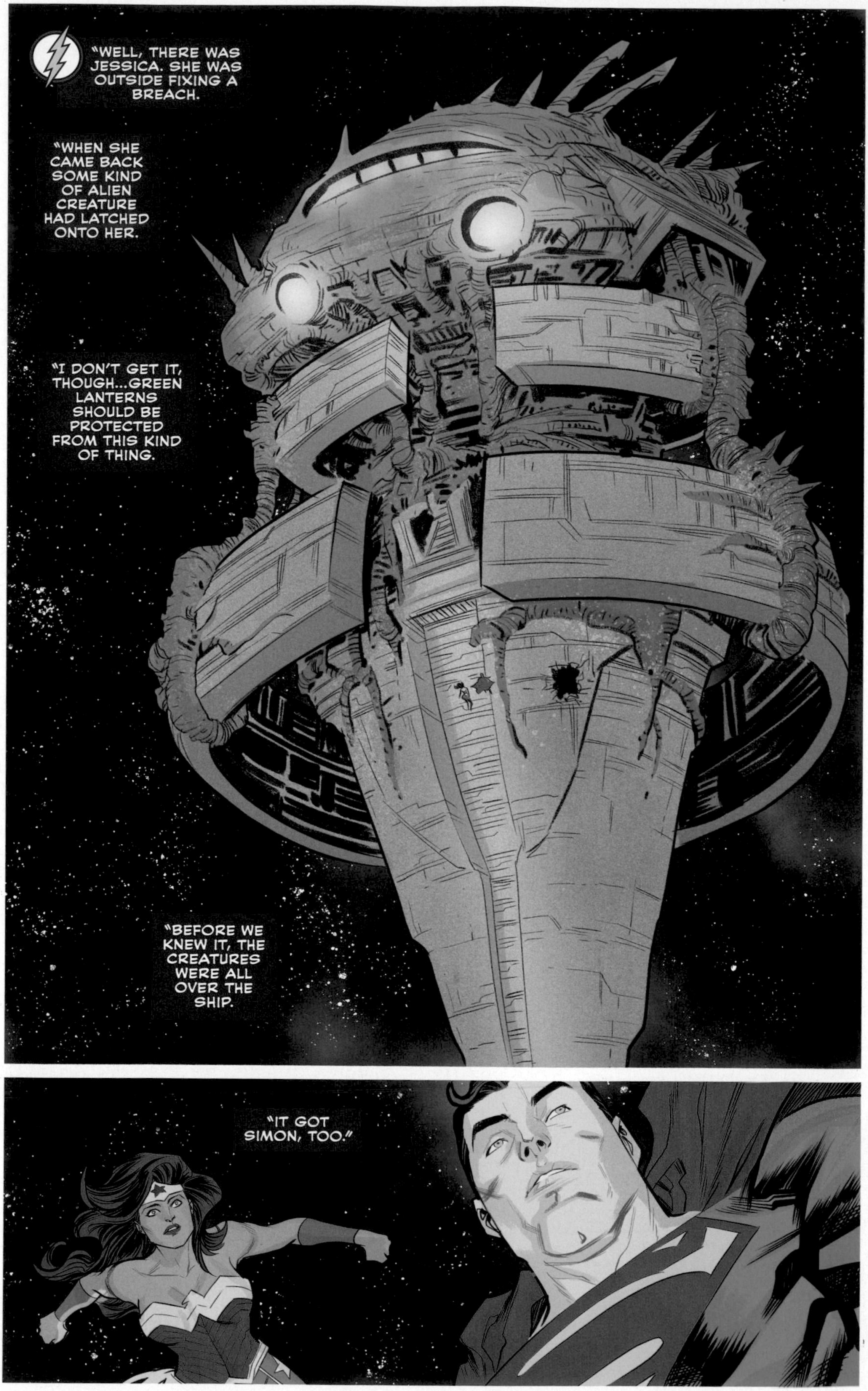
"WELL, THERE WAS JESSICA. SHE WAS OUTSIDE FIXING A BREACH.
"WHEN SHE CAME BACK SOME KIND OF ALIEN CREATURE HAD LATCHED ONTO HER.
"I DON'T GET IT, THOUGH...GREEN LANTERNS SHOULD BE PROTECTED FROM THIS KIND OF THING.
"BEFORE WE KNEW IT, THE CREATURES WERE ALL OVER THE SHIP.
"IT GOT SIMON, TOO."

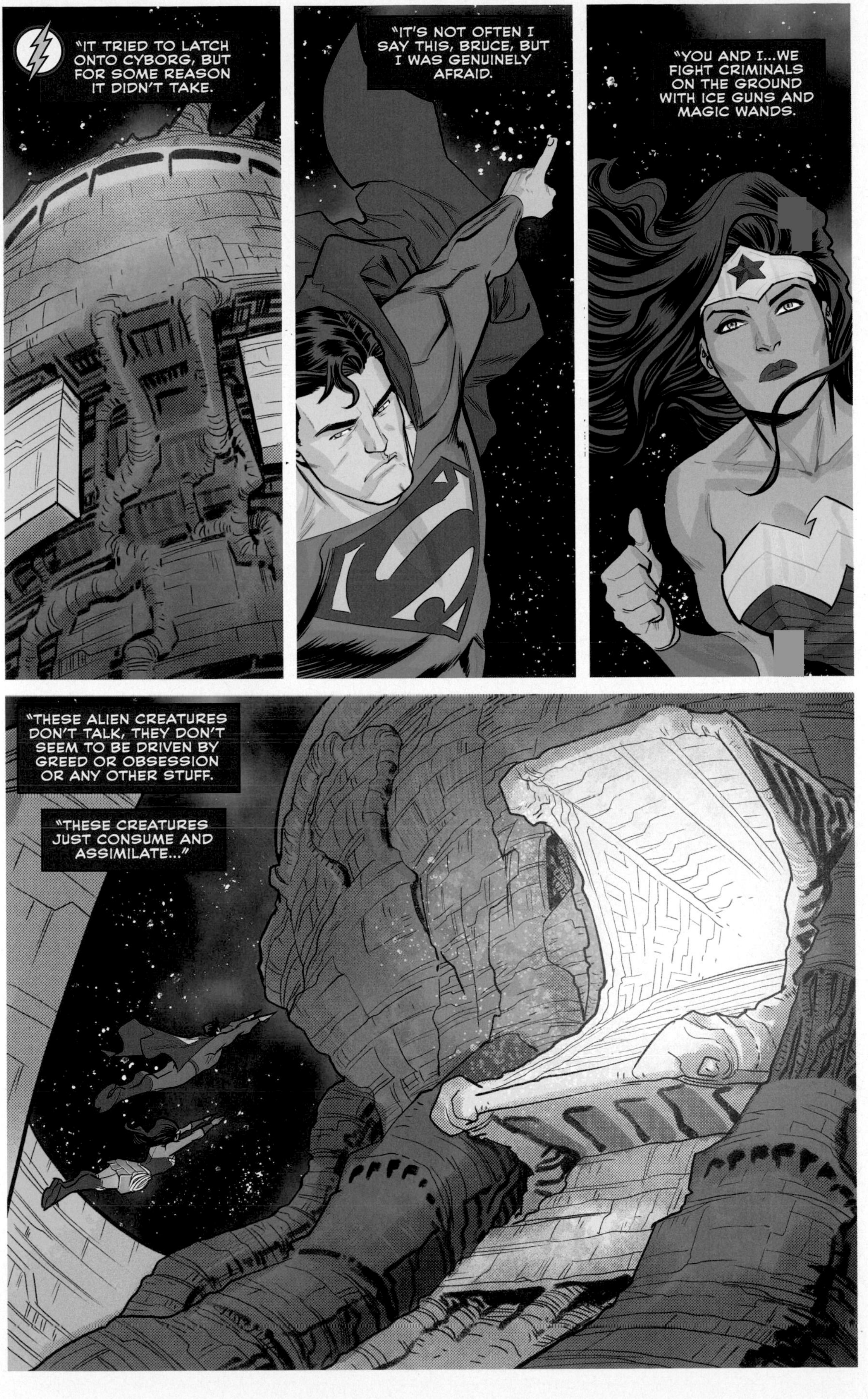
"IT TRIED TO LATCH ONTO CYBORG, BUT FOR SOME REASON IT DIDN'T TAKE.
"IT'S NOT OFTEN I SAY THIS, BRUCE, BUT I WAS GENUINELY AFRAID.
"YOU AND I...WE FIGHT CRIMINALS ON THE GROUND WITH ICE GUNS AND MAGIC WANDS.
"THESE ALIEN CREATURES DON'T TALK, THEY DON'T SEEM TO BE DRIVEN BY GREED OR OBSESSION OR ANY OTHER STUFF.
"THESE CREATURES JUST CONSUME AND ASSIMILATE..."

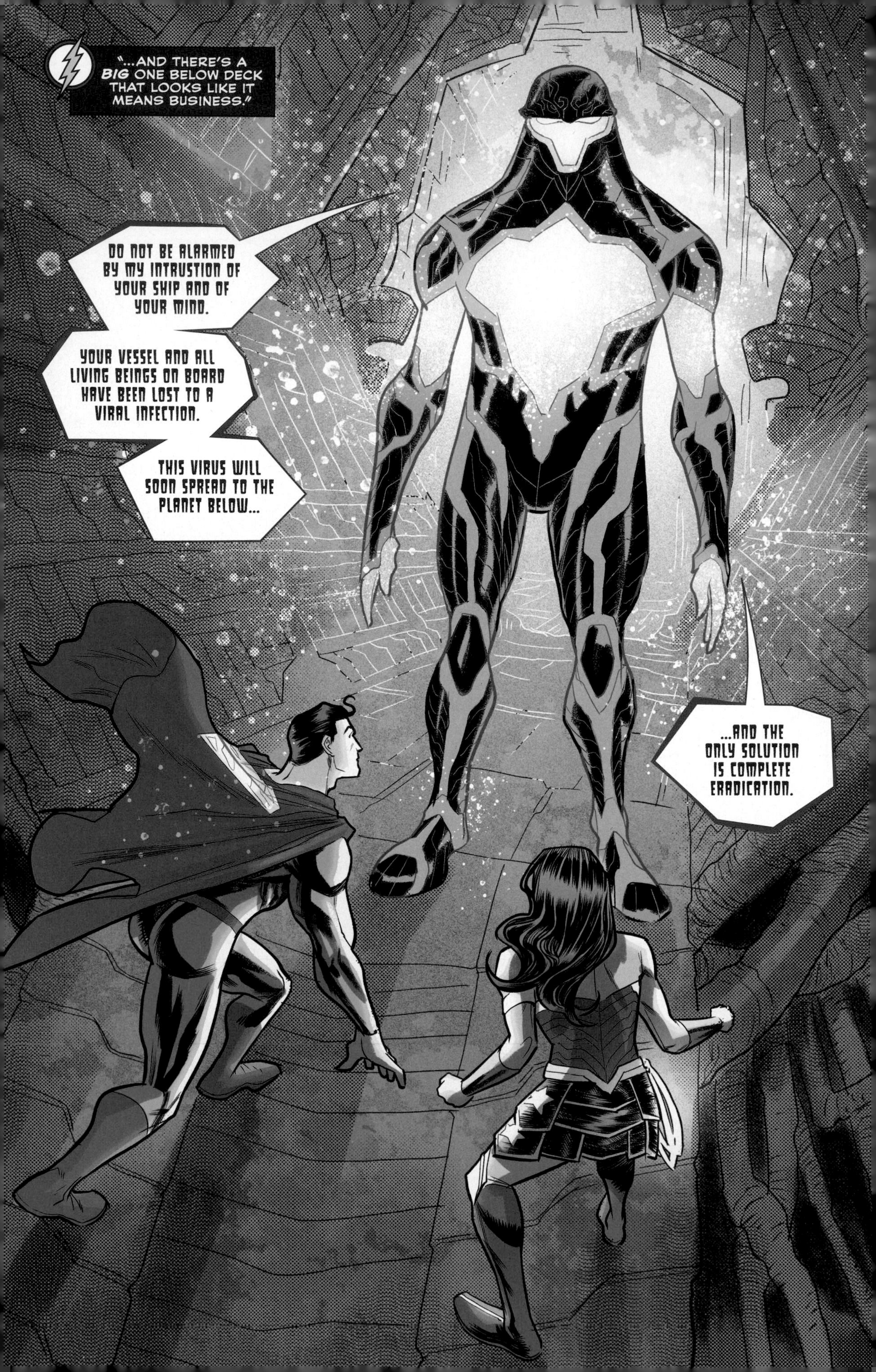

"...AND THERE'S A BIG ONE BELOW DECK THAT LOOKS LIKE IT MEANS BUSINESS."
DO NOT BE ALARMED BY MY INTRUSTION OF YOUR SHIP AND OF YOUR MIND.
YOUR VESSEL AND ALL LIVING BEINGS ON BOARD HAVE BEEN LOST TO A VIRAL INFECTION.
THIS VIRUS WILL SOON SPREAD TO THE PLANET BELOW...
...AND THE ONLY SOLUTION IS COMPLETE ERADICATION.

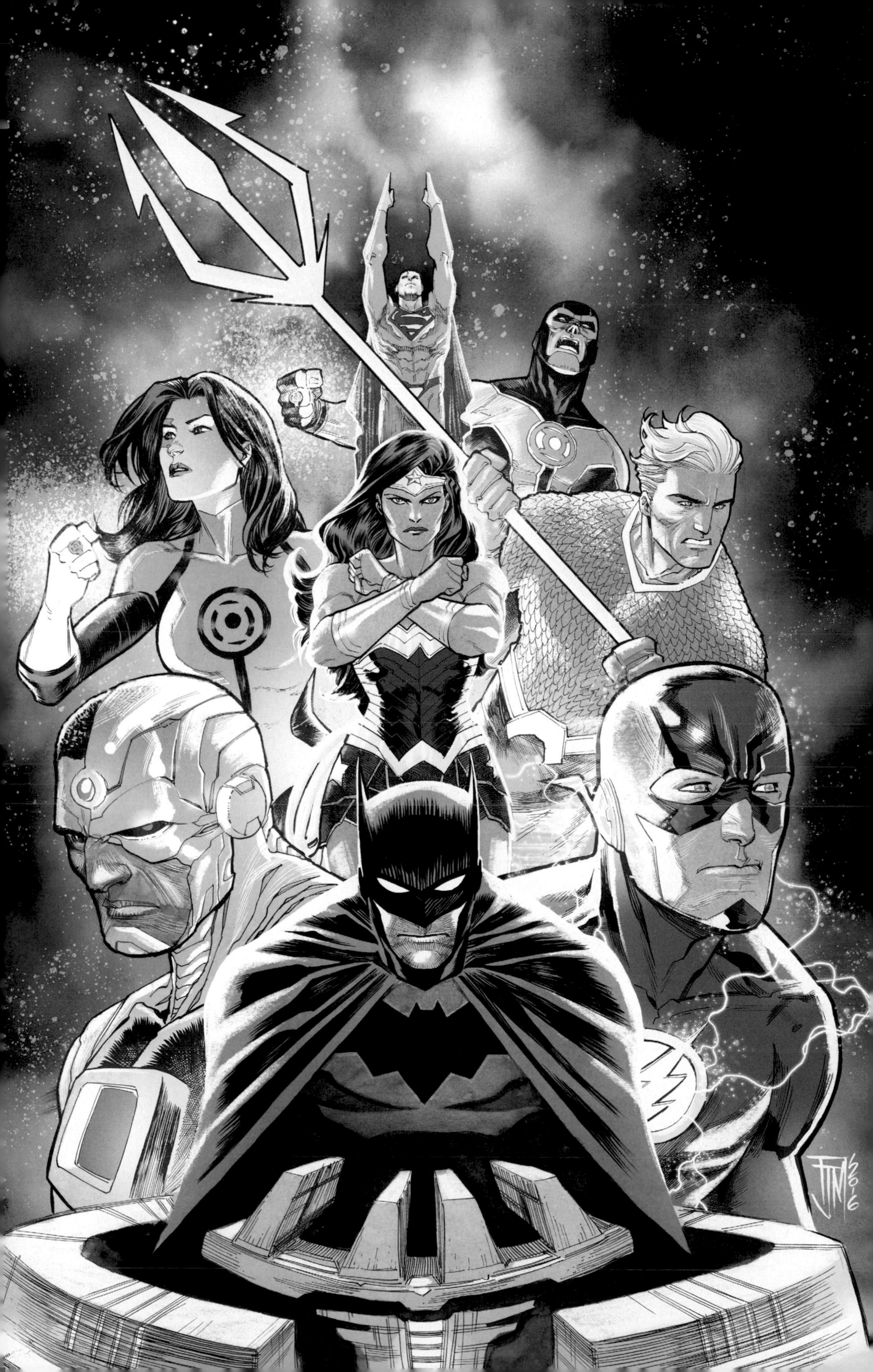

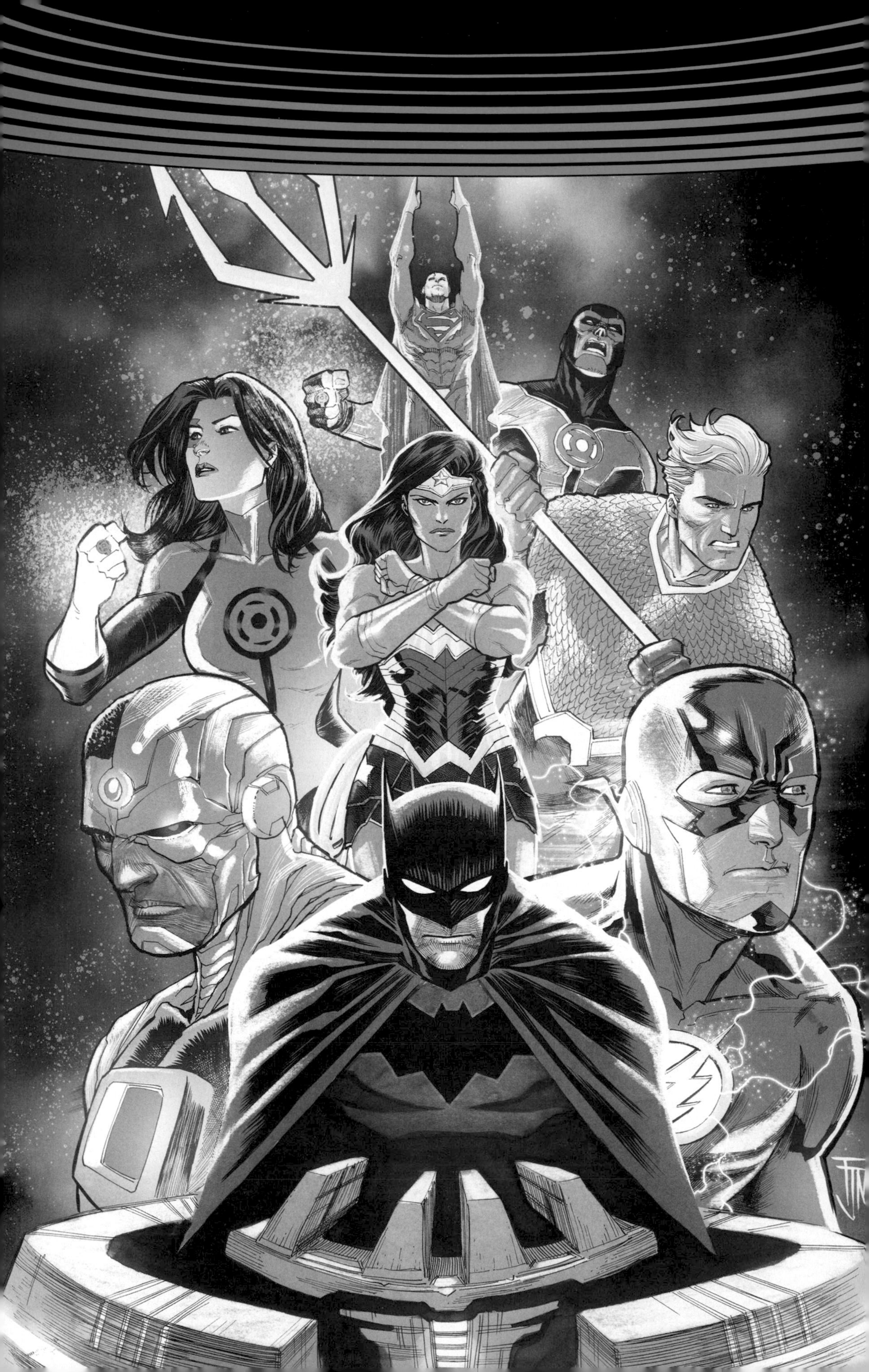

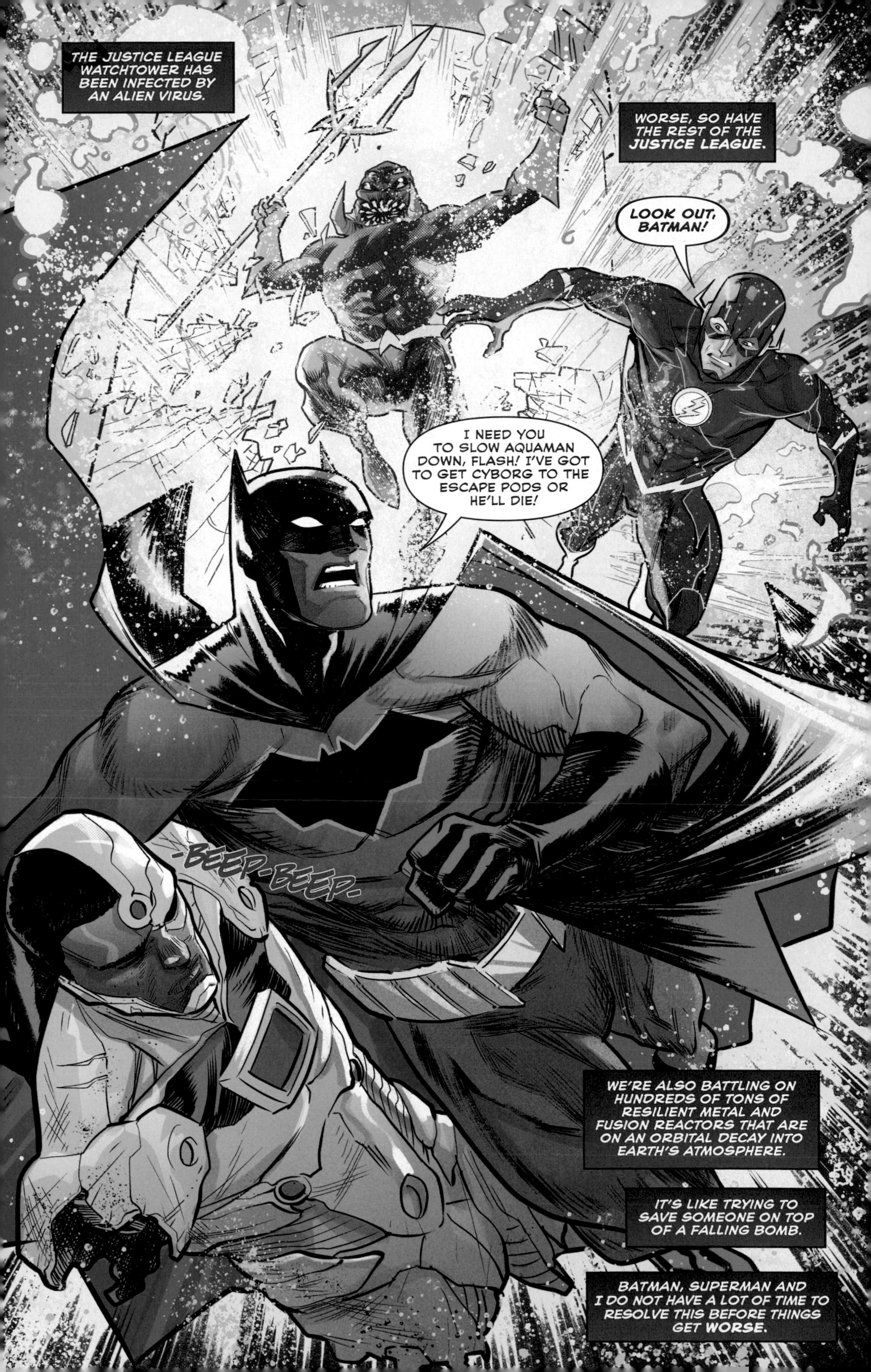
THE JUSTICE LEAGUE WATCHTOWER HAS BEEN INFECTED BY AN ALIEN VIRUS.
WORSE, SO HAVE THE REST OF THE JUSTICE LEAGUE.
LOOK OUT, BATMAN!
I NEED YOU TO SLOW AQUAMAN DOWN, FLASH! I'VE GOT TO GET CYBORG TO THE ESCAPE PODS OR HE'LL DIE!
-BEEP-BEEP-
WE'RE ALSO BATTLING ON HUNDREDS OF TONS OF RESILIENT METAL AND FUSION REACTORS THAT ARE ON AN ORBITAL DECAY INTO EARTH'S ATMOSPHERE.
IT'S LIKE TRYING TO SAVE SOMEONE ON TOP OF A FALLING BOMB.
BATMAN, SUPERMAN AND I DO NOT HAVE A LOT OF TIME TO RESOLVE THIS BEFORE THINGS GET WORSE.

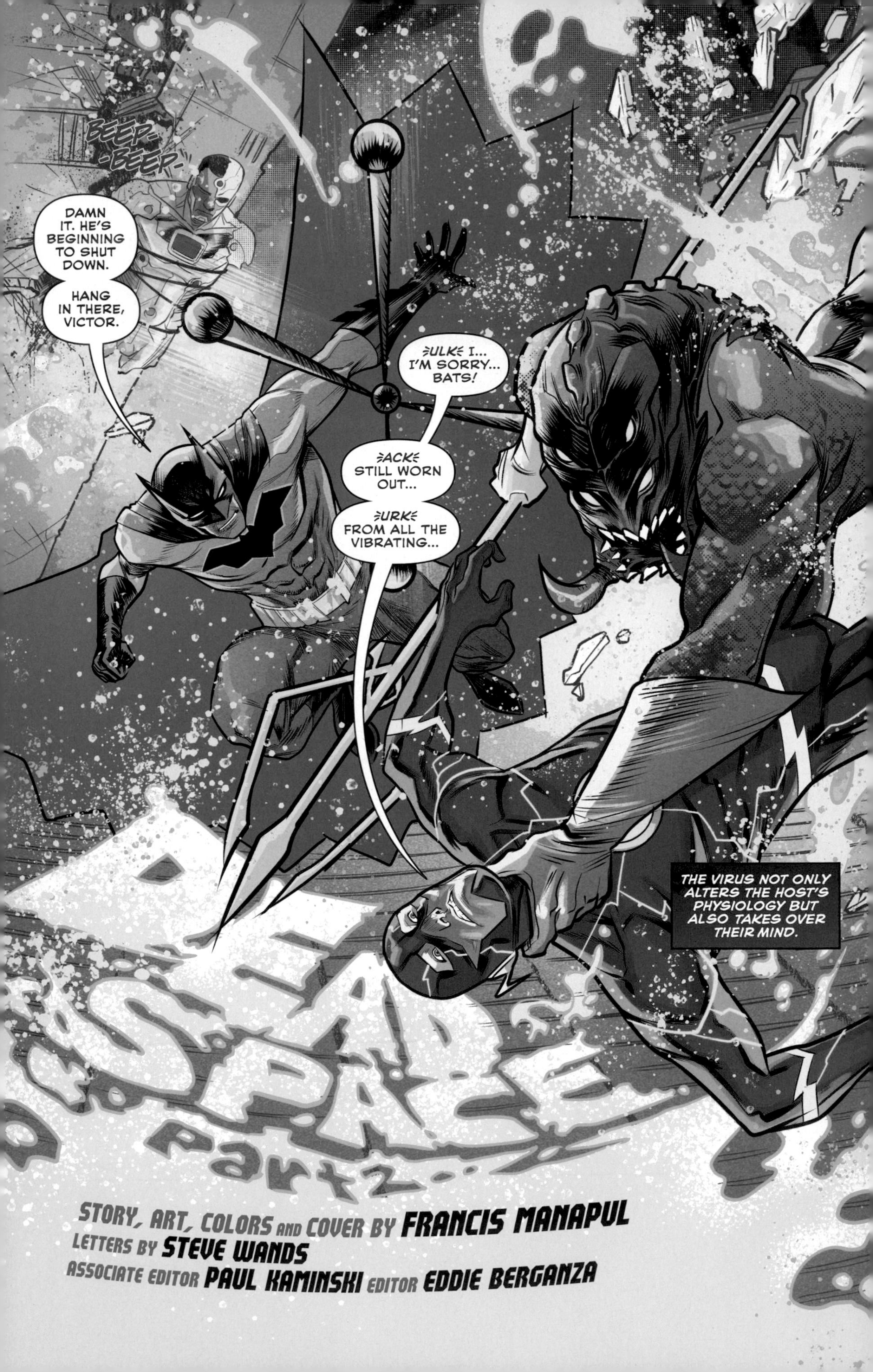
BEEP-BEEP-
DAMN IT. HE'S BEGINNING TO SHUT DOWN.
HANG IN THERE, VICTOR.
ULK I... I'M SORRY... BATS!
ACK STILL WORN OUT...
URK FROM ALL THE VIBRATING...
THE VIRUS NOT ONLY ALTERS THE HOST'S PHYSIOLOGY BUT ALSO TAKES OVER THEIR MIND.
part 2
STORY, ART, COLORS AND COVER BY FRANCIS MANAPUL
LETTERS BY STEVE WANDS
ASSOCIATE EDITOR PAUL KAMINSKI EDITOR EDDIE BERGANZA

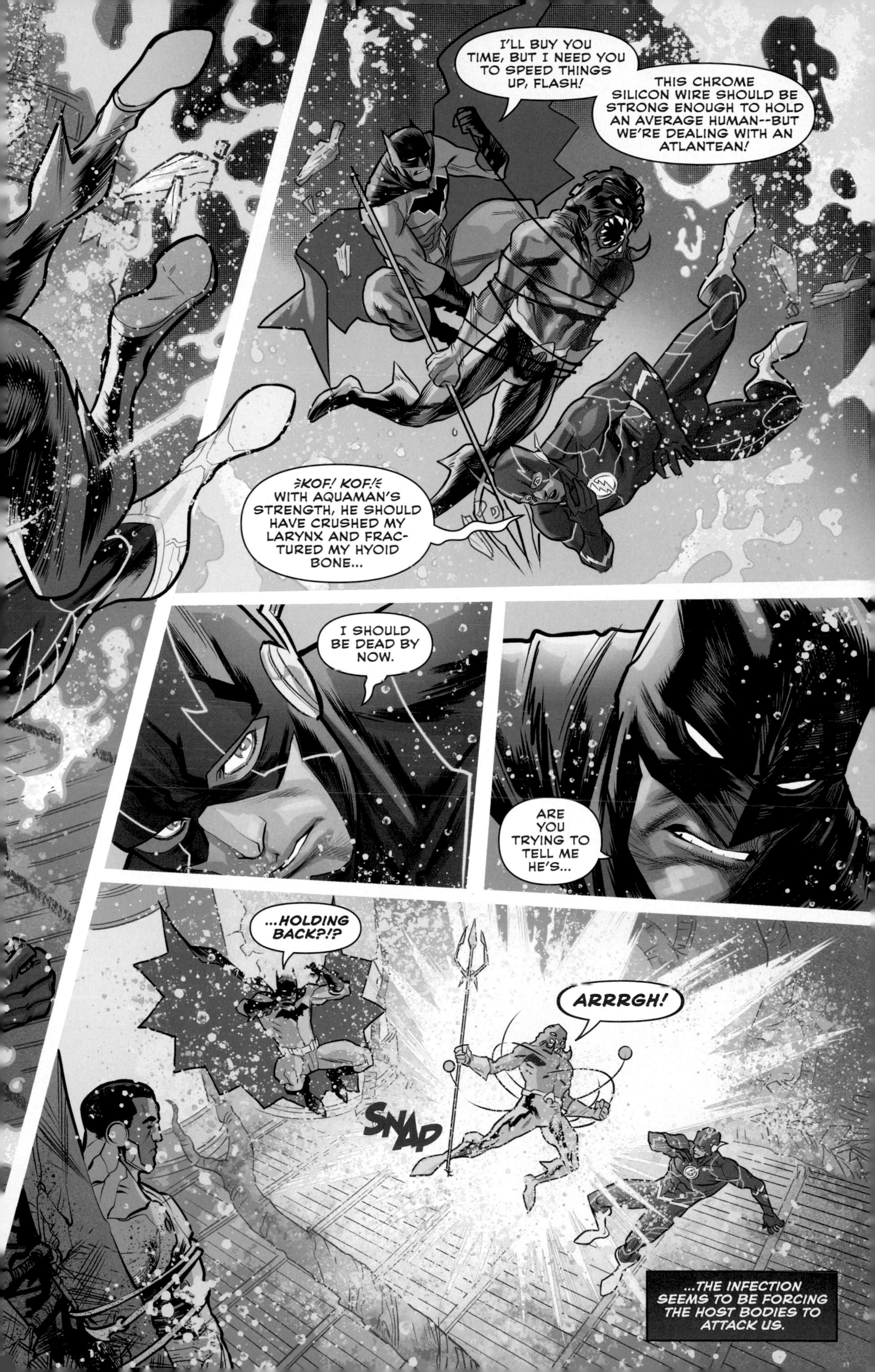
I'LL BUY YOU TIME, BUT I NEED YOU TO SPEED THINGS UP, FLASH!
THIS CHROME SILICON WIRE SHOULD BE STRONG ENOUGH TO HOLD AN AVERAGE HUMAN--BUT WE'RE DEALING WITH AN ATLANTEAN!
KOF! KOF! WITH AQUAMAN'S STRENGTH, HE SHOULD HAVE CRUSHED MY LARYNX AND FRACTURED MY HYOID BONE...
I SHOULD BE DEAD BY NOW.
ARE YOU TRYING TO TELL ME HE'S...
...HOLDING BACK?!?
ARRRGH!
SNAP
...THE INFECTION SEEMS TO BE FORCING THE HOST BODIES TO ATTACK US.

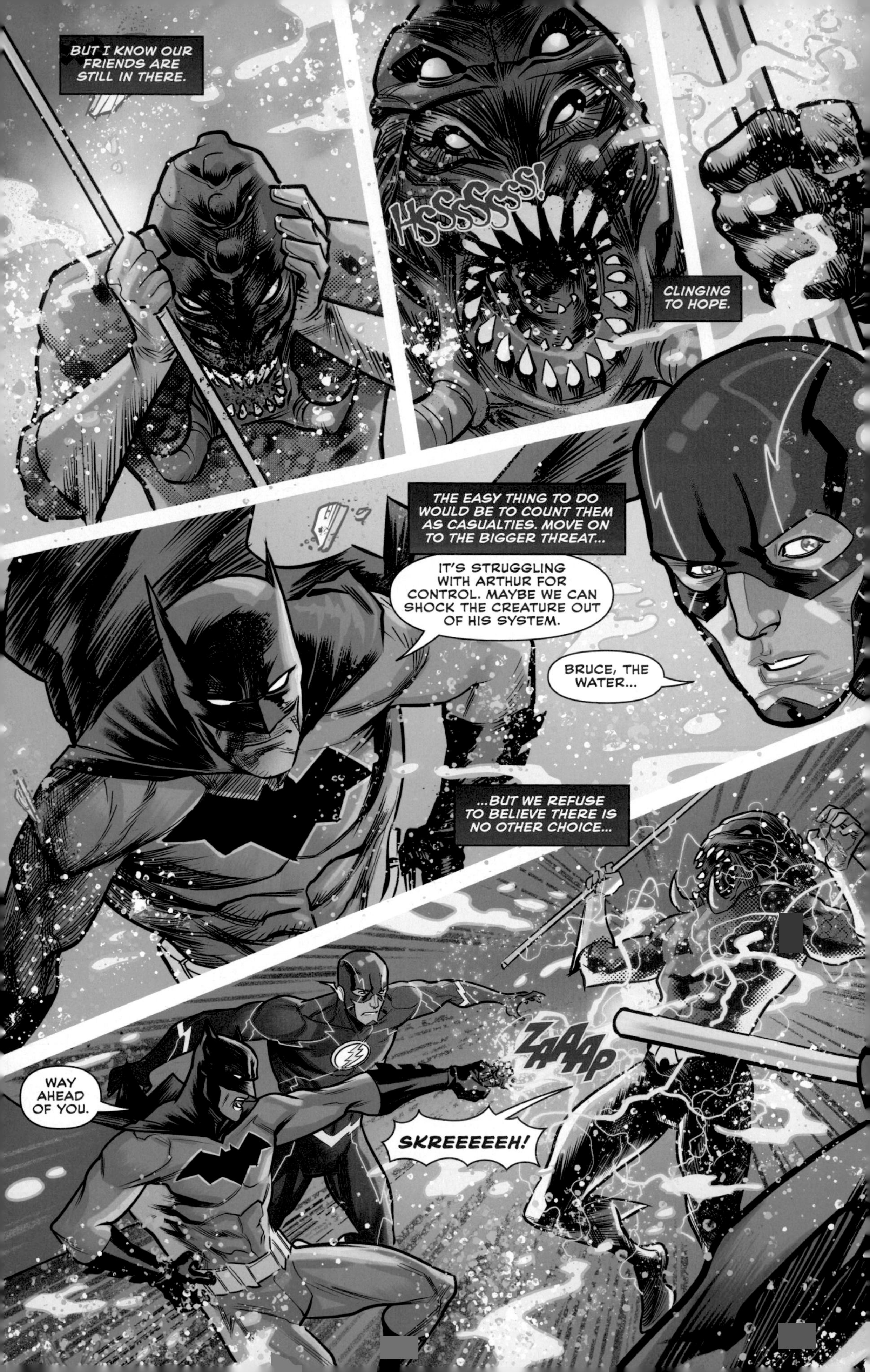
BUT I KNOW OUR FRIENDS ARE STILL IN THERE.
HSSSSSS!
CLINGING TO HOPE.
THE EASY THING TO DO WOULD BE TO COUNT THEM AS CASUALTIES. MOVE ON TO THE BIGGER THREAT...
IT'S STRUGGLING WITH ARTHUR FOR CONTROL. MAYBE WE CAN SHOCK THE CREATURE OUT OF HIS SYSTEM.
BRUCE, THE WATER...
...BUT WE REFUSE TO BELIEVE THERE IS NO OTHER CHOICE...
WAY AHEAD OF YOU.
ZAAAP
SKREEEEEH!

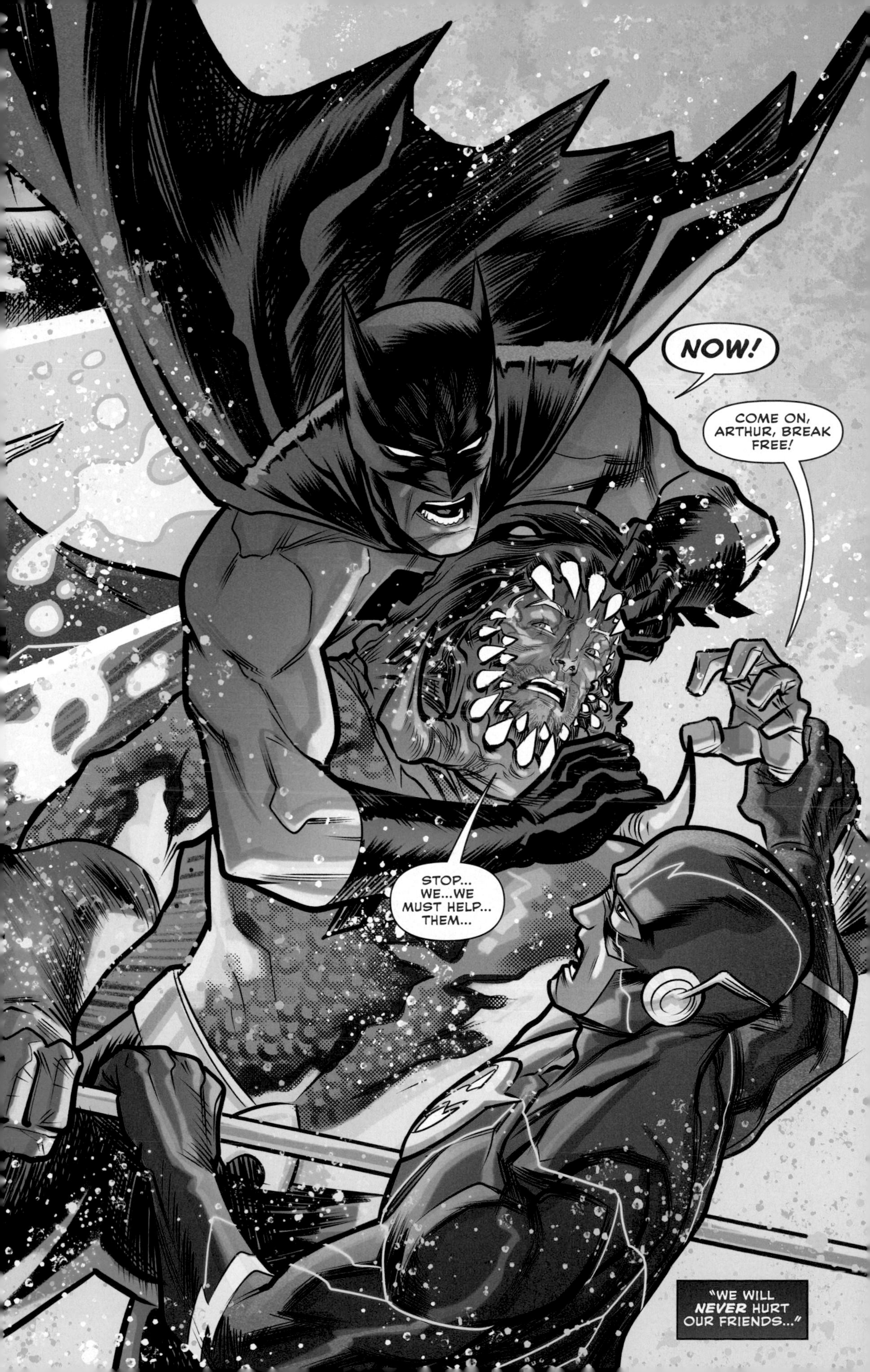
NOW!
COME ON, ARTHUR, BREAK FREE!
STOP... WE...WE MUST HELP... THEM...
"WE WILL NEVER HURT OUR FRIENDS..."

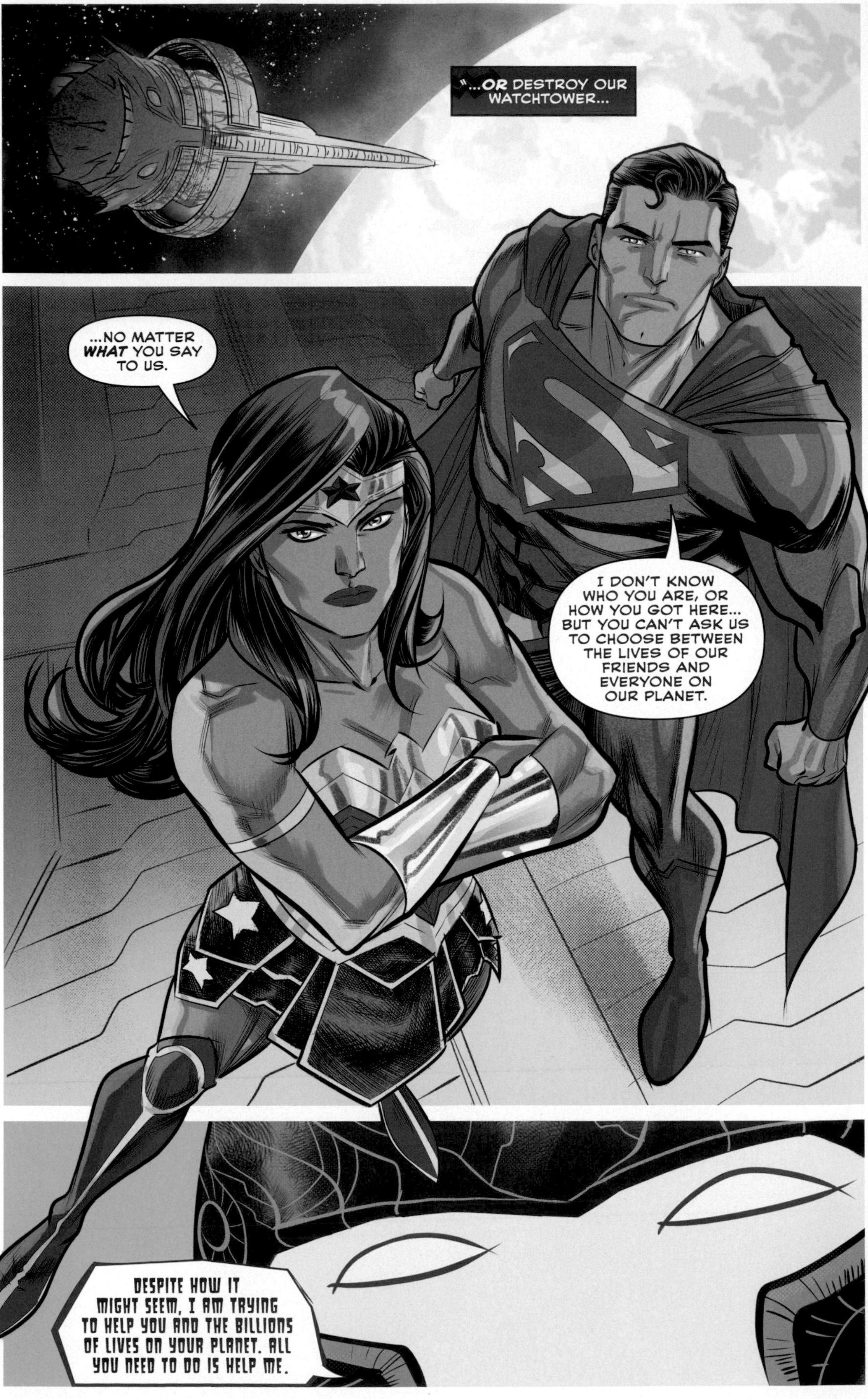
"...OR DESTROY OUR WATCHTOWER...
...NO MATTER WHAT YOU SAY TO US.
I DON'T KNOW WHO YOU ARE, OR HOW YOU GOT HERE... BUT YOU CAN'T ASK US TO CHOOSE BETWEEN THE LIVES OF OUR FRIENDS AND EVERYONE ON OUR PLANET.
DESPITE HOW IT MIGHT SEEM, I AM TRYING TO HELP YOU AND THE BILLIONS OF LIVES ON YOUR PLANET. ALL YOU NEED TO DO IS HELP ME.

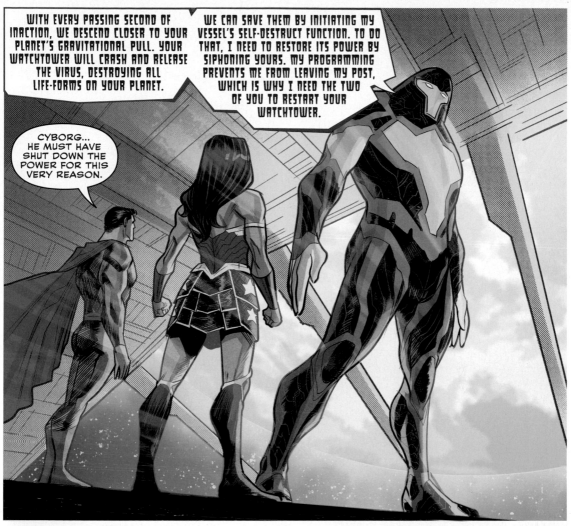

WITH EVERY PASSING SECOND OF INACTION, WE DESCEND CLOSER TO YOUR PLANET'S GRAVITATIONAL PULL. YOUR WATCHTOWER WILL CRASH AND RELEASE THE VIRUS, DESTROYING ALL LIFE-FORMS ON YOUR PLANET.

WE CAN SAVE THEM BY INITIATING MY VESSEL'S SELF-DESTRUCT FUNCTION. TO DO THAT, I NEED TO RESTORE ITS POWER BY SIPHONING YOURS. MY PROGRAMMING PREVENTS ME FROM LEAVING MY POST, WHICH IS WHY I NEED THE TWO OF YOU TO RESTART YOUR WATCHTOWER.

CYBORG... HE MUST HAVE SHUT DOWN THE POWER FOR THIS VERY REASON.

WE REJECT YOUR PROPOSAL, TRAVELER.

THERE IS ALWAYS ANOTHER WAY.

MAYBE WE CAN POWER UP THE WATCHTOWER AND STAY IN ORBIT WHILE WE FIGURE OUT WHAT TO--

NO! YOU ARE RUNNING OUT OF TIME.

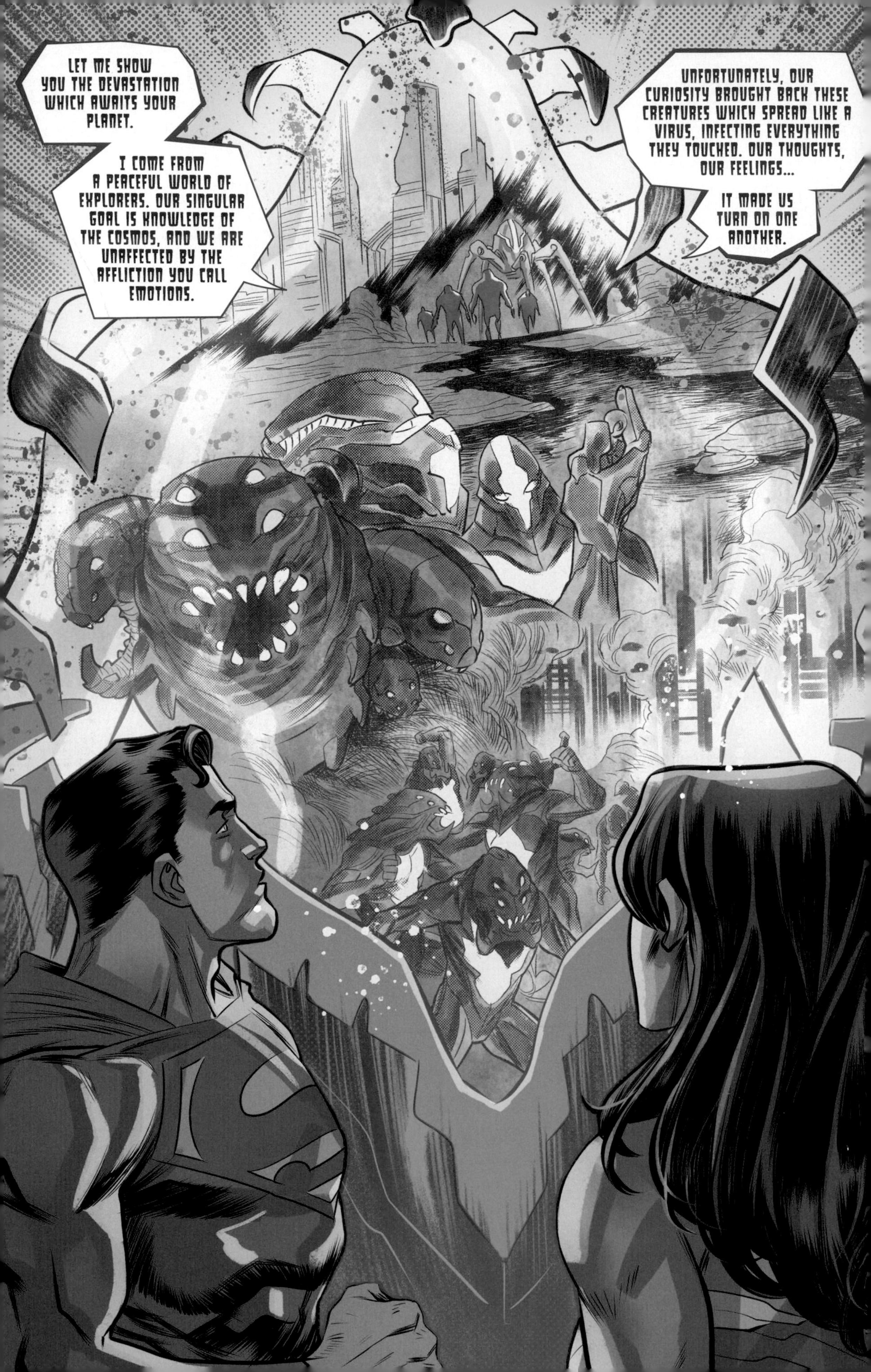
LET ME SHOW YOU THE DEVASTATION WHICH AWAITS YOUR PLANET.
I COME FROM A PEACEFUL WORLD OF EXPLORERS. OUR SINGULAR GOAL IS KNOWLEDGE OF THE COSMOS, AND WE ARE UNAFFECTED BY THE AFFLICTION YOU CALL EMOTIONS.
UNFORTUNATELY, OUR CURIOSITY BROUGHT BACK THESE CREATURES WHICH SPREAD LIKE A VIRUS, INFECTING EVERYTHING THEY TOUCHED. OUR THOUGHTS, OUR FEELINGS...
IT MADE US TURN ON ONE ANOTHER.

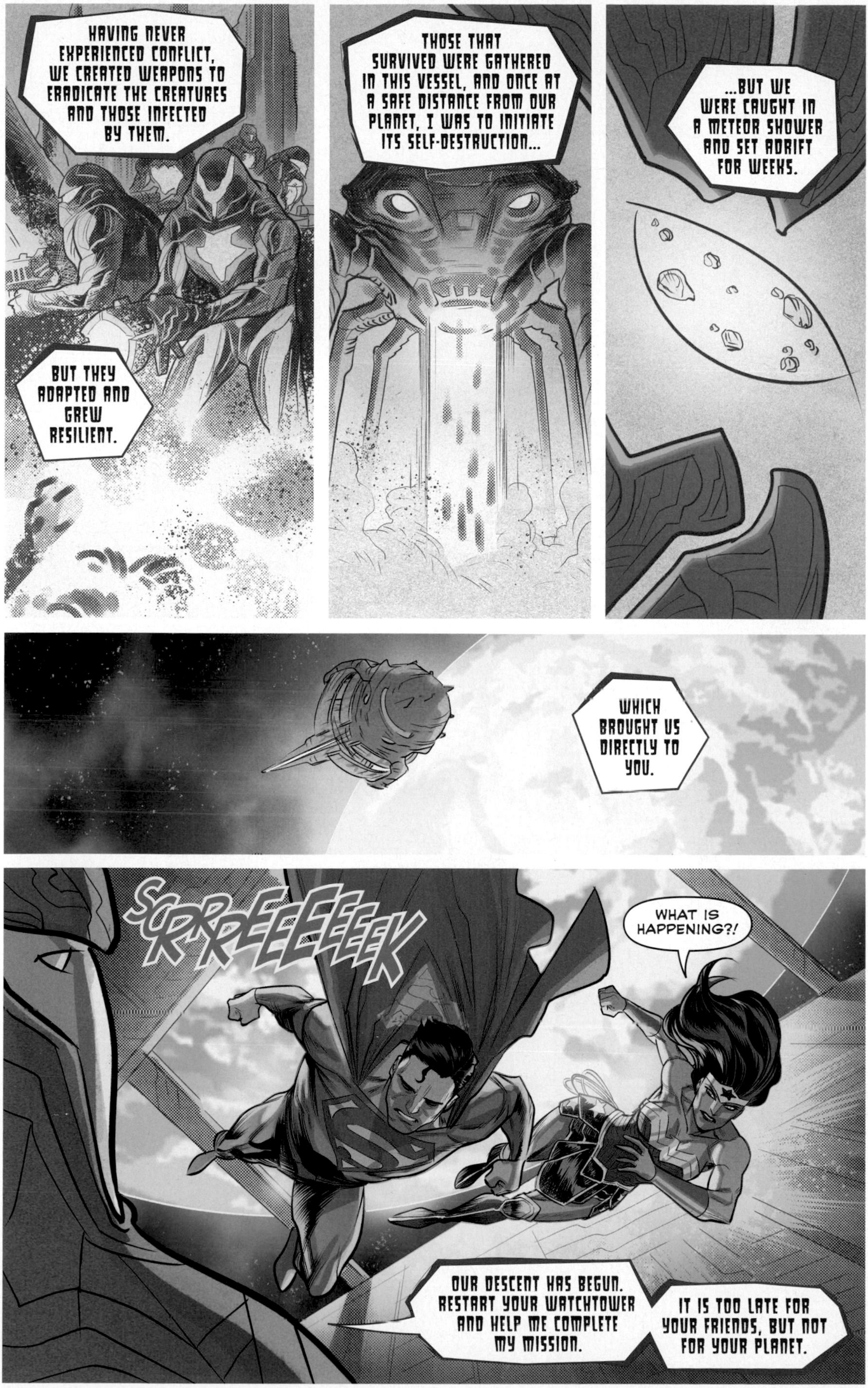
HAVING NEVER EXPERIENCED CONFLICT, WE CREATED WEAPONS TO ERADICATE THE CREATURES AND THOSE INFECTED BY THEM.
BUT THEY ADAPTED AND GREW RESILIENT.
THOSE THAT SURVIVED WERE GATHERED IN THIS VESSEL, AND ONCE AT A SAFE DISTANCE FROM OUR PLANET, I WAS TO INITIATE ITS SELF-DESTRUCTION...
...BUT WE WERE CAUGHT IN A METEOR SHOWER AND SET ADRIFT FOR WEEKS.
WHICH BROUGHT US DIRECTLY TO YOU.
SCRRREEEEEEEK
WHAT IS HAPPENING?!
OUR DESCENT HAS BEGUN. RESTART YOUR WATCHTOWER AND HELP ME COMPLETE MY MISSION.
IT IS TOO LATE FOR YOUR FRIENDS, BUT NOT FOR YOUR PLANET.

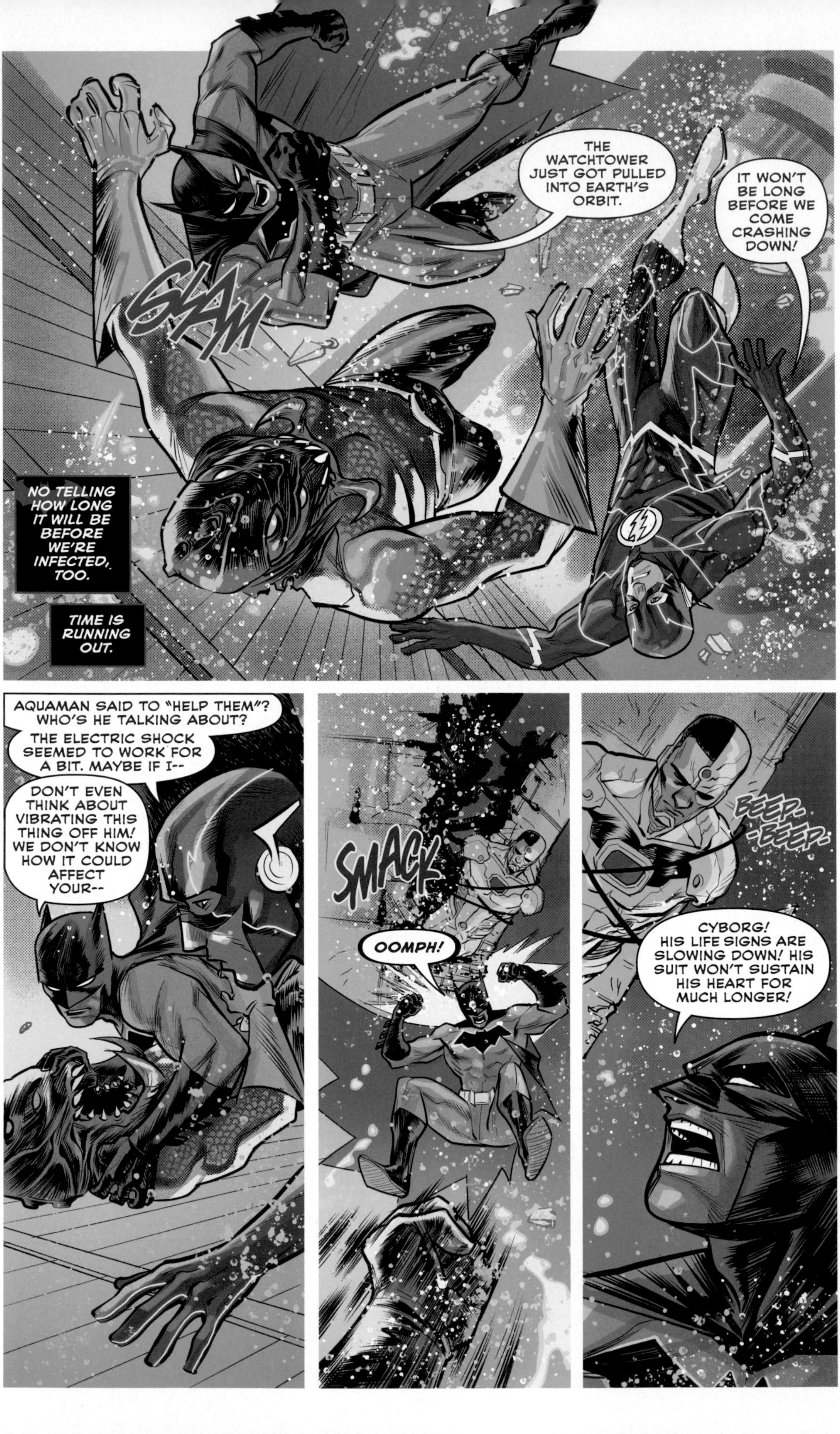
SLAM
THE WATCHTOWER JUST GOT PULLED INTO EARTH'S ORBIT.
IT WON'T BE LONG BEFORE WE COME CRASHING DOWN!
NO TELLING HOW LONG IT WILL BE BEFORE WE'RE INFECTED, TOO.
TIME IS RUNNING OUT.
AQUAMAN SAID TO "HELP THEM"? WHO'S HE TALKING ABOUT?
THE ELECTRIC SHOCK SEEMED TO WORK FOR A BIT. MAYBE IF I--
DON'T EVEN THINK ABOUT VIBRATING THIS THING OFF HIM! WE DON'T KNOW HOW IT COULD AFFECT YOUR--
SMACK
OOMPH!
BEEP-BEEP-
CYBORG! HIS LIFE SIGNS ARE SLOWING DOWN! HIS SUIT WON'T SUSTAIN HIS HEART FOR MUCH LONGER!

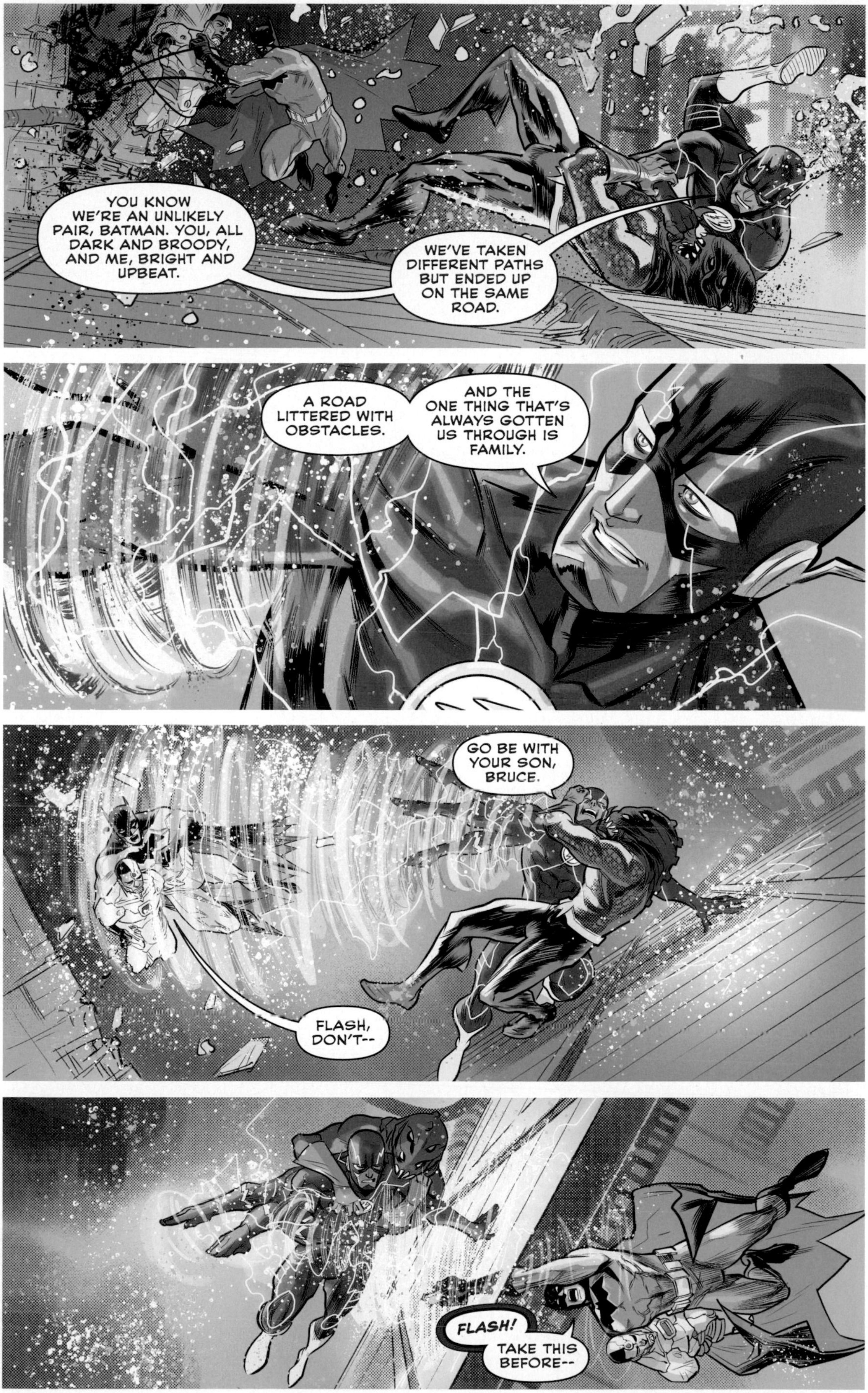
YOU KNOW WE'RE AN UNLIKELY PAIR, BATMAN. YOU, ALL DARK AND BROODY, AND ME, BRIGHT AND UPBEAT.
WE'VE TAKEN DIFFERENT PATHS BUT ENDED UP ON THE SAME ROAD.
A ROAD LITTERED WITH OBSTACLES.
AND THE ONE THING THAT'S ALWAYS GOTTEN US THROUGH IS FAMILY.
GO BE WITH YOUR SON, BRUCE.
FLASH, DON'T--
FLASH!
TAKE THIS BEFORE--

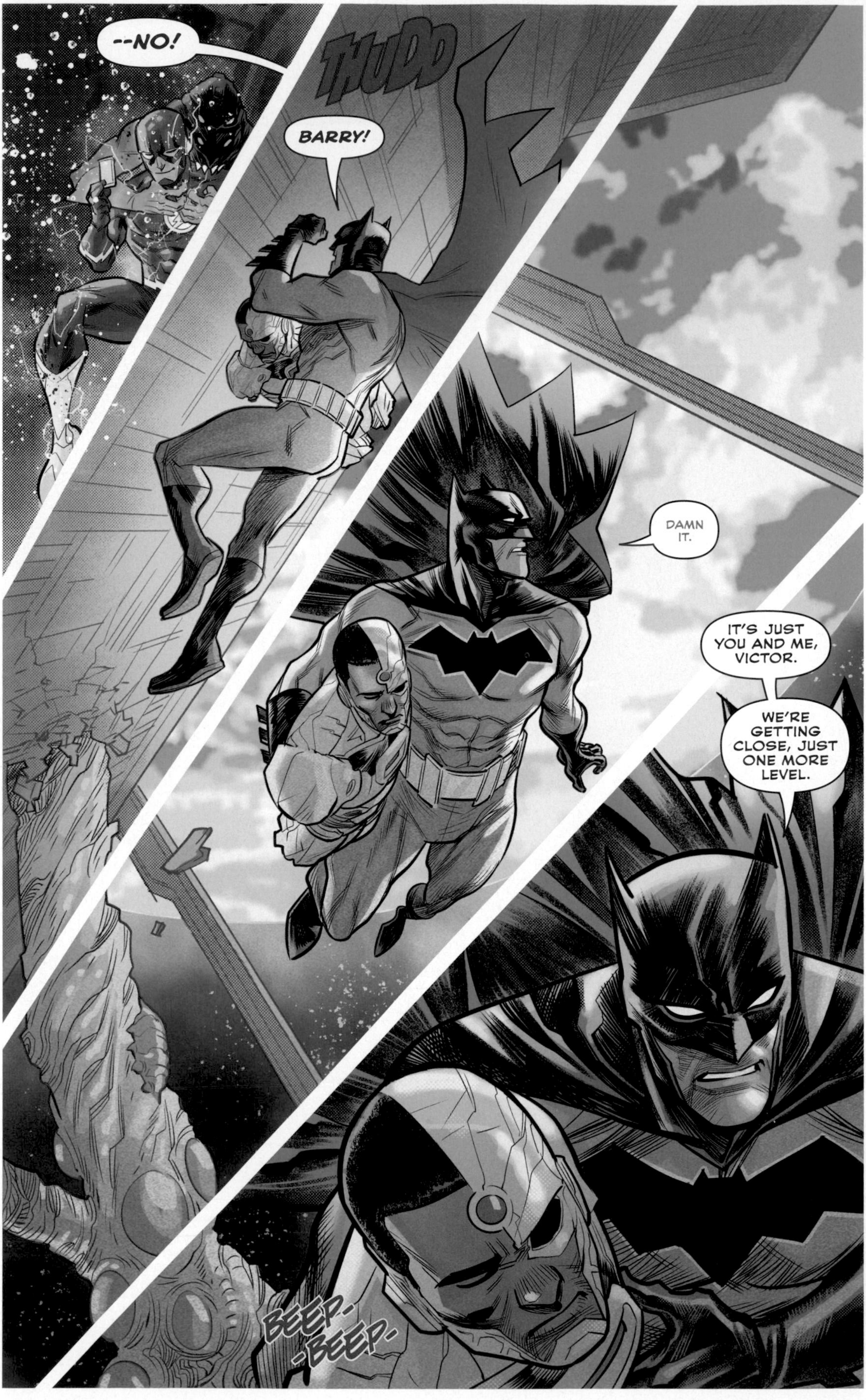
--NO!
THUDD
BARRY!
DAMN IT.
IT'S JUST YOU AND ME, VICTOR.
WE'RE GETTING CLOSE, JUST ONE MORE LEVEL.
BEEP- -BEEP-

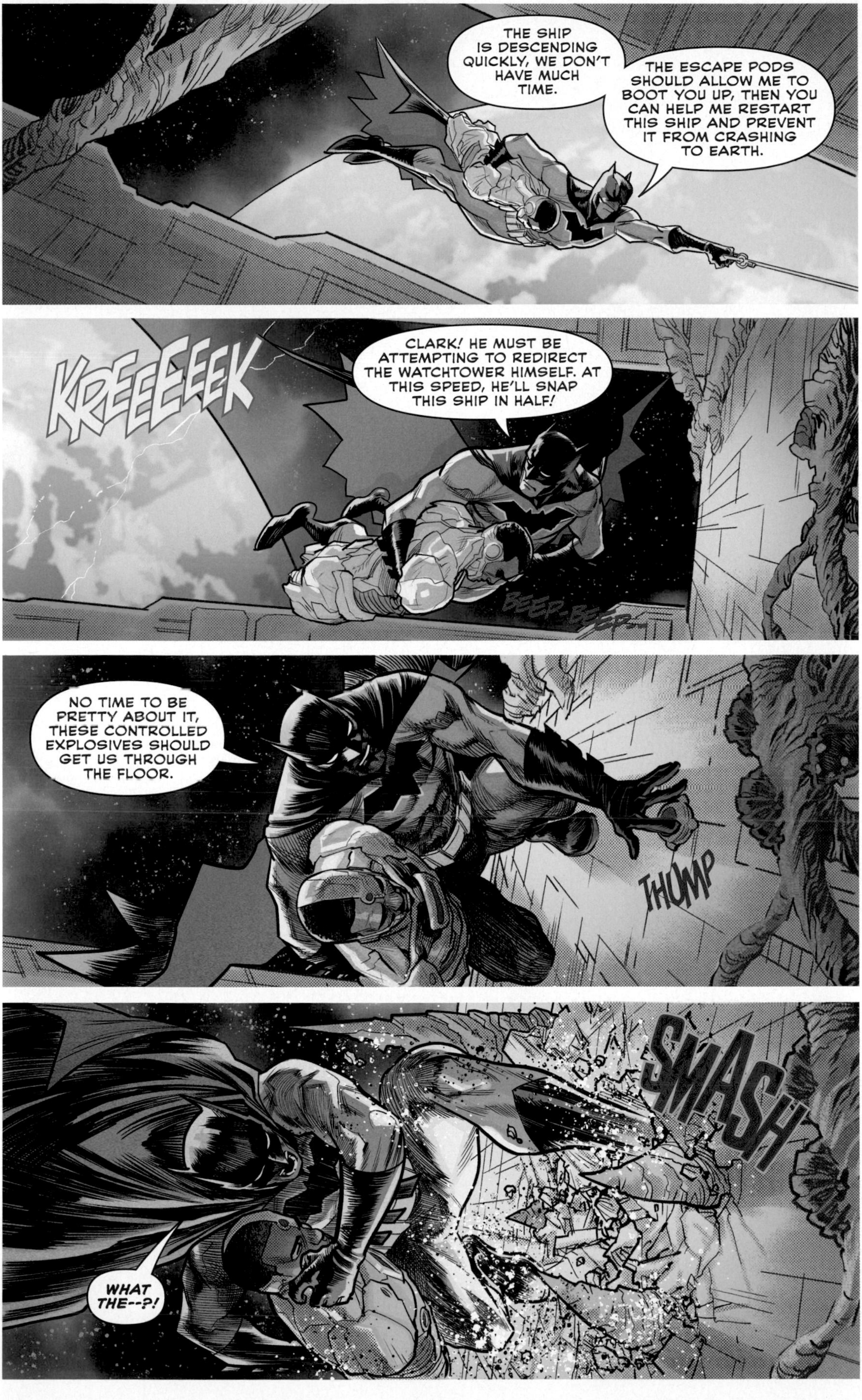
THE SHIP IS DESCENDING QUICKLY, WE DON'T HAVE MUCH TIME.
THE ESCAPE PODS SHOULD ALLOW ME TO BOOT YOU UP, THEN YOU CAN HELP ME RESTART THIS SHIP AND PREVENT IT FROM CRASHING TO EARTH.
KREEEEEK
CLARK! HE MUST BE ATTEMPTING TO REDIRECT THE WATCHTOWER HIMSELF. AT THIS SPEED, HE'LL SNAP THIS SHIP IN HALF!
BEEP-BEEP...
NO TIME TO BE PRETTY ABOUT IT, THESE CONTROLLED EXPLOSIVES SHOULD GET US THROUGH THE FLOOR.
THUMP
SMASH
WHAT THE--?!

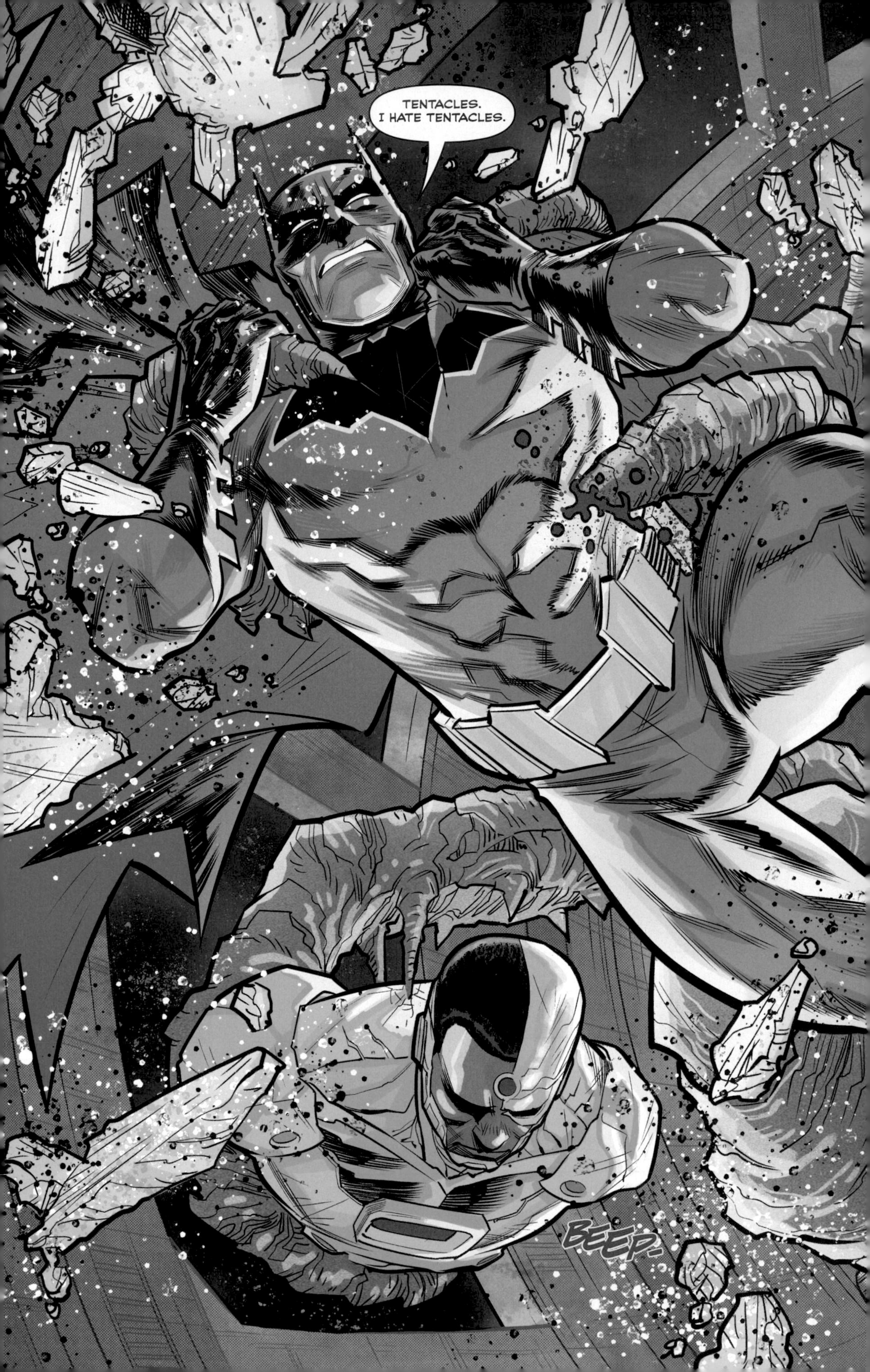
TENTACLES.
I HATE TENTACLES.
BEEP-

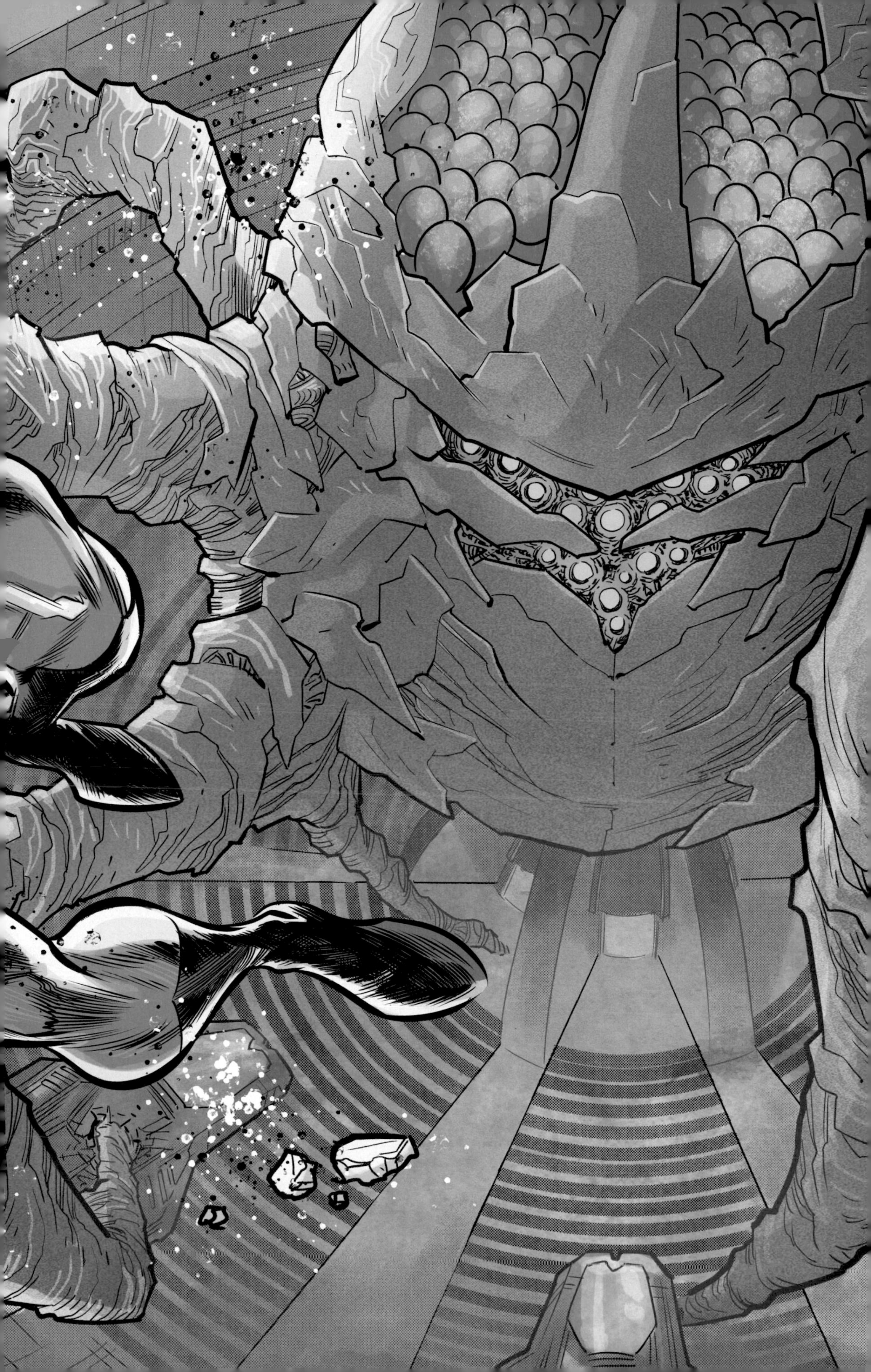

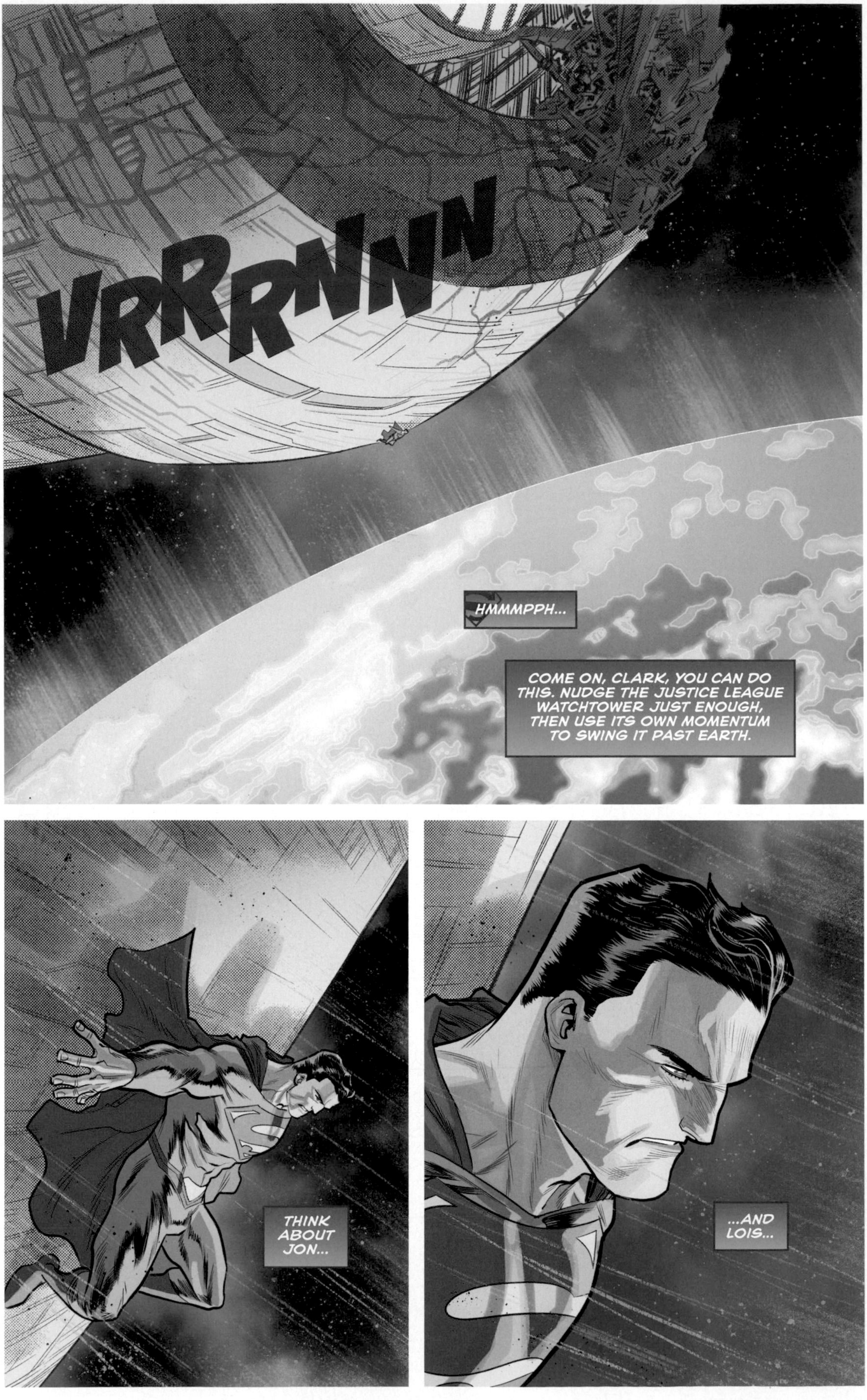

VRRRNNN
HMMMPPH...
COME ON, CLARK, YOU CAN DO THIS. NUDGE THE JUSTICE LEAGUE WATCHTOWER JUST ENOUGH, THEN USE ITS OWN MOMENTUM TO SWING IT PAST EARTH.
THINK ABOUT JON...
...AND LOIS...

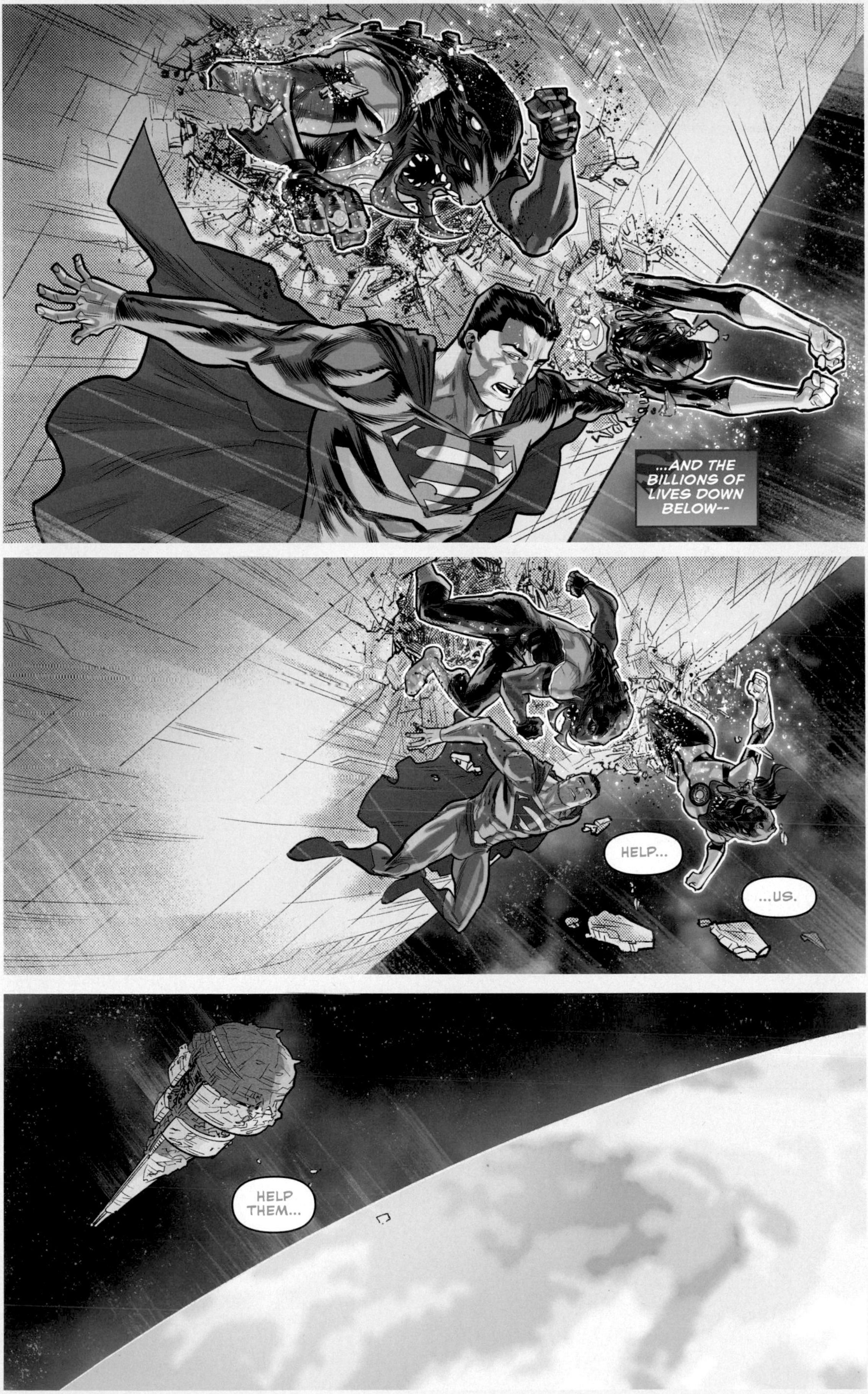
...AND THE BILLIONS OF LIVES DOWN BELOW--
HELP...
...US.
HELP THEM...

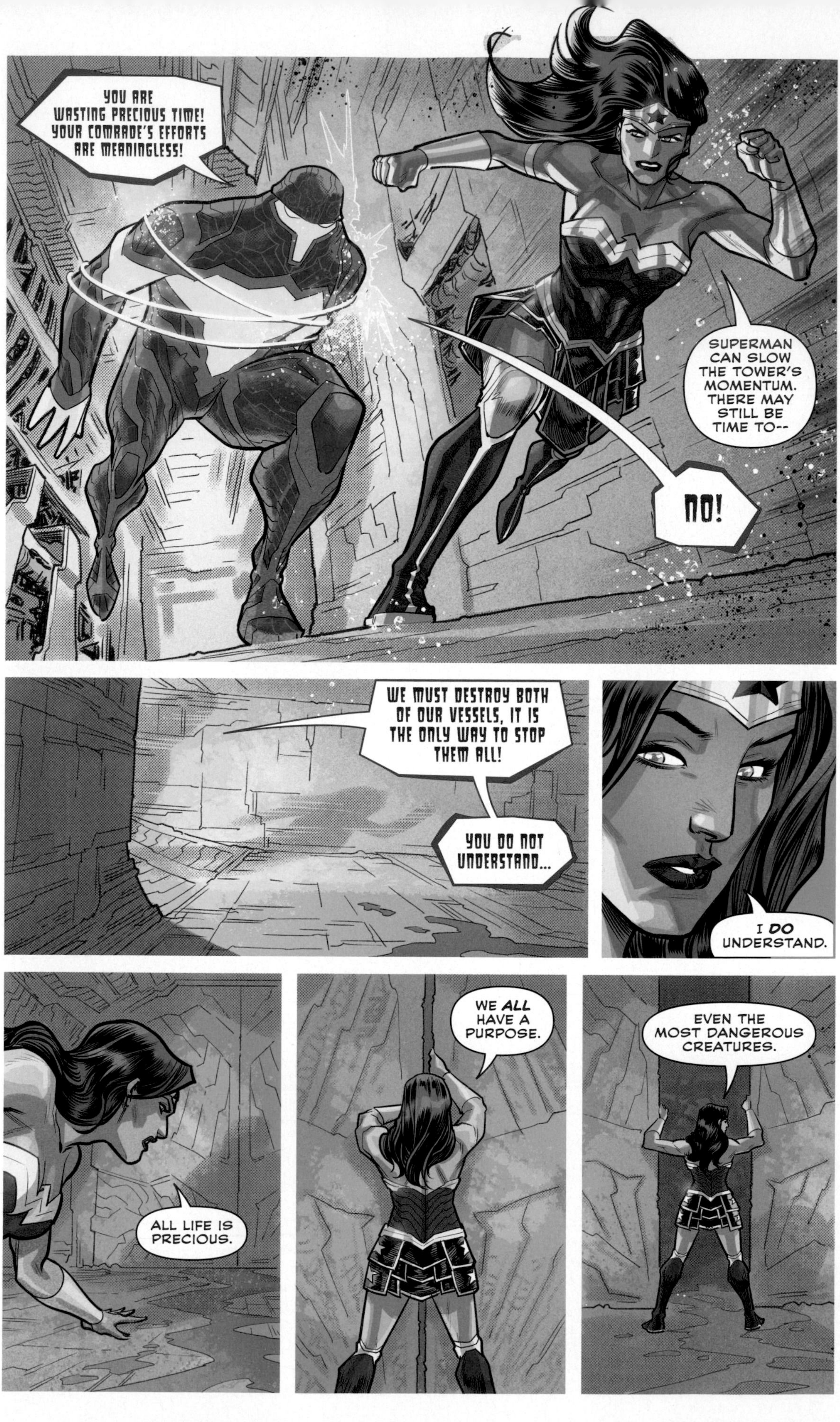
YOU ARE WASTING PRECIOUS TIME! YOUR COMRADE'S EFFORTS ARE MEANINGLESS!
SUPERMAN CAN SLOW THE TOWER'S MOMENTUM. THERE MAY STILL BE TIME TO--
NO!
WE MUST DESTROY BOTH OF OUR VESSELS, IT IS THE ONLY WAY TO STOP THEM ALL!
YOU DO NOT UNDERSTAND...
I DO UNDERSTAND.
ALL LIFE IS PRECIOUS.
WE ALL HAVE A PURPOSE.
EVEN THE MOST DANGEROUS CREATURES.

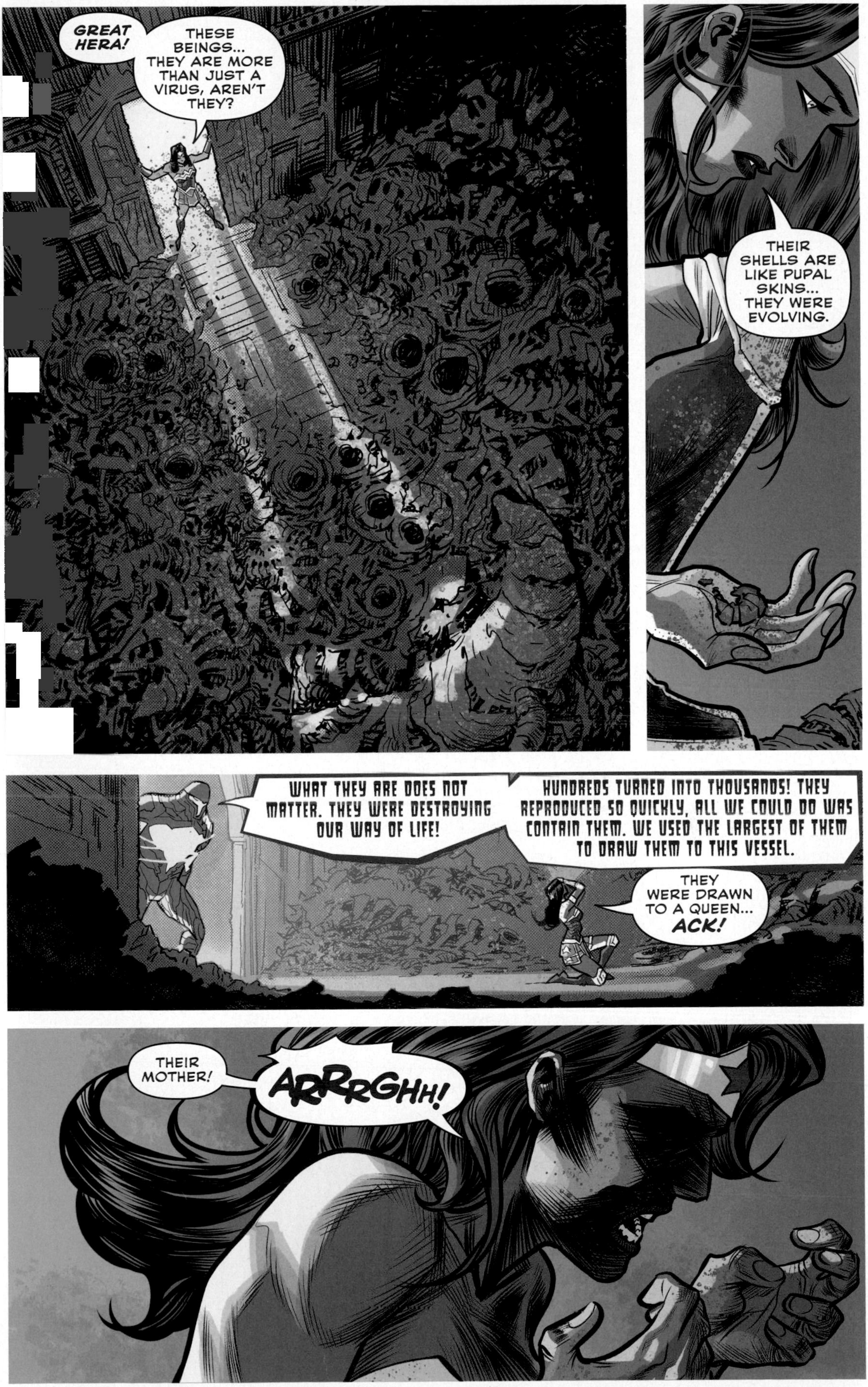
GREAT HERA!
THESE BEINGS... THEY ARE MORE THAN JUST A VIRUS, AREN'T THEY?
THEIR SHELLS ARE LIKE PUPAL SKINS... THEY WERE EVOLVING.
WHAT THEY ARE DOES NOT MATTER. THEY WERE DESTROYING OUR WAY OF LIFE!
HUNDREDS TURNED INTO THOUSANDS! THEY REPRODUCED SO QUICKLY, ALL WE COULD DO WAS CONTAIN THEM. WE USED THE LARGEST OF THEM TO DRAW THEM TO THIS VESSEL.
THEY WERE DRAWN TO A QUEEN... ACK!
THEIR MOTHER!
ARRRGHH!

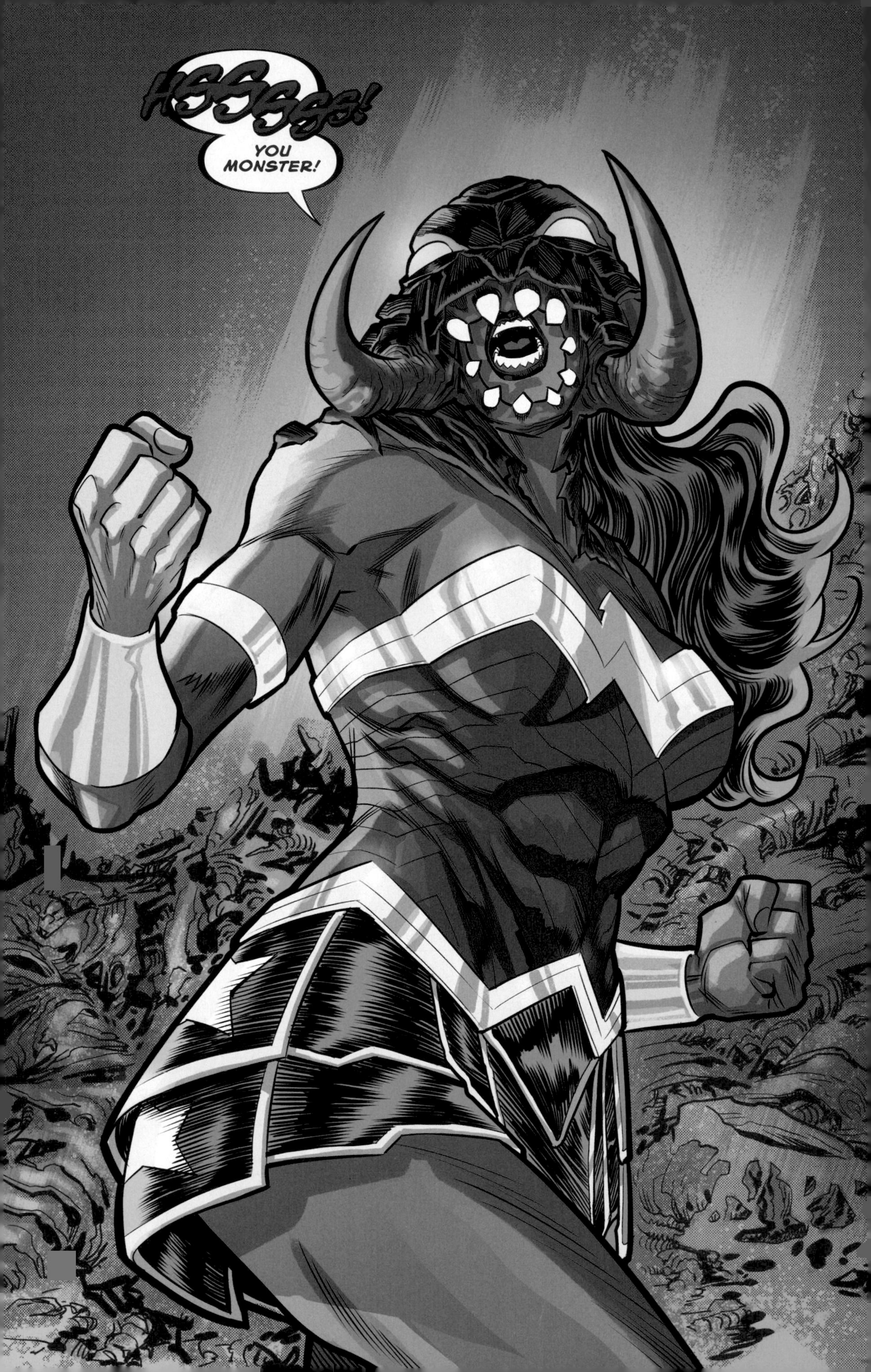
HSSSSSS!
YOU MONSTER!

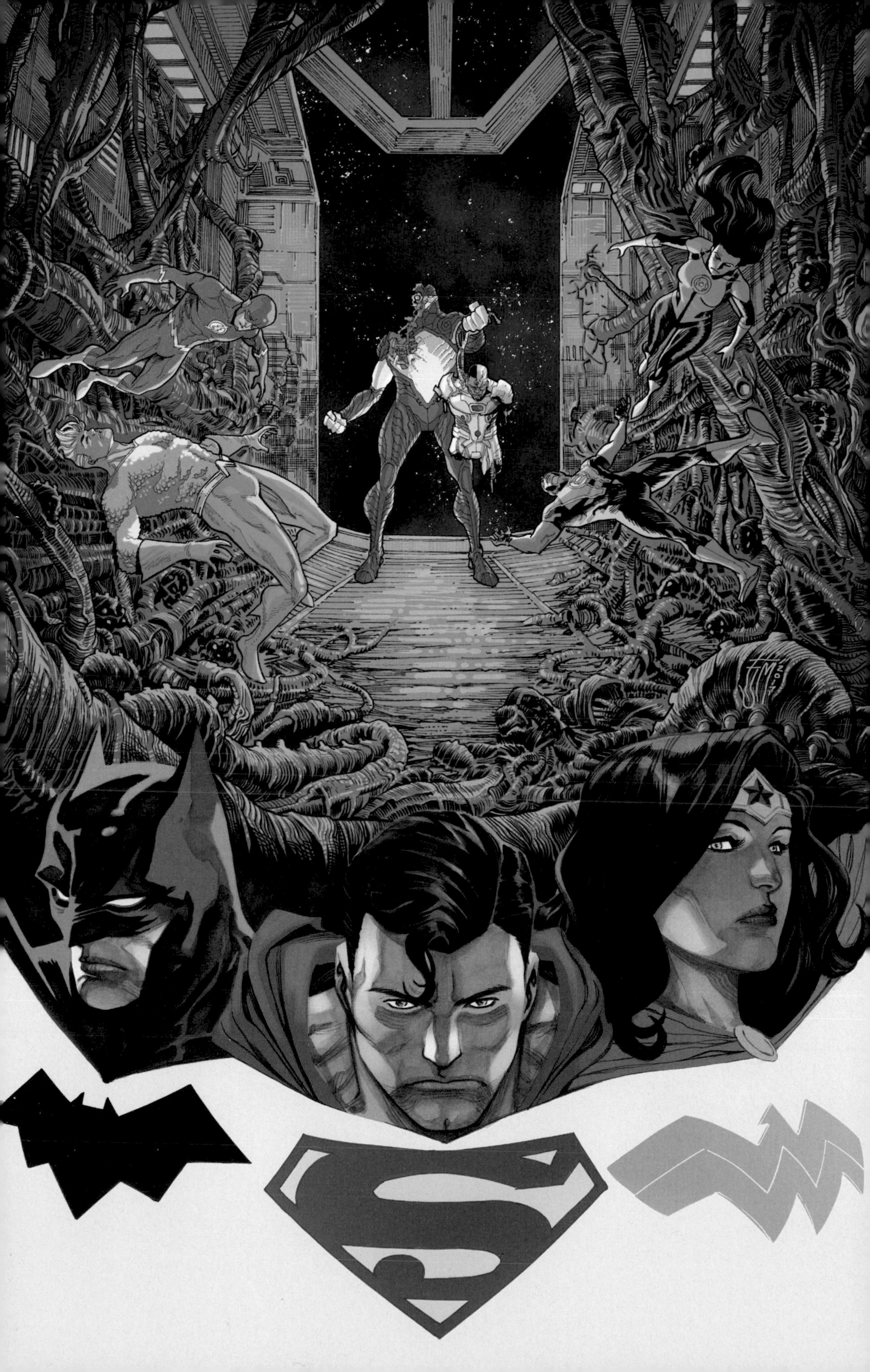

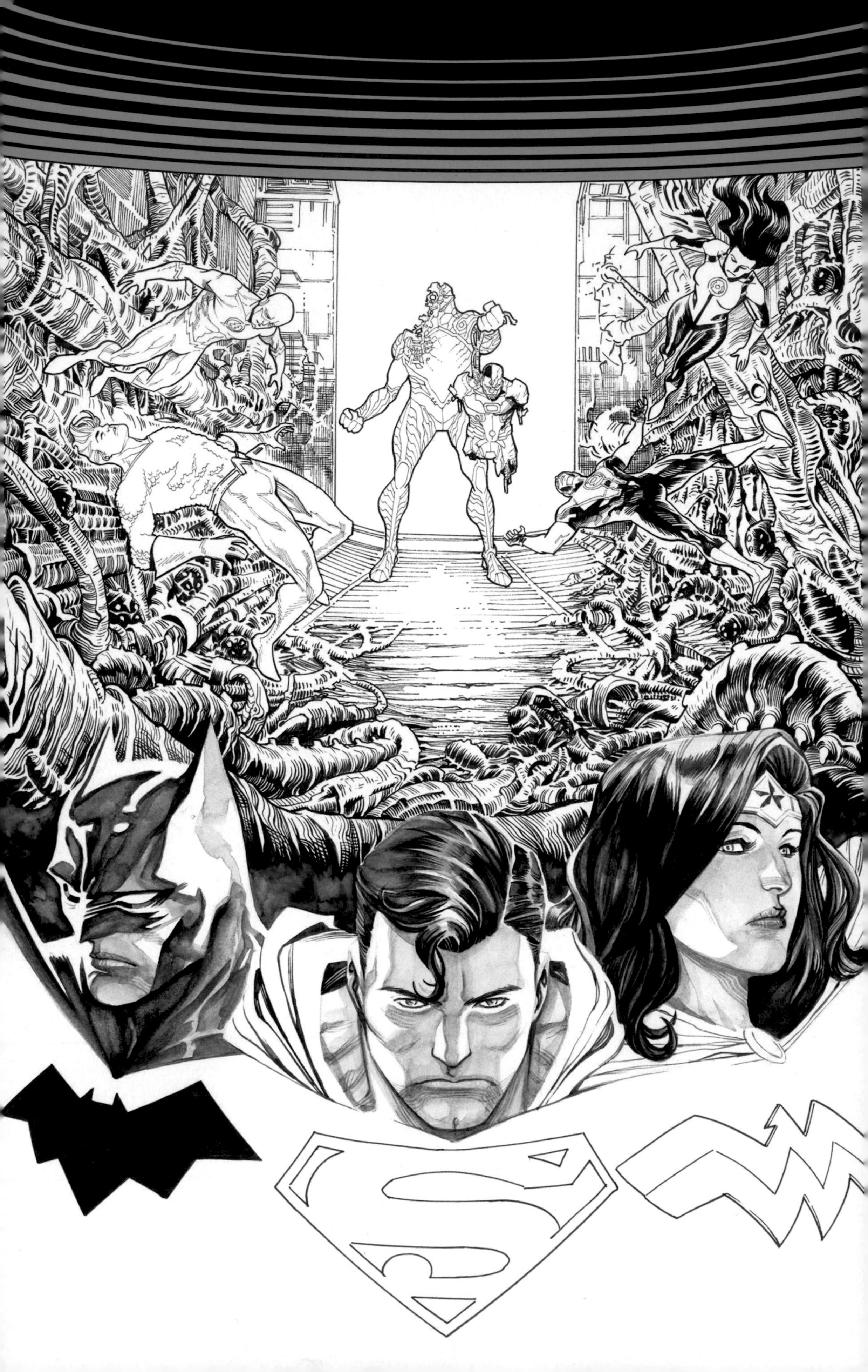

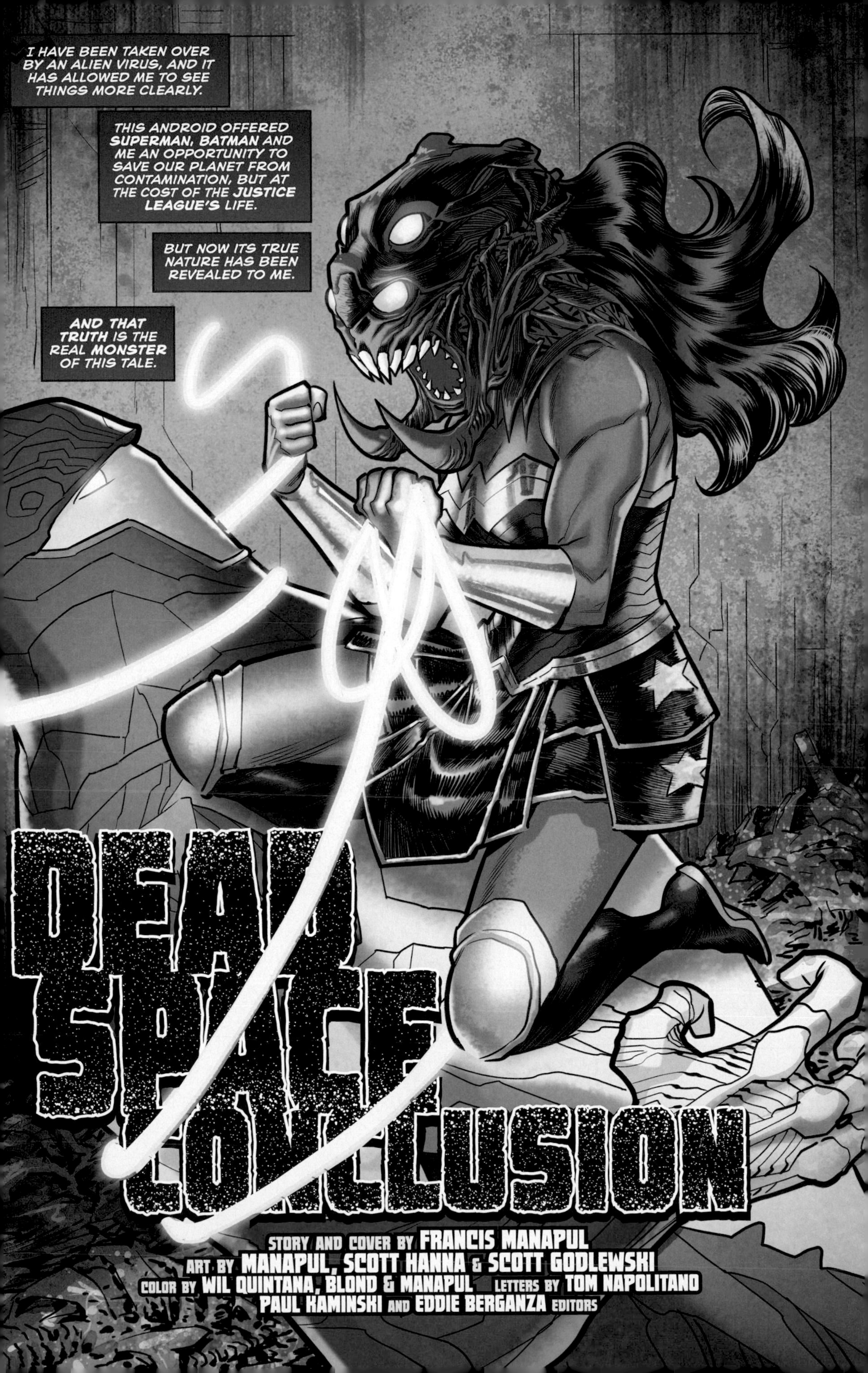
I HAVE BEEN TAKEN OVER BY AN ALIEN VIRUS, AND IT HAS ALLOWED ME TO SEE THINGS MORE CLEARLY.
THIS ANDROID OFFERED SUPERMAN, BATMAN AND ME AN OPPORTUNITY TO SAVE OUR PLANET FROM CONTAMINATION, BUT AT THE COST OF THE JUSTICE LEAGUE'S LIFE.
BUT NOW ITS TRUE NATURE HAS BEEN REVEALED TO ME.
AND THAT TRUTH IS THE REAL MONSTER OF THIS TALE.
DEAD SPACE CONCLUSION
STORY AND COVER BY FRANCIS MANAPUL
ART BY MANAPUL, SCOTT HANNA & SCOTT GODLEWSKI
COLOR BY WIL QUINTANA, BLOND & MANAPUL LETTERS BY TOM NAPOLITANO
PAUL KAMINSKI AND EDDIE BERGANZA EDITORS

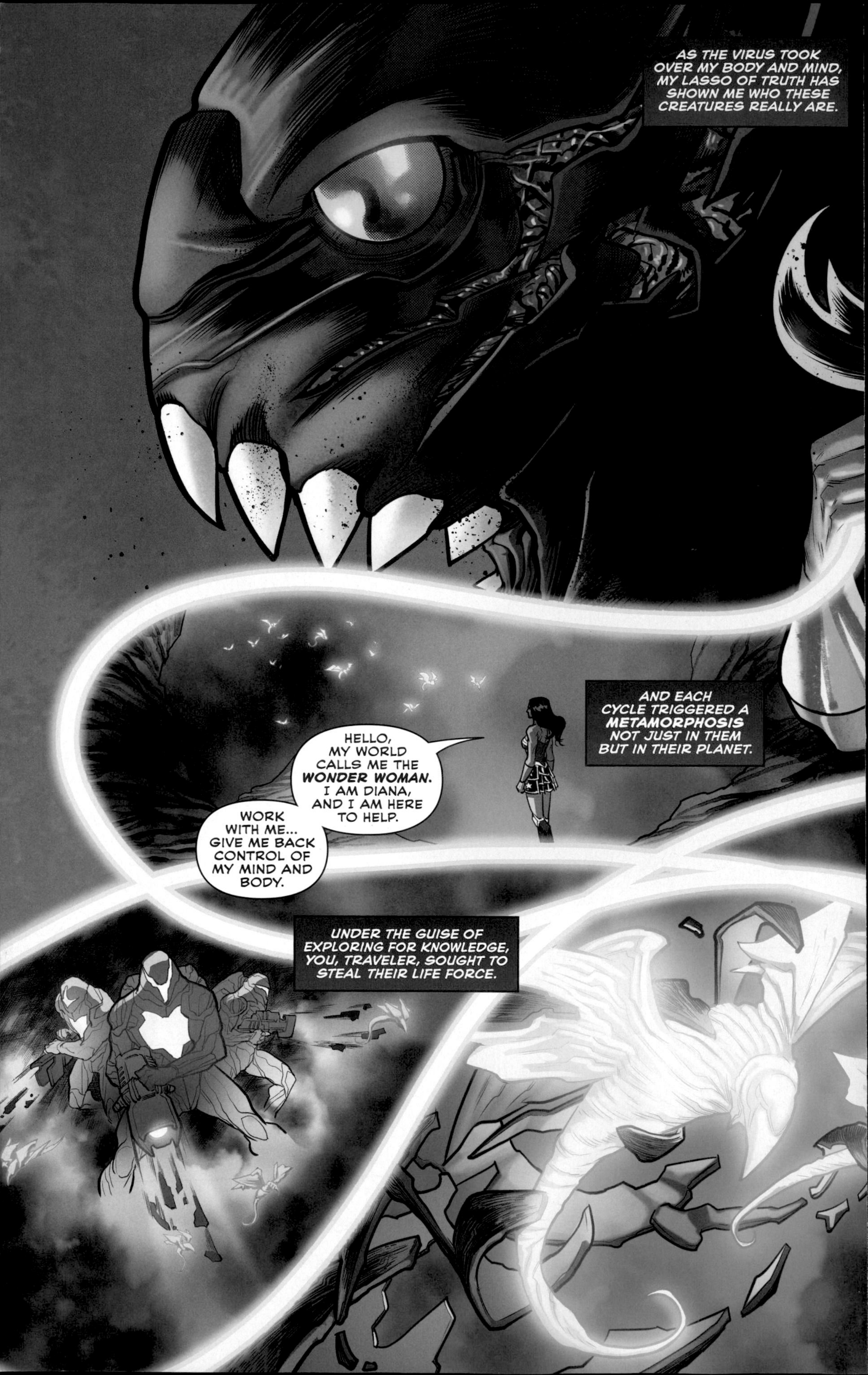
AS THE VIRUS TOOK OVER MY BODY AND MIND, MY LASSO OF TRUTH HAS SHOWN ME WHO THESE CREATURES REALLY ARE.
AND EACH CYCLE TRIGGERED A **METAMORPHOSIS** NOT JUST IN THEM BUT IN THEIR PLANET.
HELLO, MY WORLD CALLS ME THE **WONDER WOMAN.** I AM DIANA, AND I AM HERE TO HELP.
WORK WITH ME... GIVE ME BACK CONTROL OF MY MIND AND BODY.
UNDER THE GUISE OF EXPLORING FOR KNOWLEDGE, YOU, TRAVELER, SOUGHT TO STEAL THEIR LIFE FORCE.

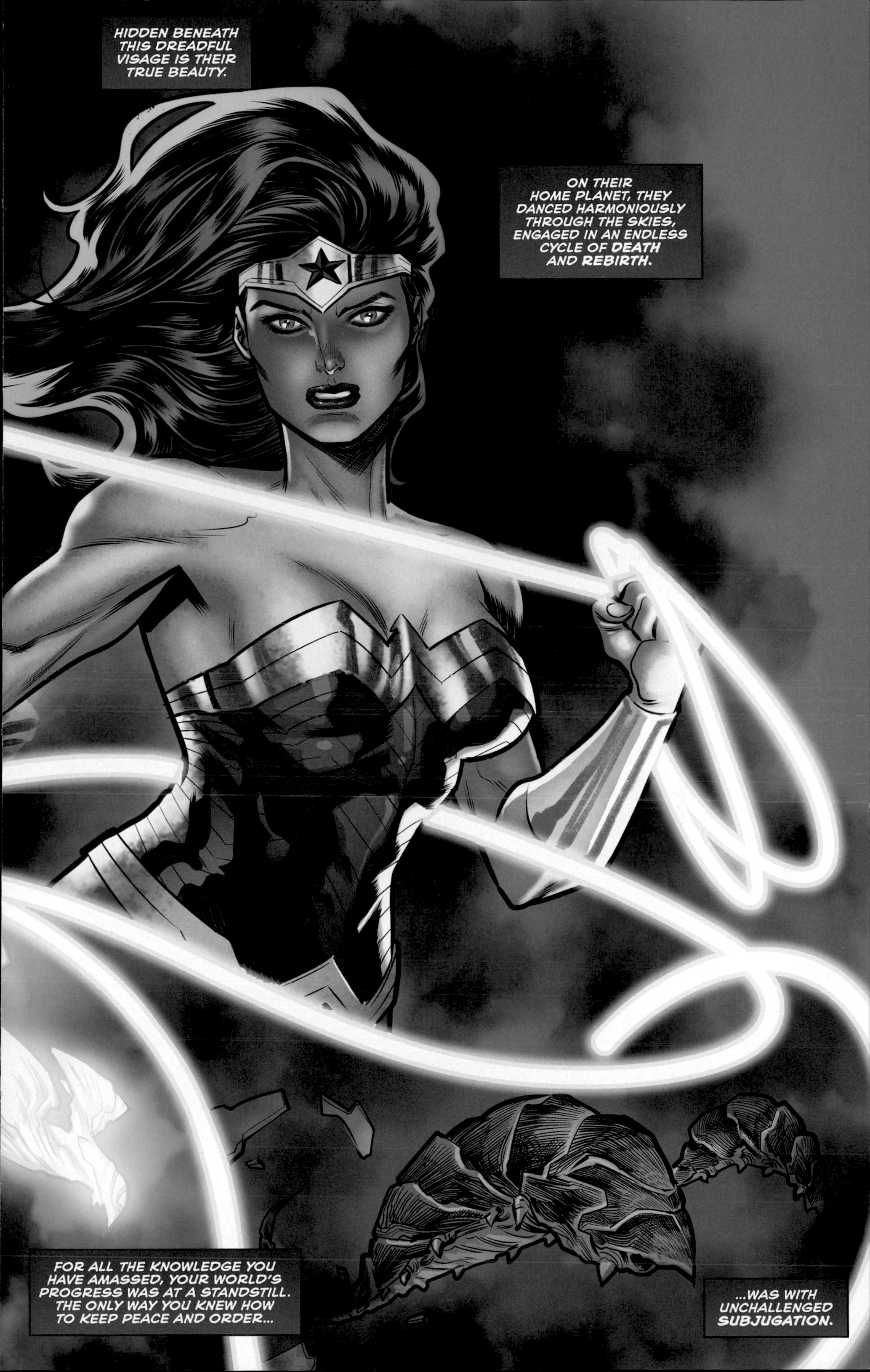
HIDDEN BENEATH THIS DREADFUL VISAGE IS THEIR TRUE BEAUTY.
ON THEIR HOME PLANET, THEY DANCED HARMONIOUSLY THROUGH THE SKIES, ENGAGED IN AN ENDLESS CYCLE OF DEATH AND REBIRTH.
FOR ALL THE KNOWLEDGE YOU HAVE AMASSED, YOUR WORLD'S PROGRESS WAS AT A STANDSTILL. THE ONLY WAY YOU KNEW HOW TO KEEP PEACE AND ORDER...
...WAS WITH UNCHALLENGED SUBJUGATION.

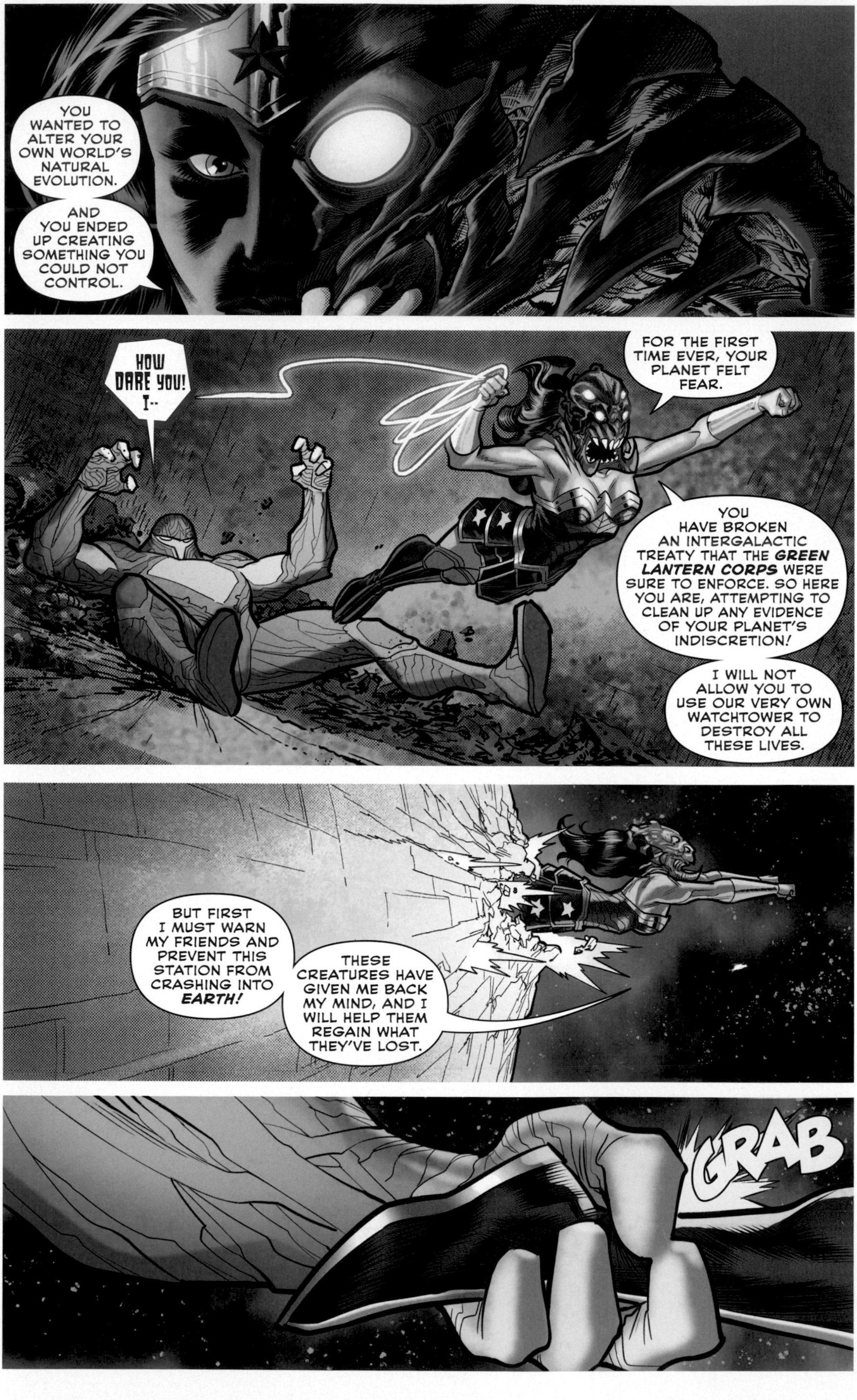
YOU WANTED TO ALTER YOUR OWN WORLD'S NATURAL EVOLUTION.
AND YOU ENDED UP CREATING SOMETHING YOU COULD NOT CONTROL.
HOW DARE YOU! I--
FOR THE FIRST TIME EVER, YOUR PLANET FELT FEAR.
YOU HAVE BROKEN AN INTERGALACTIC TREATY THAT THE GREEN LANTERN CORPS WERE SURE TO ENFORCE. SO HERE YOU ARE, ATTEMPTING TO CLEAN UP ANY EVIDENCE OF YOUR PLANET'S INDISCRETION!
I WILL NOT ALLOW YOU TO USE OUR VERY OWN WATCHTOWER TO DESTROY ALL THESE LIVES.
BUT FIRST I MUST WARN MY FRIENDS AND PREVENT THIS STATION FROM CRASHING INTO EARTH!
THESE CREATURES HAVE GIVEN ME BACK MY MIND, AND I WILL HELP THEM REGAIN WHAT THEY'VE LOST.
GRAB

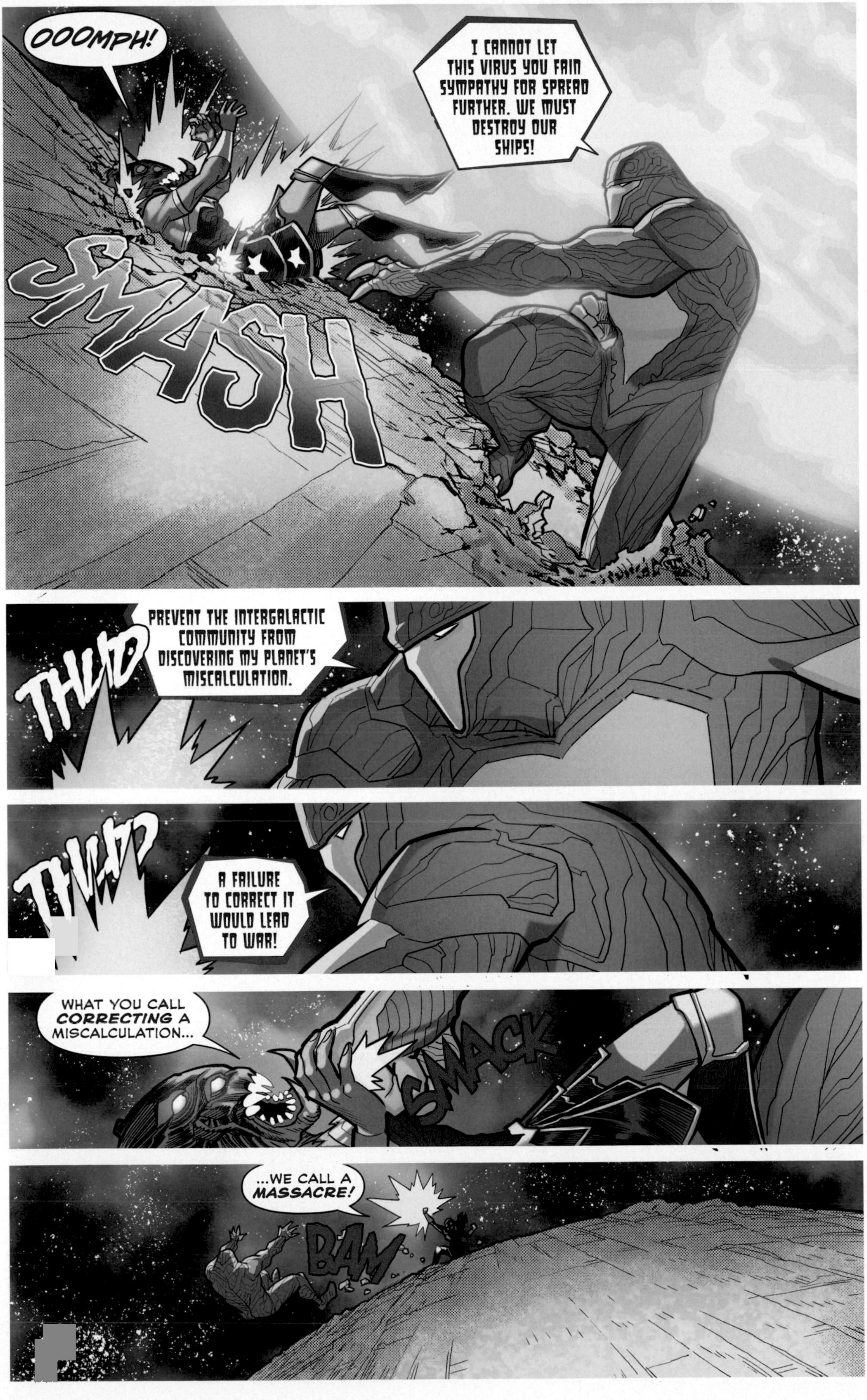

OOOMPH!
I CANNOT LET THIS VIRUS YOU FAIN SYMPATHY FOR SPREAD FURTHER. WE MUST DESTROY OUR SHIPS!
SMASH
THUD
PREVENT THE INTERGALACTIC COMMUNITY FROM DISCOVERING MY PLANET'S MISCALCULATION.
THUD
A FAILURE TO CORRECT IT WOULD LEAD TO WAR!
WHAT YOU CALL *CORRECTING* A MISCALCULATION...
SMACK
...WE CALL A *MASSACRE!*
BAM

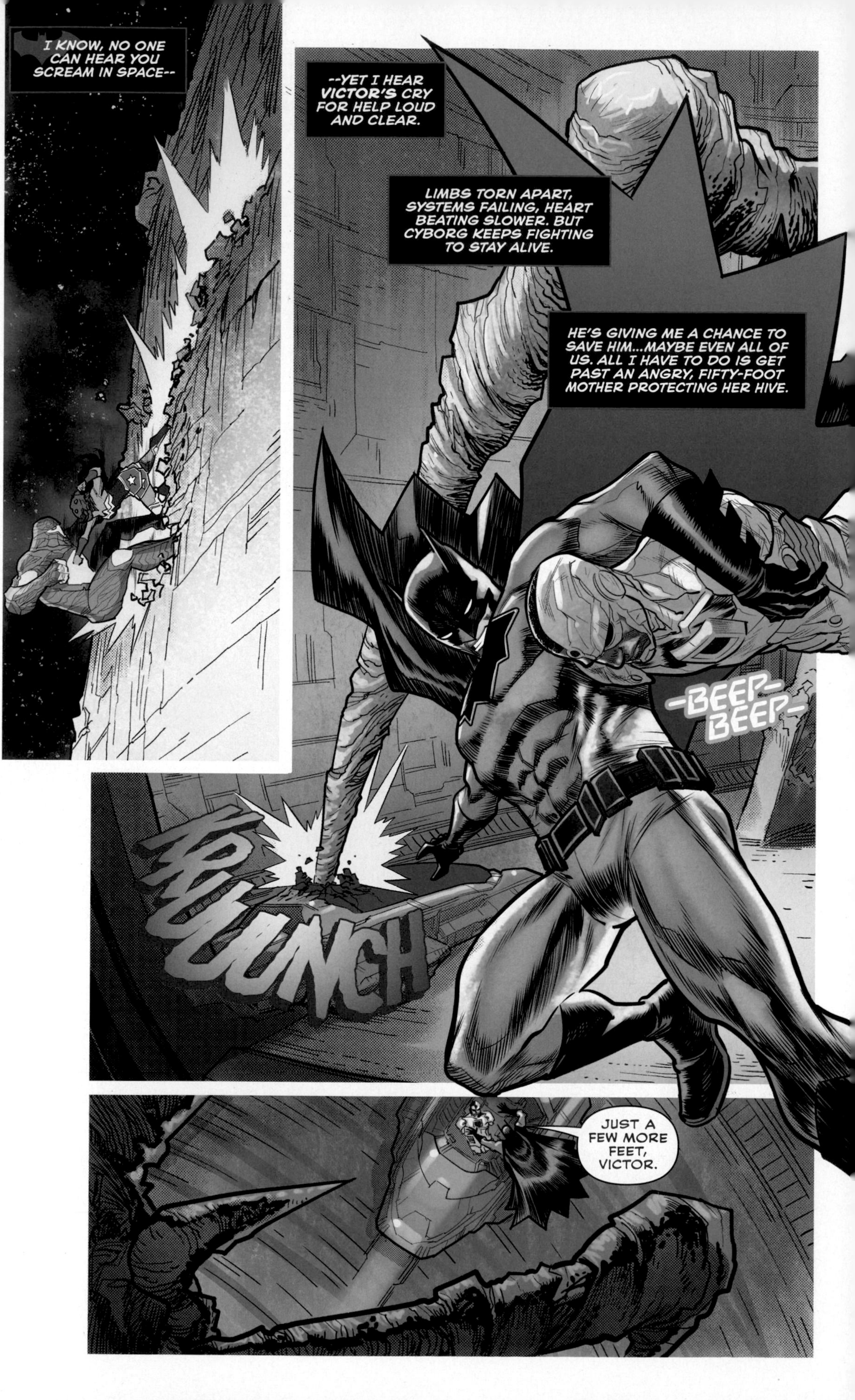
I KNOW, NO ONE CAN HEAR YOU SCREAM IN SPACE--
--YET I HEAR VICTOR'S CRY FOR HELP LOUD AND CLEAR.
LIMBS TORN APART, SYSTEMS FAILING, HEART BEATING SLOWER. BUT CYBORG KEEPS FIGHTING TO STAY ALIVE.
HE'S GIVING ME A CHANCE TO SAVE HIM...MAYBE EVEN ALL OF US. ALL I HAVE TO DO IS GET PAST AN ANGRY, FIFTY-FOOT MOTHER PROTECTING HER HIVE.
-BEEP- BEEP-
KRUUUNCH
JUST A FEW MORE FEET, VICTOR.

THESE PODS ARE POWERED INDEPENDENTLY FROM THE REST OF THE WATCHTOWER. IT SHOULD HAVE ENOUGH ENERGY TO REBOOT YOUR SYSTEM...

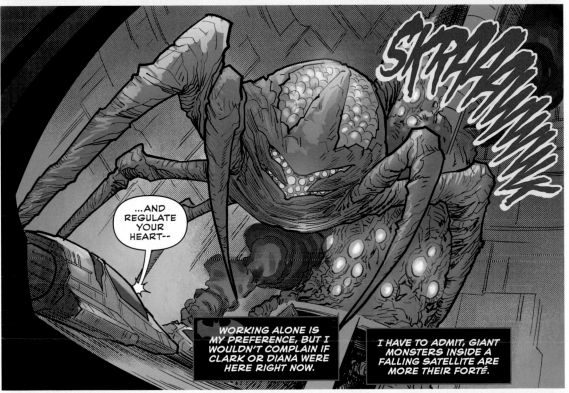

SKRRRRWWWWK

...AND REGULATE YOUR HEART--

WORKING ALONE IS MY PREFERENCE, BUT I WOULDN'T COMPLAIN IF CLARK OR DIANA WERE HERE RIGHT NOW.

I HAVE TO ADMIT, GIANT MONSTERS INSIDE A FALLING SATELLITE ARE MORE THEIR FORTÉ.

BUT I SURE AS HELL CAN SAVE VICTOR...

SPLURCH

SPLURCH

...AND TRUST MY FRIENDS NOT TO LET US FALL.

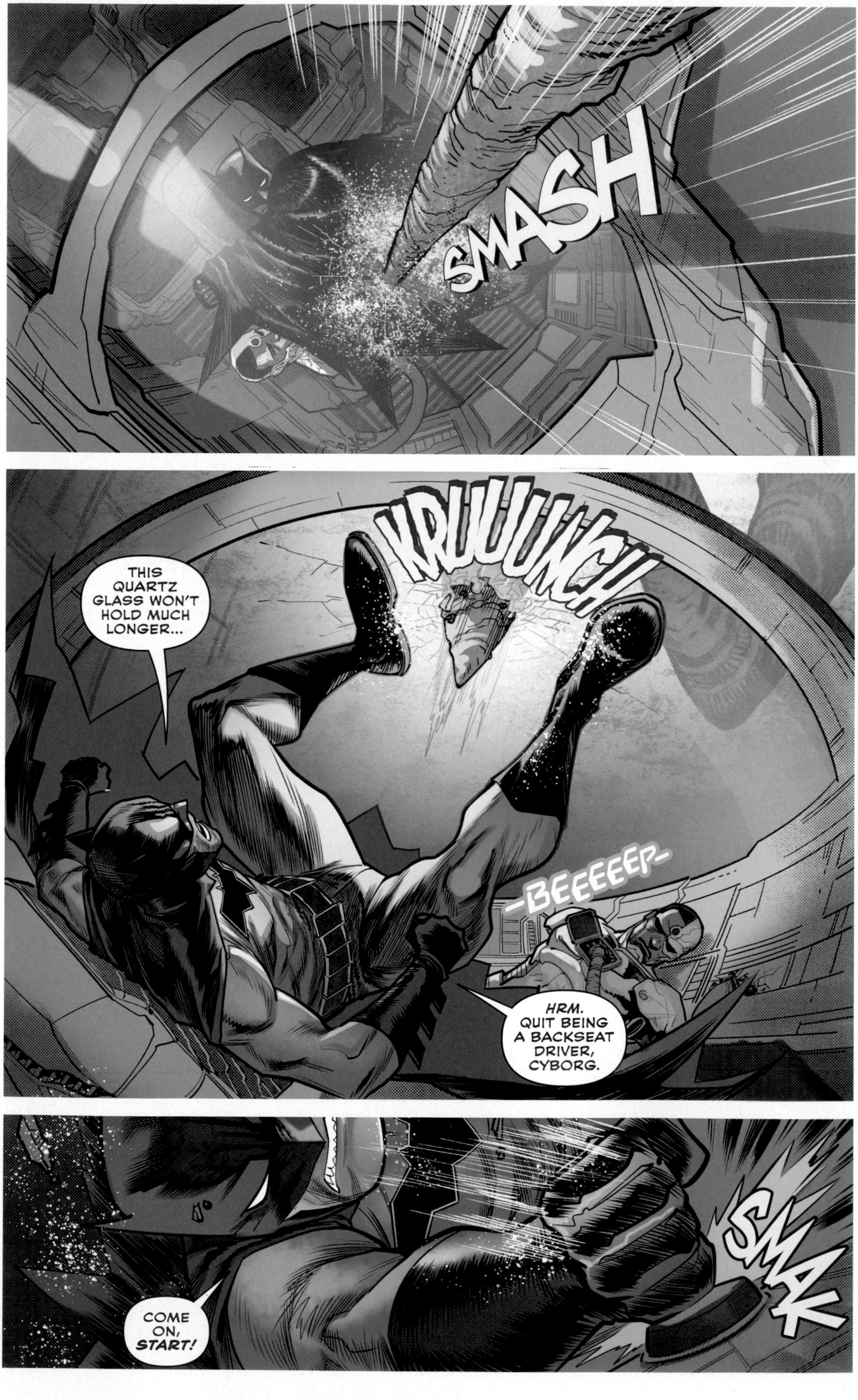
SMASH
KRUUUNCH
THIS QUARTZ GLASS WON'T HOLD MUCH LONGER...
-BEEEEEP-
HRM. QUIT BEING A BACKSEAT DRIVER, CYBORG.
SMAK
COME ON, ***START!***

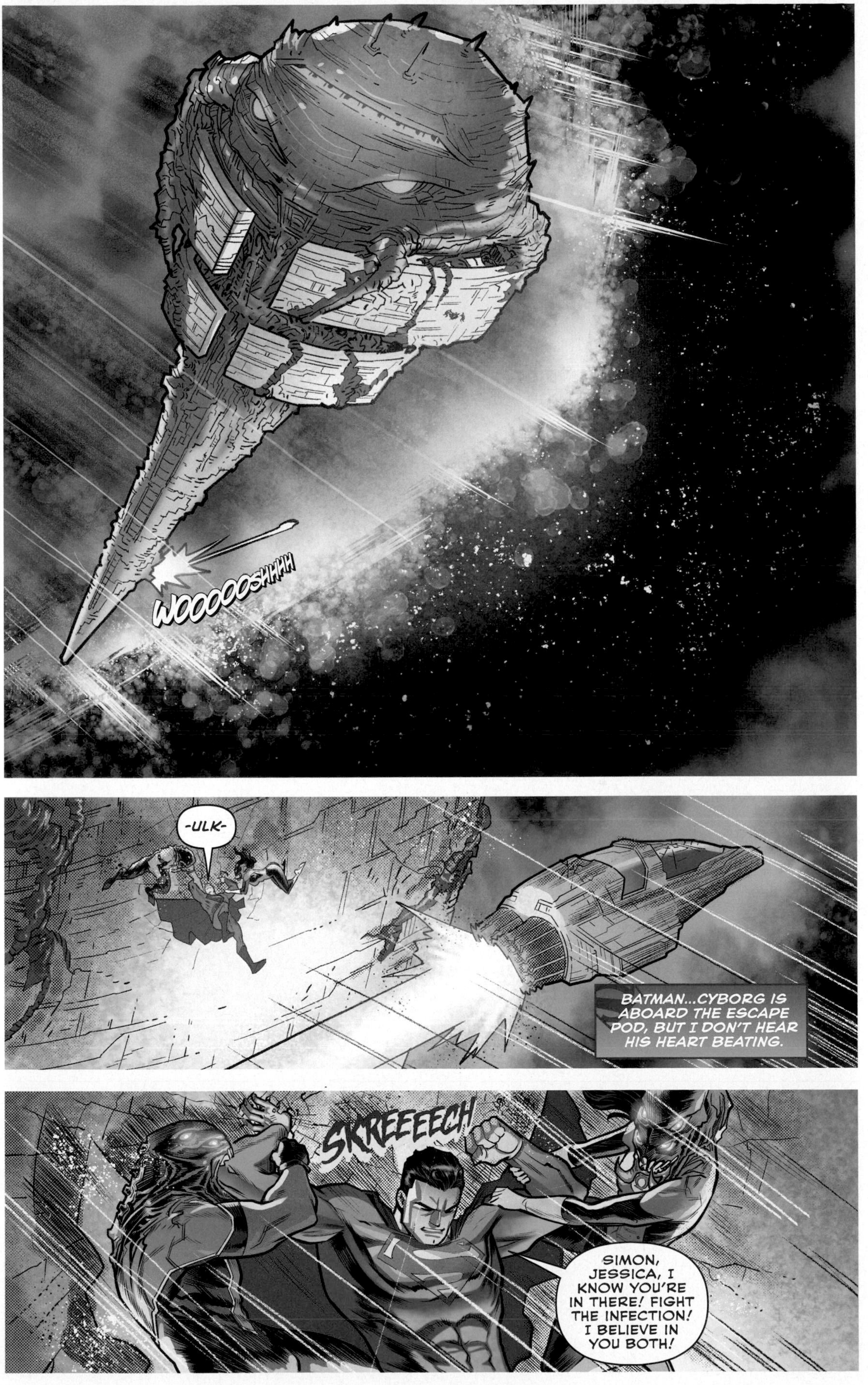
WOOOOOSHHHH
-ULK-
BATMAN...CYBORG IS ABOARD THE ESCAPE POD, BUT I DON'T HEAR HIS HEART BEATING.
SKREEEECH
SIMON, JESSICA, I KNOW YOU'RE IN THERE! FIGHT THE INFECTION! I BELIEVE IN YOU BOTH!

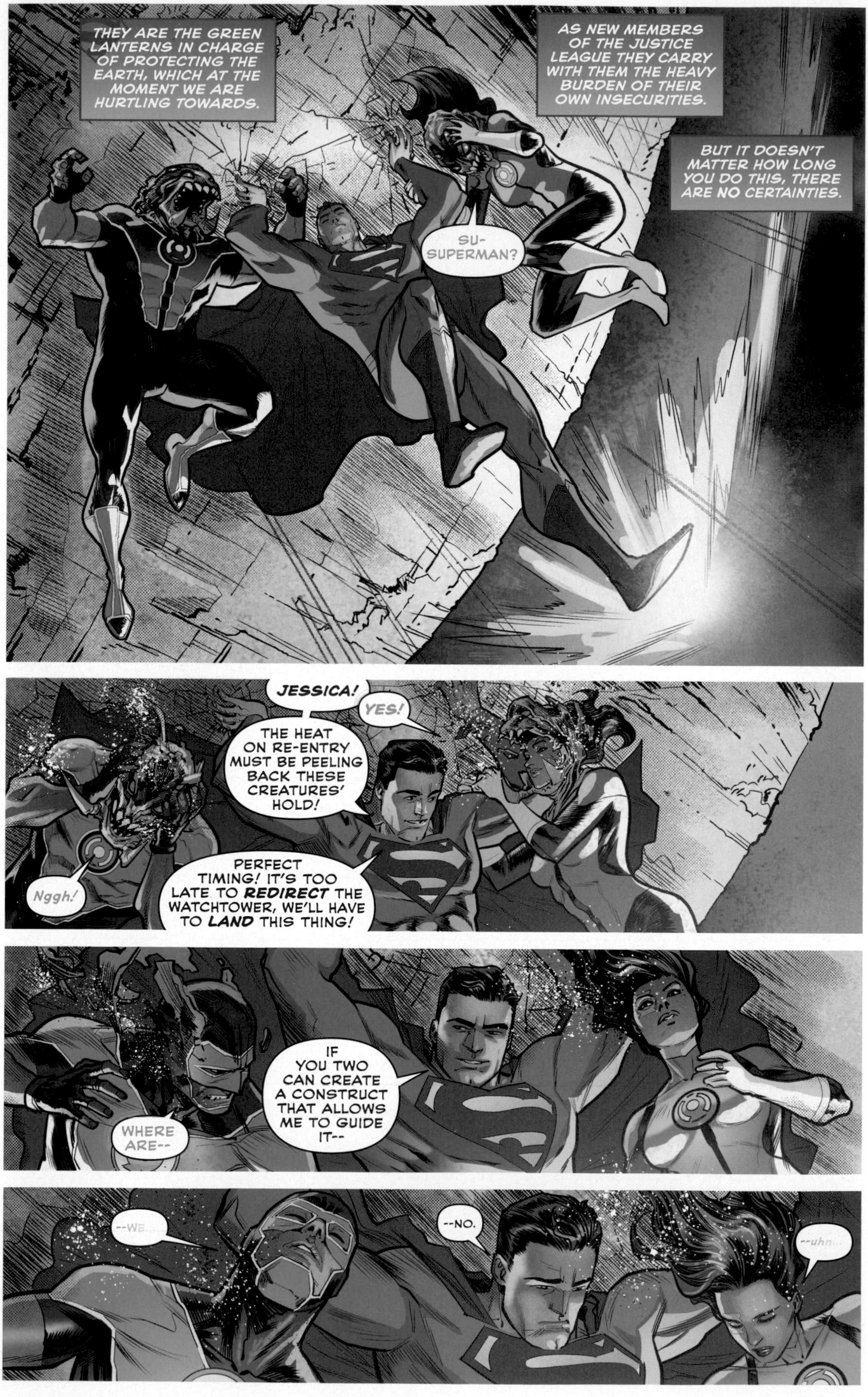
THEY ARE THE GREEN LANTERNS IN CHARGE OF PROTECTING THE EARTH, WHICH AT THE MOMENT WE ARE HURTLING TOWARDS.
AS NEW MEMBERS OF THE JUSTICE LEAGUE THEY CARRY WITH THEM THE HEAVY BURDEN OF THEIR OWN INSECURITIES.
BUT IT DOESN'T MATTER HOW LONG YOU DO THIS, THERE ARE NO CERTAINTIES.
SU-SUPERMAN?
JESSICA!
YES!
THE HEAT ON RE-ENTRY MUST BE PEELING BACK THESE CREATURES' HOLD!
PERFECT TIMING! IT'S TOO LATE TO REDIRECT THE WATCHTOWER, WE'LL HAVE TO LAND THIS THING!
Nggh!
IF YOU TWO CAN CREATE A CONSTRUCT THAT ALLOWS ME TO GUIDE IT--
WHERE ARE--
--WE...
--NO.
--uhn...

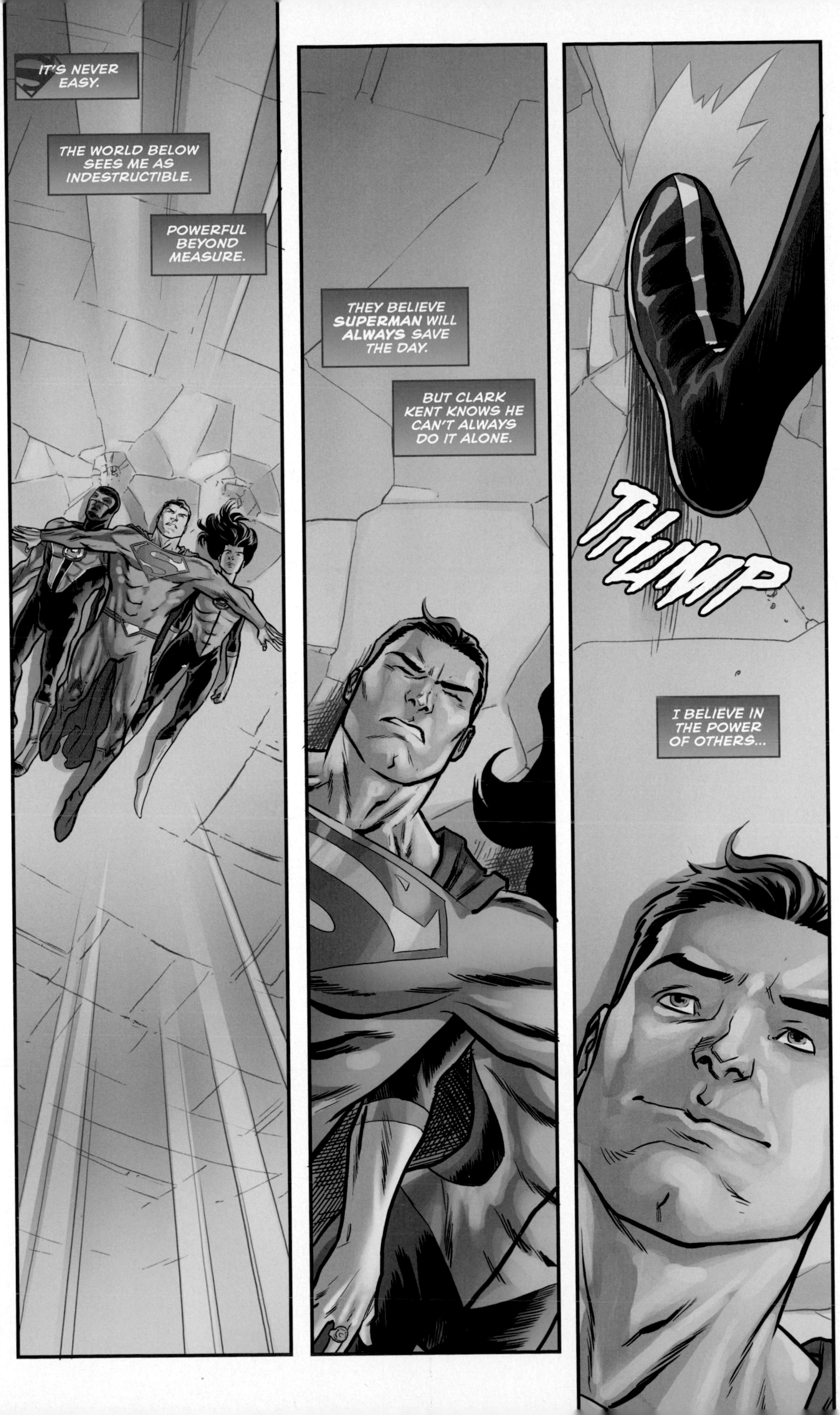
IT'S NEVER EASY.
THE WORLD BELOW SEES ME AS INDESTRUCTIBLE.
POWERFUL BEYOND MEASURE.
THEY BELIEVE SUPERMAN WILL ALWAYS SAVE THE DAY.
BUT CLARK KENT KNOWS HE CAN'T ALWAYS DO IT ALONE.
THUMP
I BELIEVE IN THE POWER OF OTHERS...

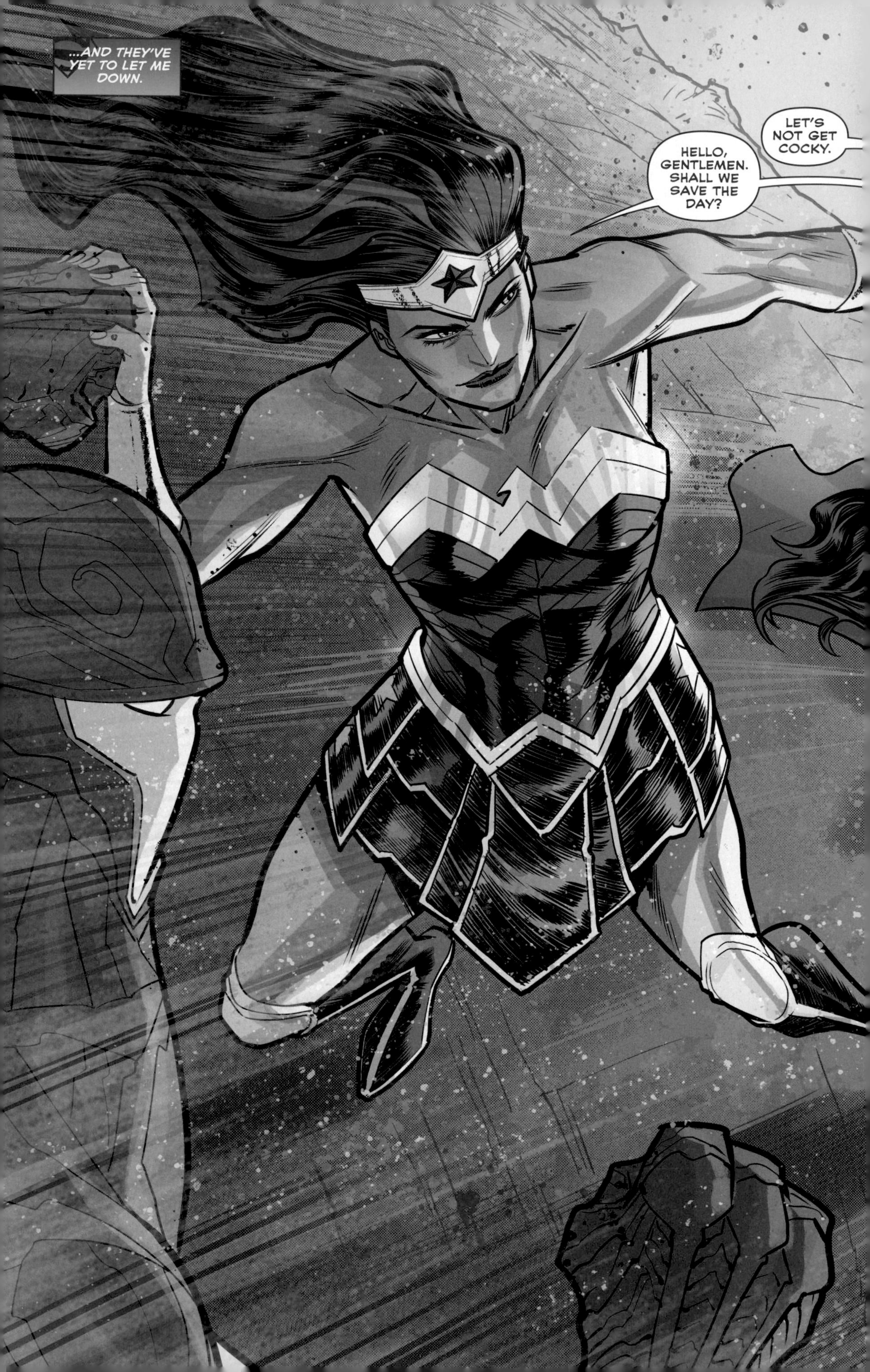
...AND THEY'VE YET TO LET ME DOWN.
HELLO, GENTLEMEN. SHALL WE SAVE THE DAY?
LET'S NOT GET COCKY.

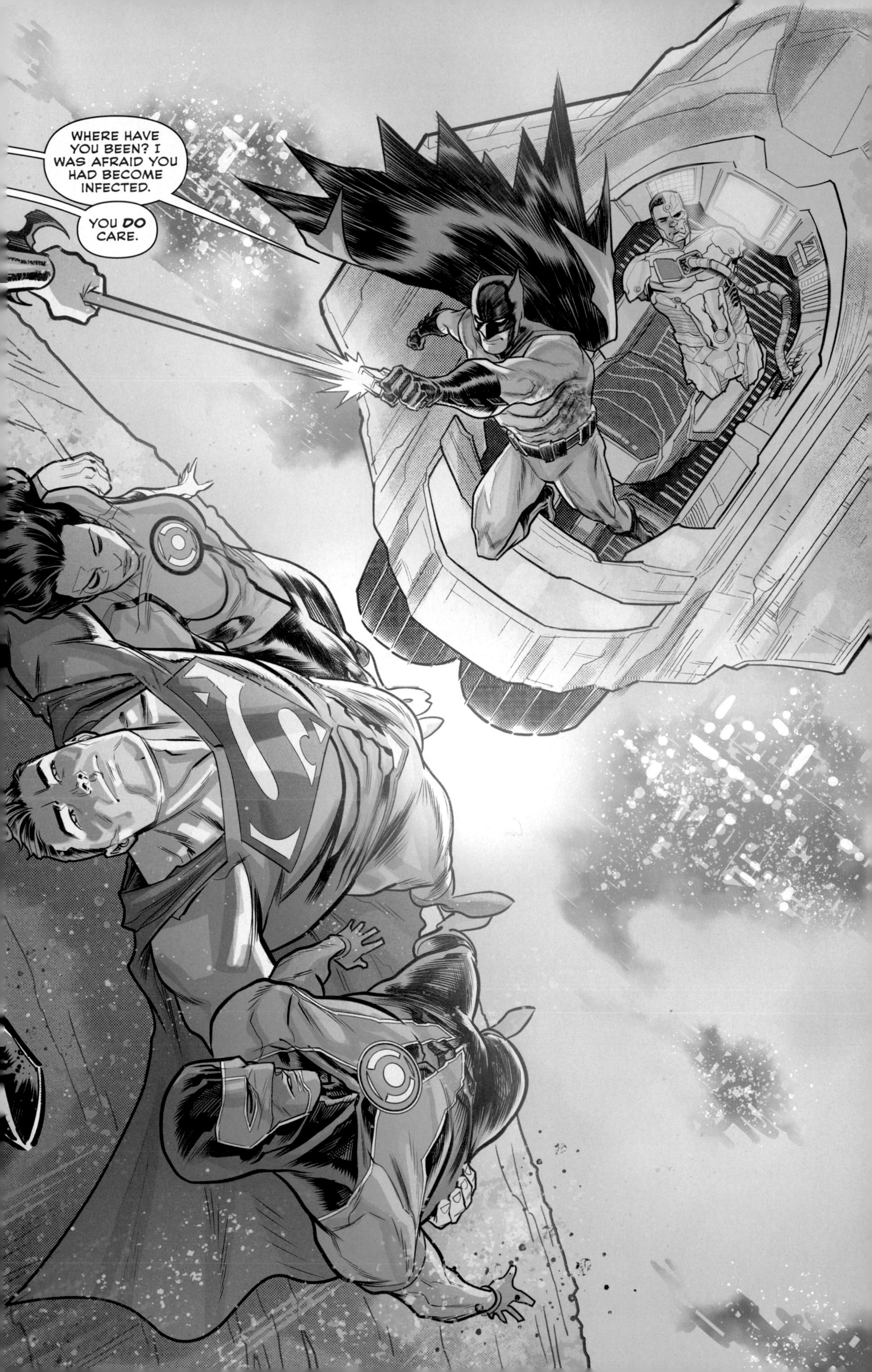
WHERE HAVE YOU BEEN? I WAS AFRAID YOU HAD BECOME INFECTED.
YOU DO CARE.

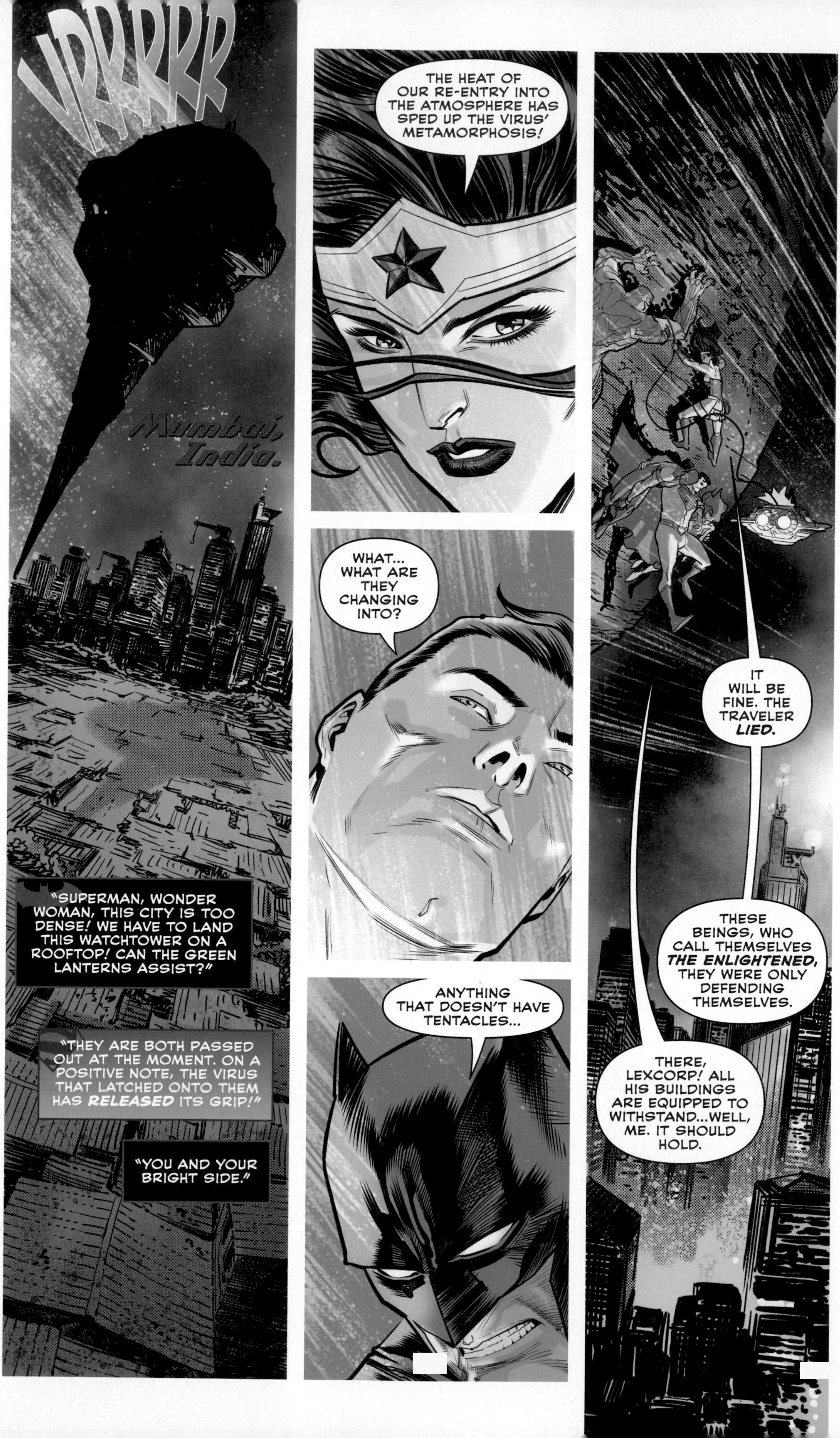
VRRRRR
Mumbai, India.
"SUPERMAN, WONDER WOMAN, THIS CITY IS TOO DENSE! WE HAVE TO LAND THIS WATCHTOWER ON A ROOFTOP! CAN THE GREEN LANTERNS ASSIST?"
"THEY ARE BOTH PASSED OUT AT THE MOMENT. ON A POSITIVE NOTE, THE VIRUS THAT LATCHED ONTO THEM HAS *RELEASED* ITS GRIP!"
"YOU AND YOUR BRIGHT SIDE."
THE HEAT OF OUR RE-ENTRY INTO THE ATMOSPHERE HAS SPED UP THE VIRUS' METAMORPHOSIS!
WHAT... WHAT ARE THEY CHANGING INTO?
ANYTHING THAT DOESN'T HAVE TENTACLES...
IT WILL BE FINE. THE TRAVELER *LIED.*
THESE BEINGS, WHO CALL THEMSELVES *THE ENLIGHTENED,* THEY WERE ONLY DEFENDING THEMSELVES.
THERE, LEXCORP! ALL HIS BUILDINGS ARE EQUIPPED TO WITHSTAND...WELL, ME. IT SHOULD HOLD.

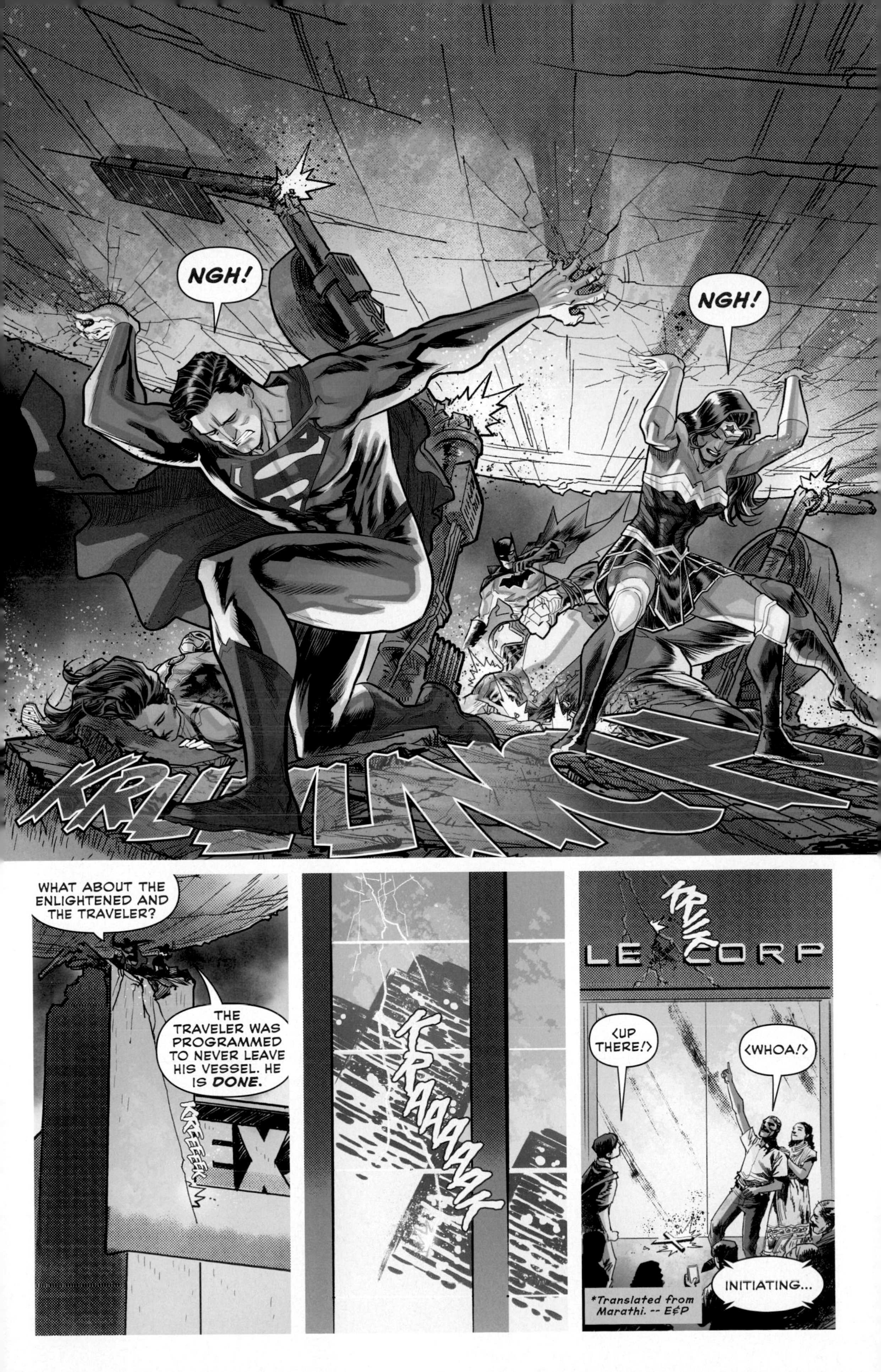
NGH!
NGH!
WHAT ABOUT THE ENLIGHTENED AND THE TRAVELER?
THE TRAVELER WAS PROGRAMMED TO NEVER LEAVE HIS VESSEL. HE IS *DONE*.
LE CORP
⟨UP THERE!⟩
⟨WHOA!⟩
INITIATING...
*Translated from Marathi. -- E&P

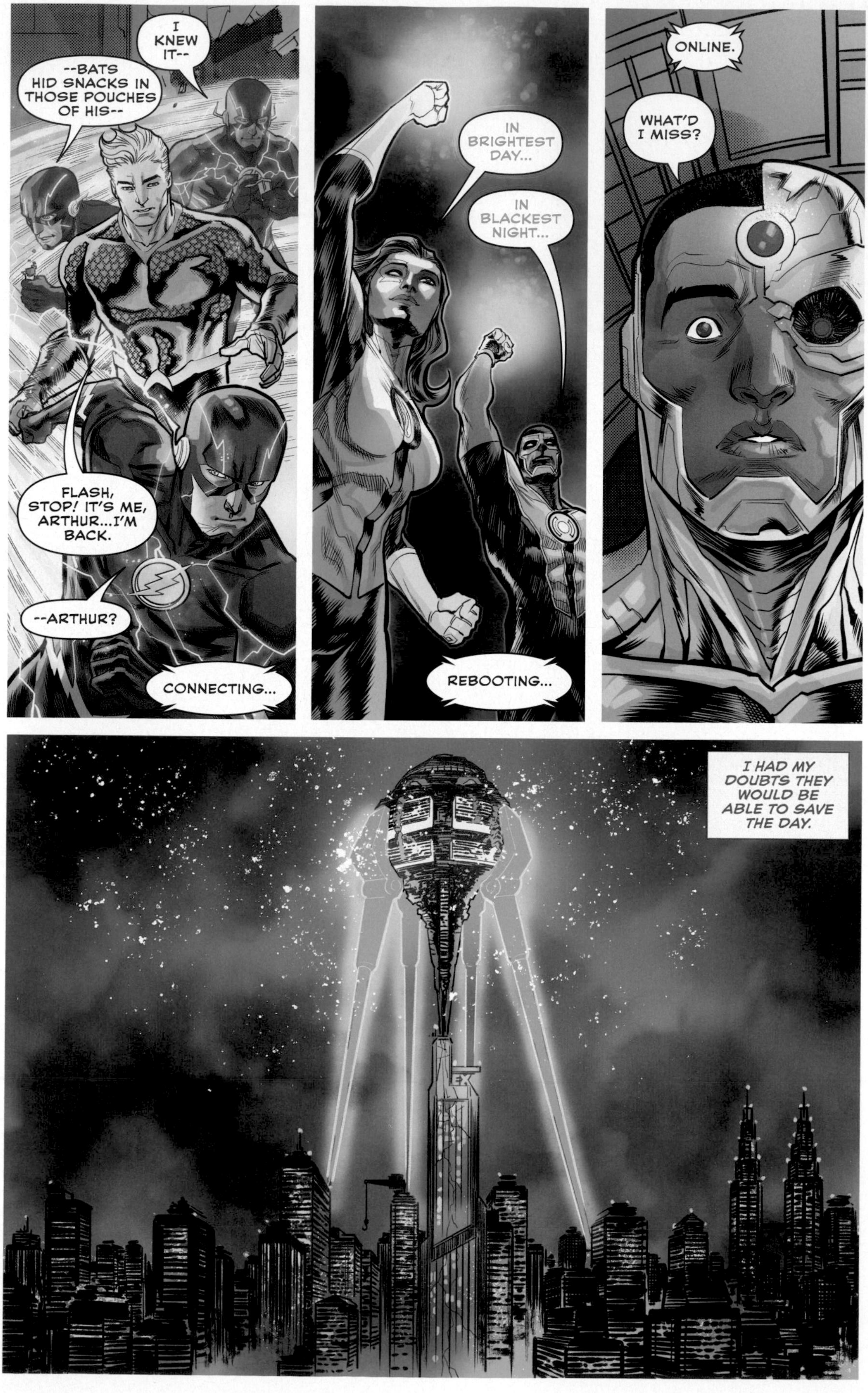
I KNEW IT--
--BATS HID SNACKS IN THOSE POUCHES OF HIS--
FLASH, STOP! IT'S ME, ARTHUR...I'M BACK.
--ARTHUR?
CONNECTING...
IN BRIGHTEST DAY...
IN BLACKEST NIGHT...
REBOOTING...
ONLINE.
WHAT'D I MISS?
I HAD MY DOUBTS THEY WOULD BE ABLE TO SAVE THE DAY.

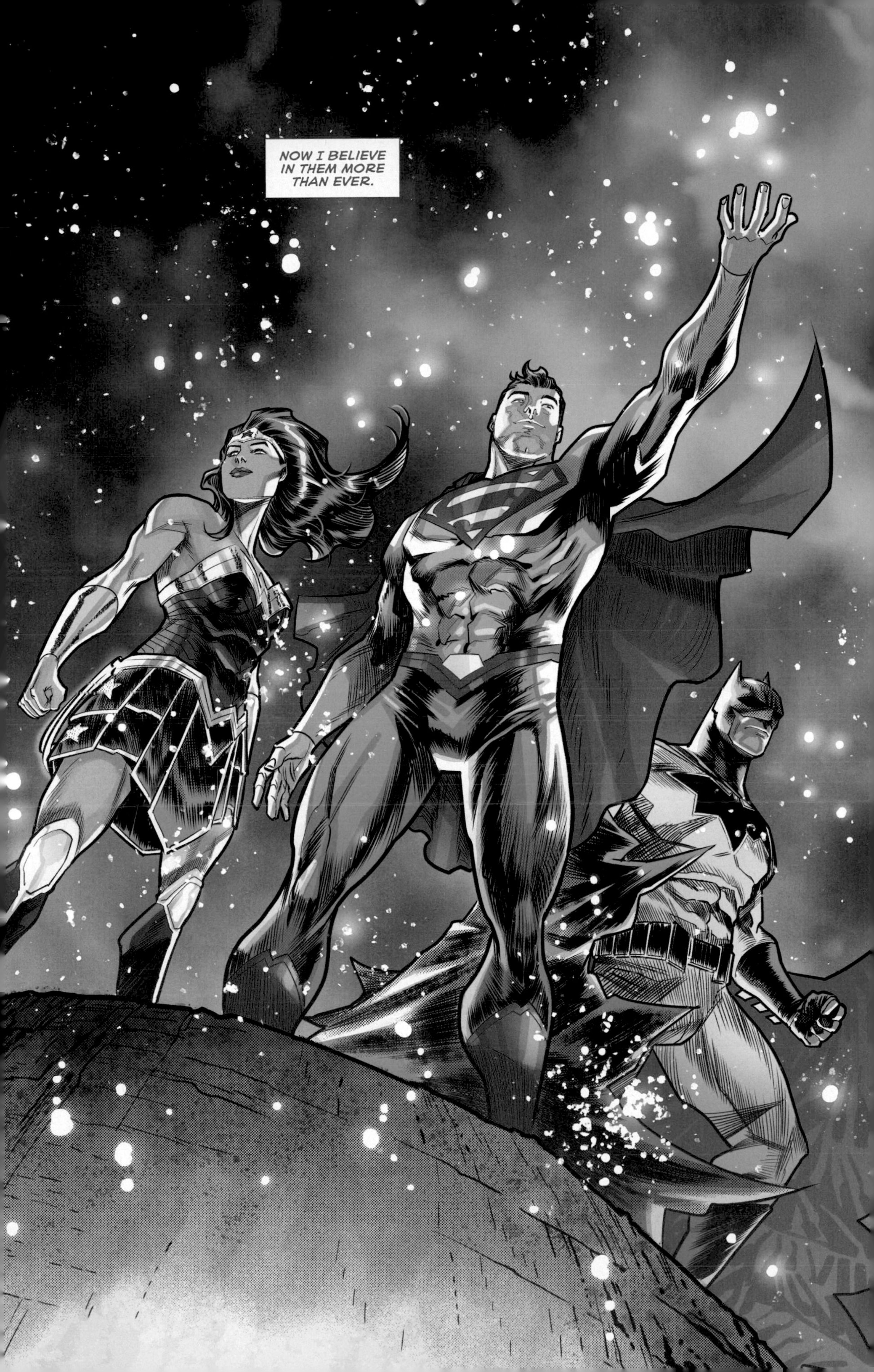
NOW I BELIEVE IN THEM MORE THAN EVER.

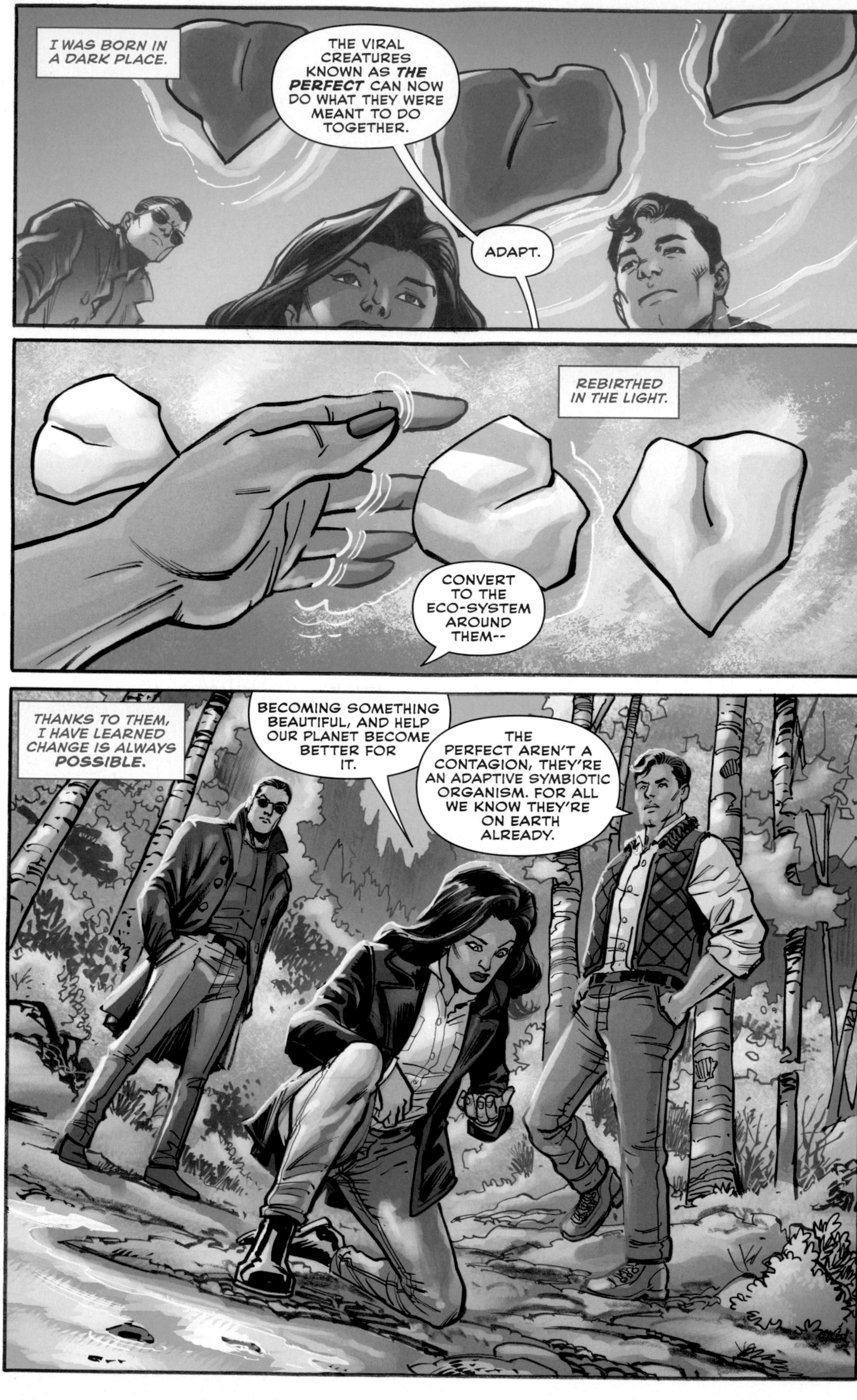
I WAS BORN IN A DARK PLACE.
THE VIRAL CREATURES KNOWN AS THE PERFECT CAN NOW DO WHAT THEY WERE MEANT TO DO TOGETHER.
ADAPT.
REBIRTHED IN THE LIGHT.
CONVERT TO THE ECO-SYSTEM AROUND THEM--
THANKS TO THEM, I HAVE LEARNED CHANGE IS ALWAYS POSSIBLE.
BECOMING SOMETHING BEAUTIFUL, AND HELP OUR PLANET BECOME BETTER FOR IT.
THE PERFECT AREN'T A CONTAGION, THEY'RE AN ADAPTIVE SYMBIOTIC ORGANISM. FOR ALL WE KNOW THEY'RE ON EARTH ALREADY.

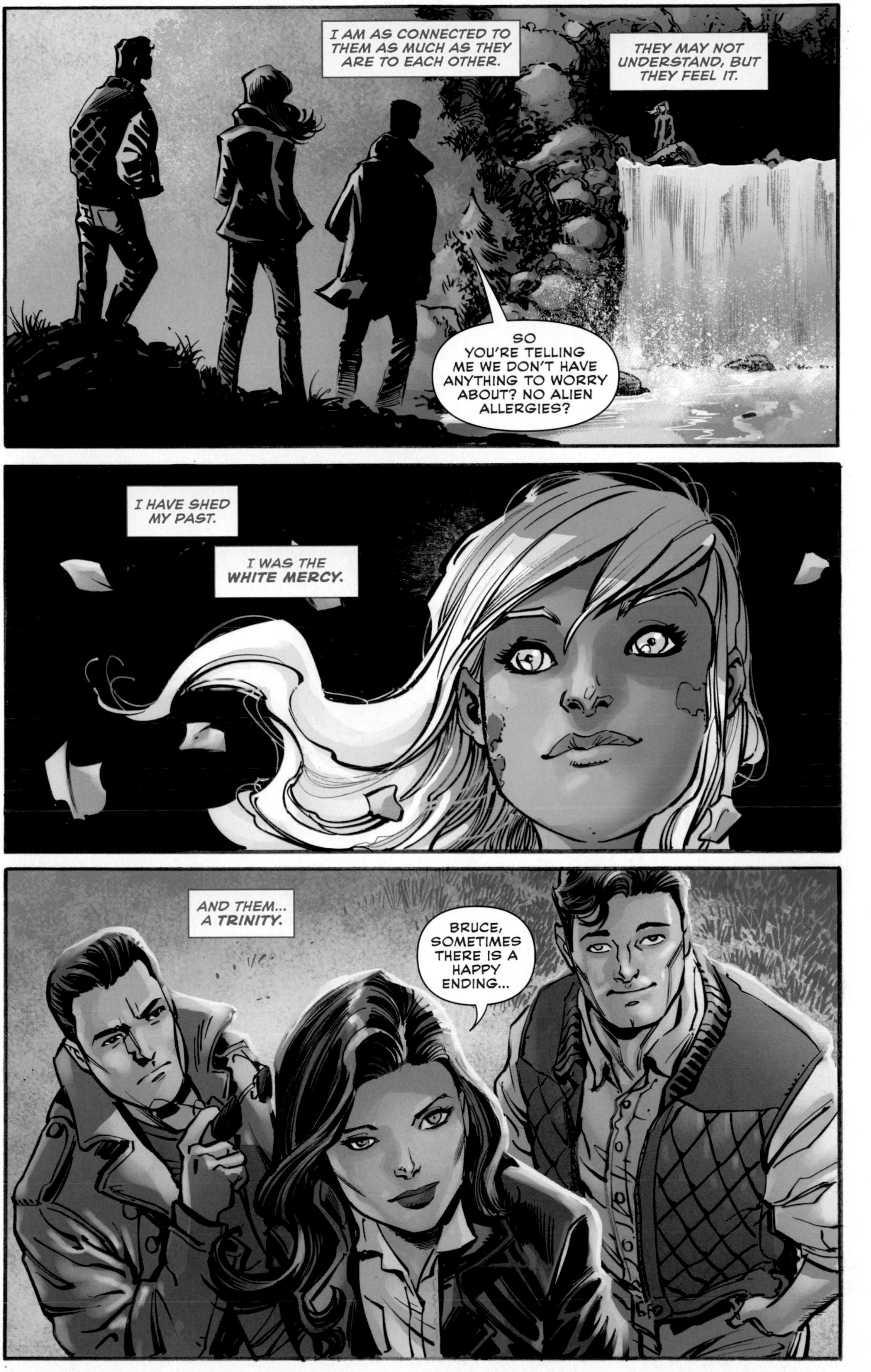
I AM AS CONNECTED TO THEM AS MUCH AS THEY ARE TO EACH OTHER.
THEY MAY NOT UNDERSTAND, BUT THEY FEEL IT.
SO YOU'RE TELLING ME WE DON'T HAVE ANYTHING TO WORRY ABOUT? NO ALIEN ALLERGIES?
I HAVE SHED MY PAST.
I WAS THE WHITE MERCY.
AND THEM... A TRINITY.
BRUCE, SOMETIMES THERE IS A HAPPY ENDING...

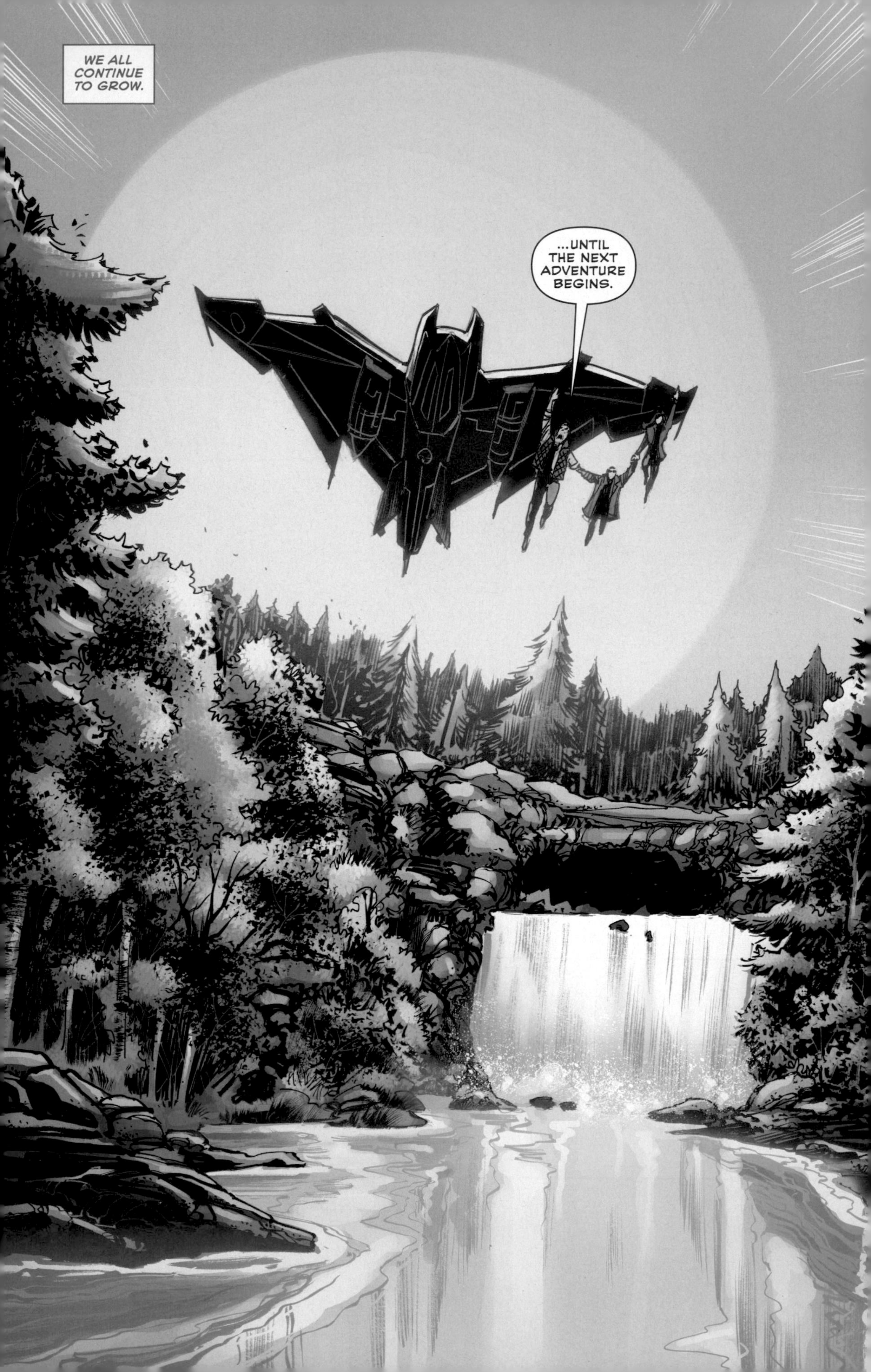
WE ALL CONTINUE TO GROW.
...UNTIL THE NEXT ADVENTURE BEGINS.

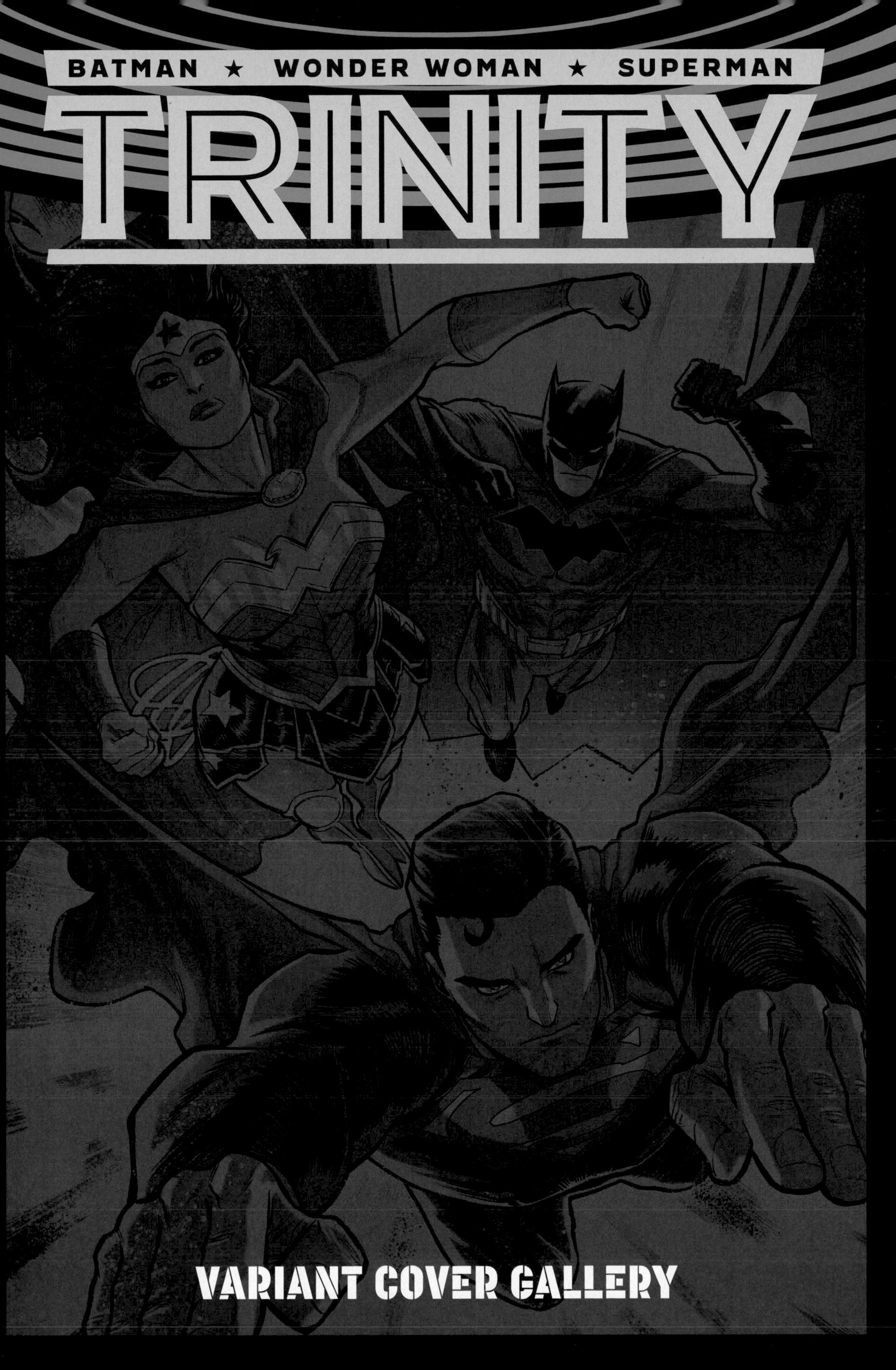
BATMAN ★ WONDER WOMAN ★ SUPERMAN
TRINITY
VARIANT COVER GALLERY

TRINITY #7 Variant Cover by BILL SIENKIEWICZ

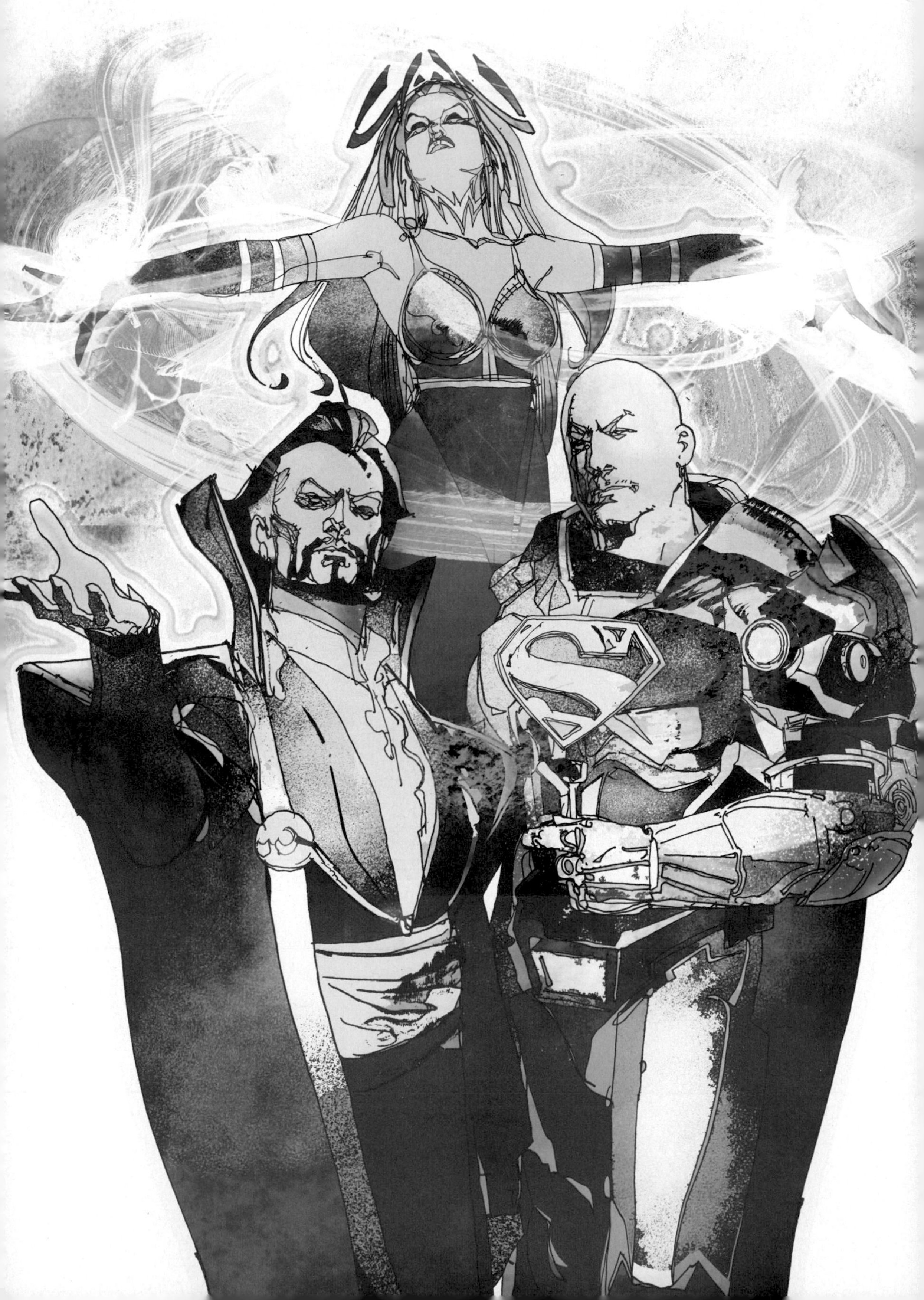

TRINITY #8 variant cover by BILL SIENKIEWICZ

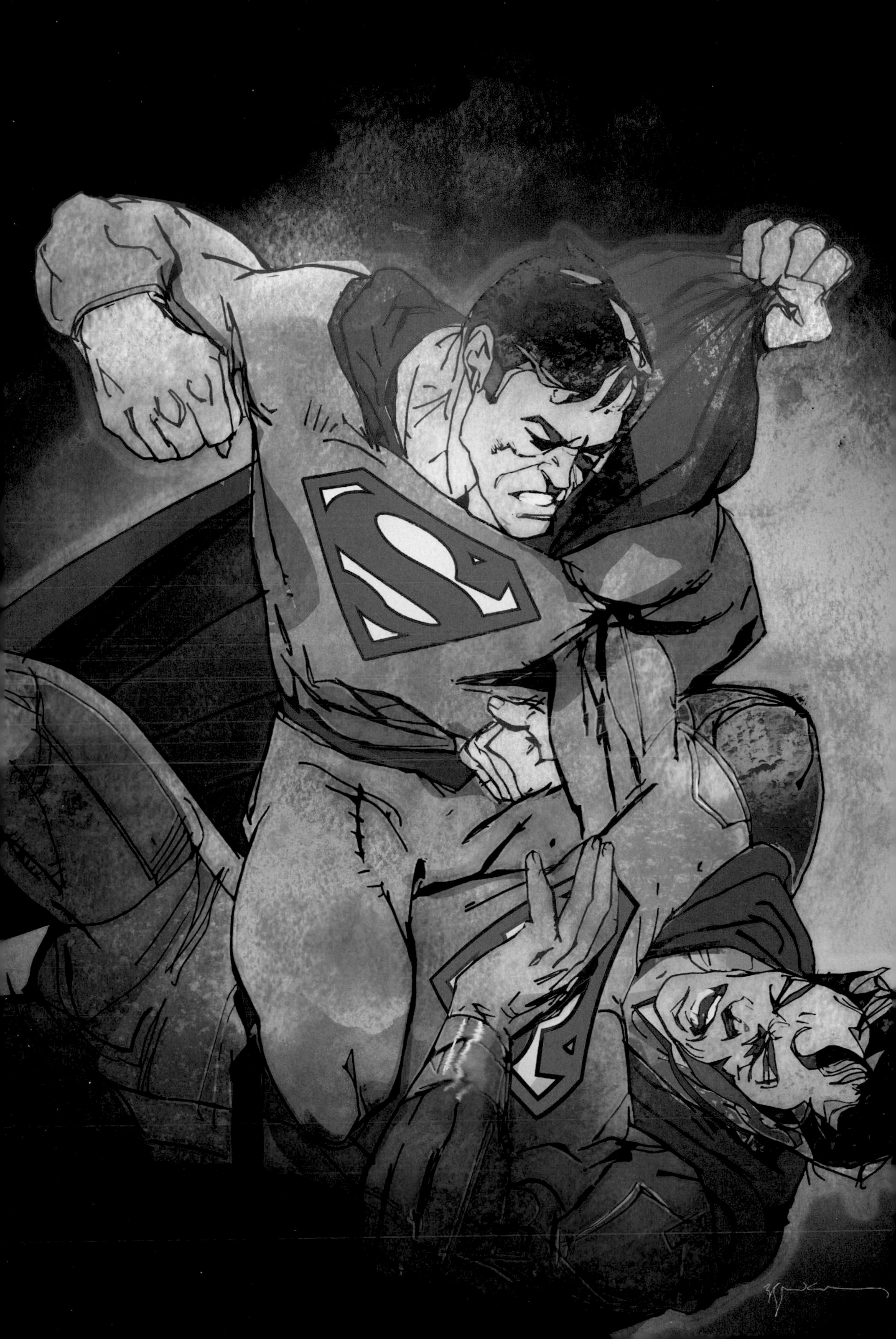

TRINITY #9 Variant Cover by
BILL SIENKIEWICZ

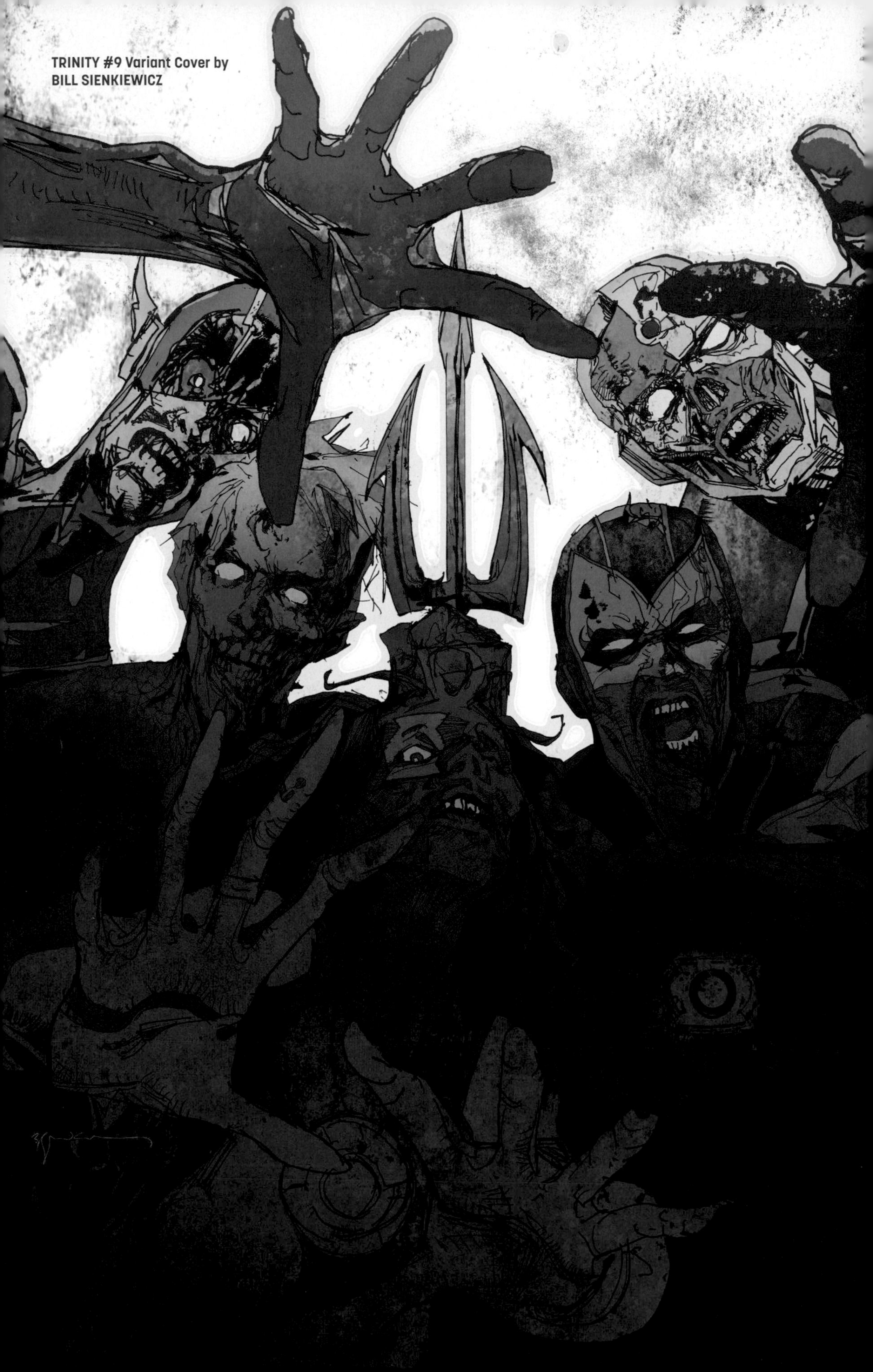

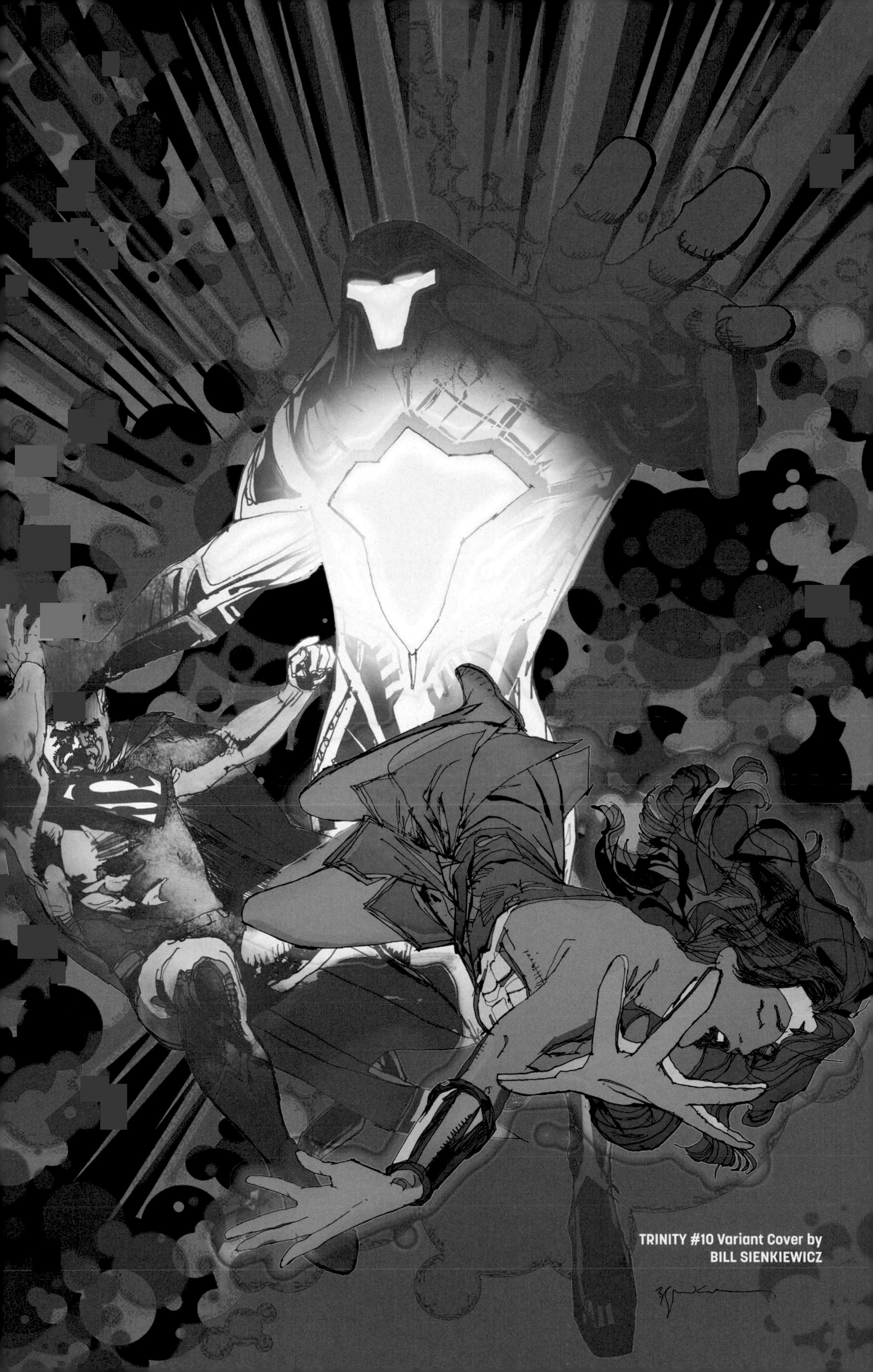

TRINITY #10 Variant Cover by
BILL SIENKIEWICZ

TRINITY #11
Variant Cover by
BILL SIENKIEWICZ

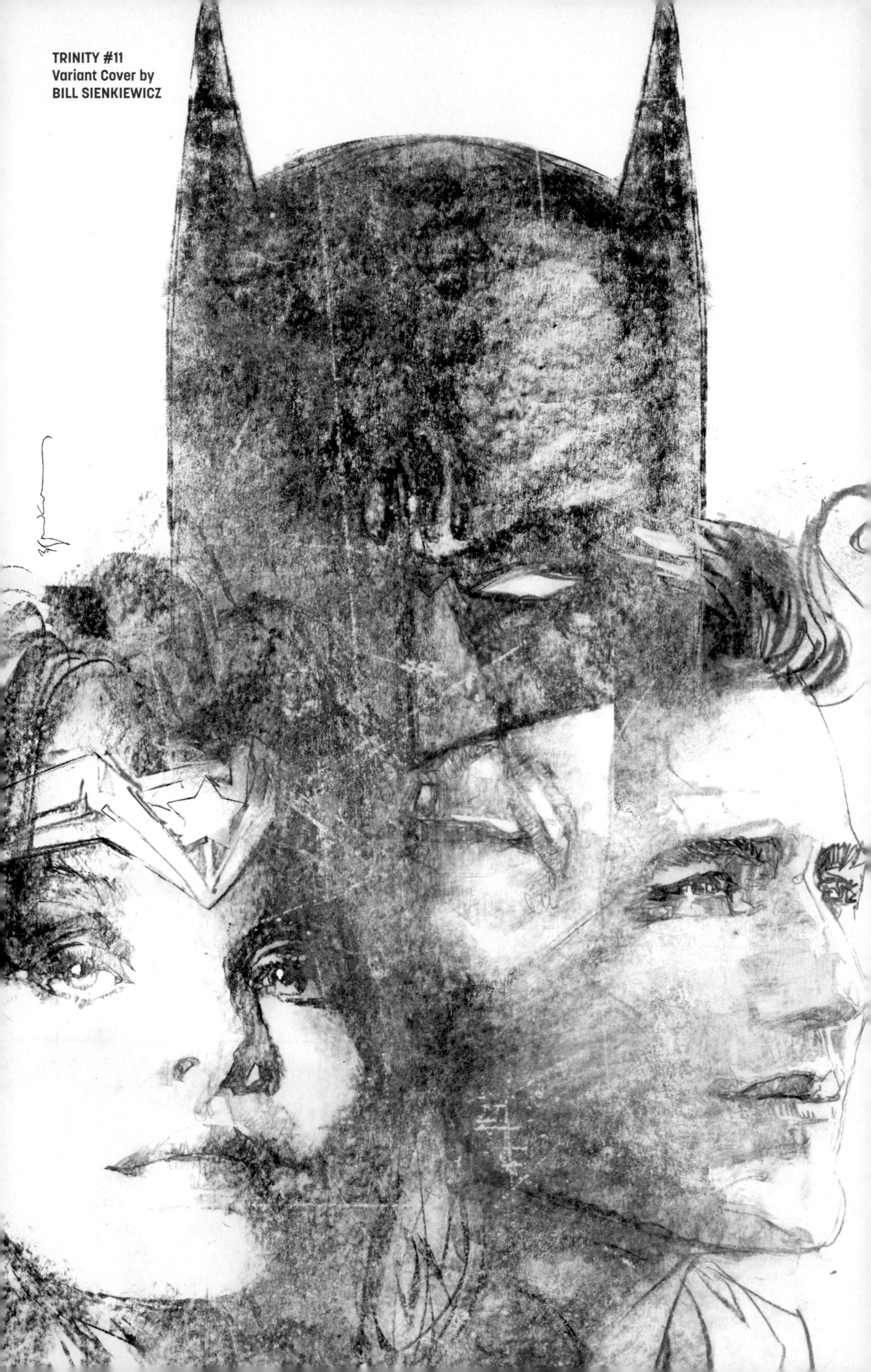

A

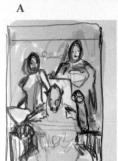

RA'S in throne, Circe at his side, Lex on his other

B

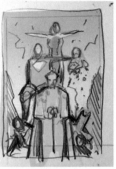

Ra's in front. Lex stands on rubble,skulls AND the Trinity in crumbles. LEX hold out superman as he breaks apart. Circe in back doing a spell

C

CIRCE
LEX
RA'S

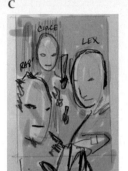

the three bad guys up close and the trinity falling into RA'S hand

COVER SKETCHES FOR TRINITY #7 AND #8

BY Clay Mann

TRINITY #8 mann

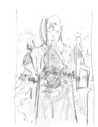

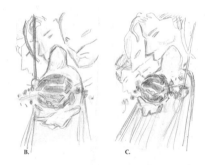

A. gotham behind Batman, Themyscira behind WW

B.

C.

COVER SKETCHES FOR TRINITY #9 AND #10

by Francis Manapul

#9

TRAPPED
IN THE
WATCHTOWER!

#10 A

WHO
IS THE
TRAITOR?

#10 B

WHO
IS THE
TRAITOR?

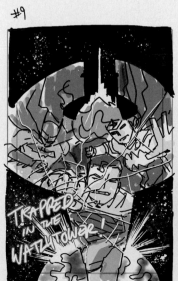

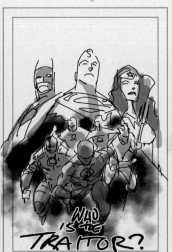

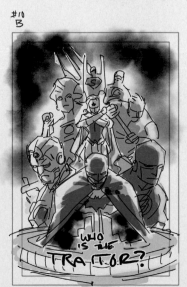

COVER SKETCHES FOR TRINITY #11
by Francis Manapul

A

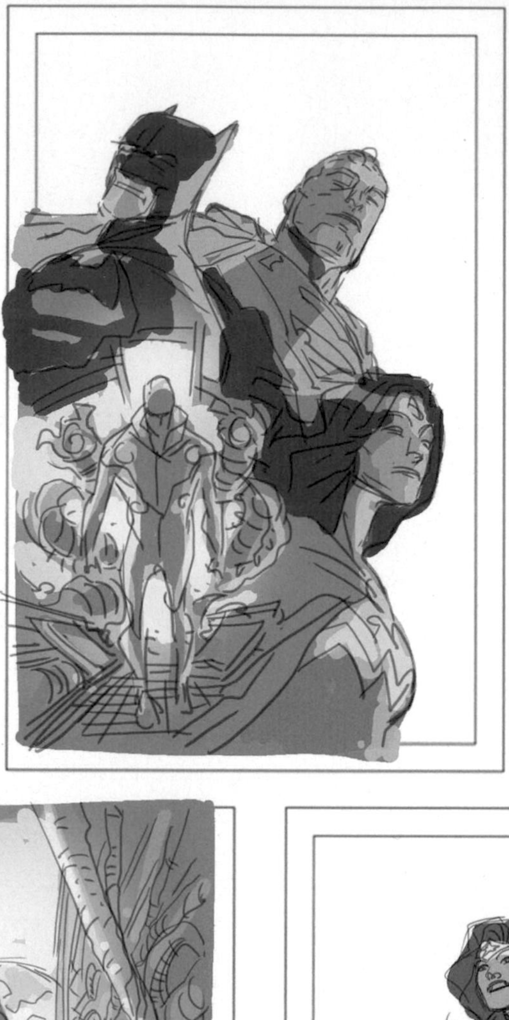

B

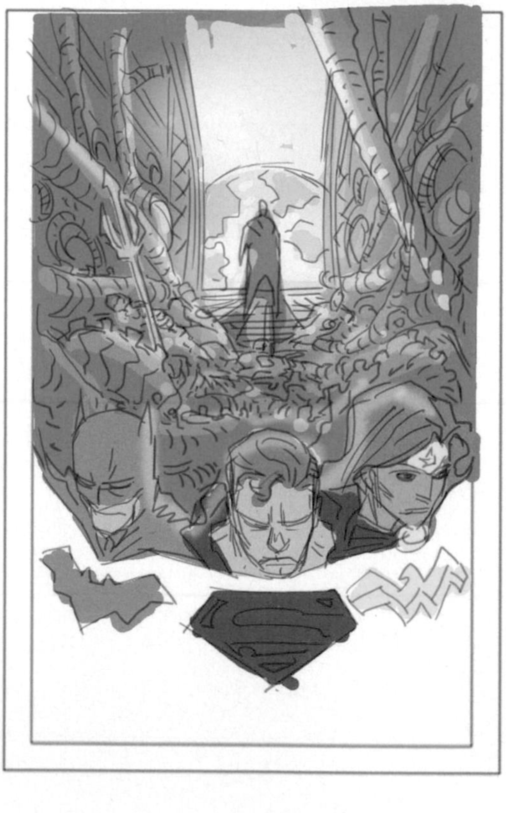

C

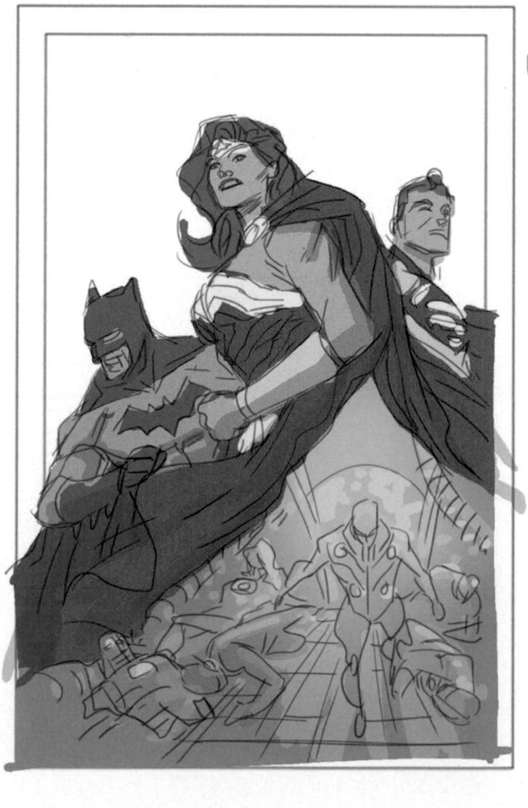

COVER PENCILS FOR TRINITY #11
by Francis Manapul

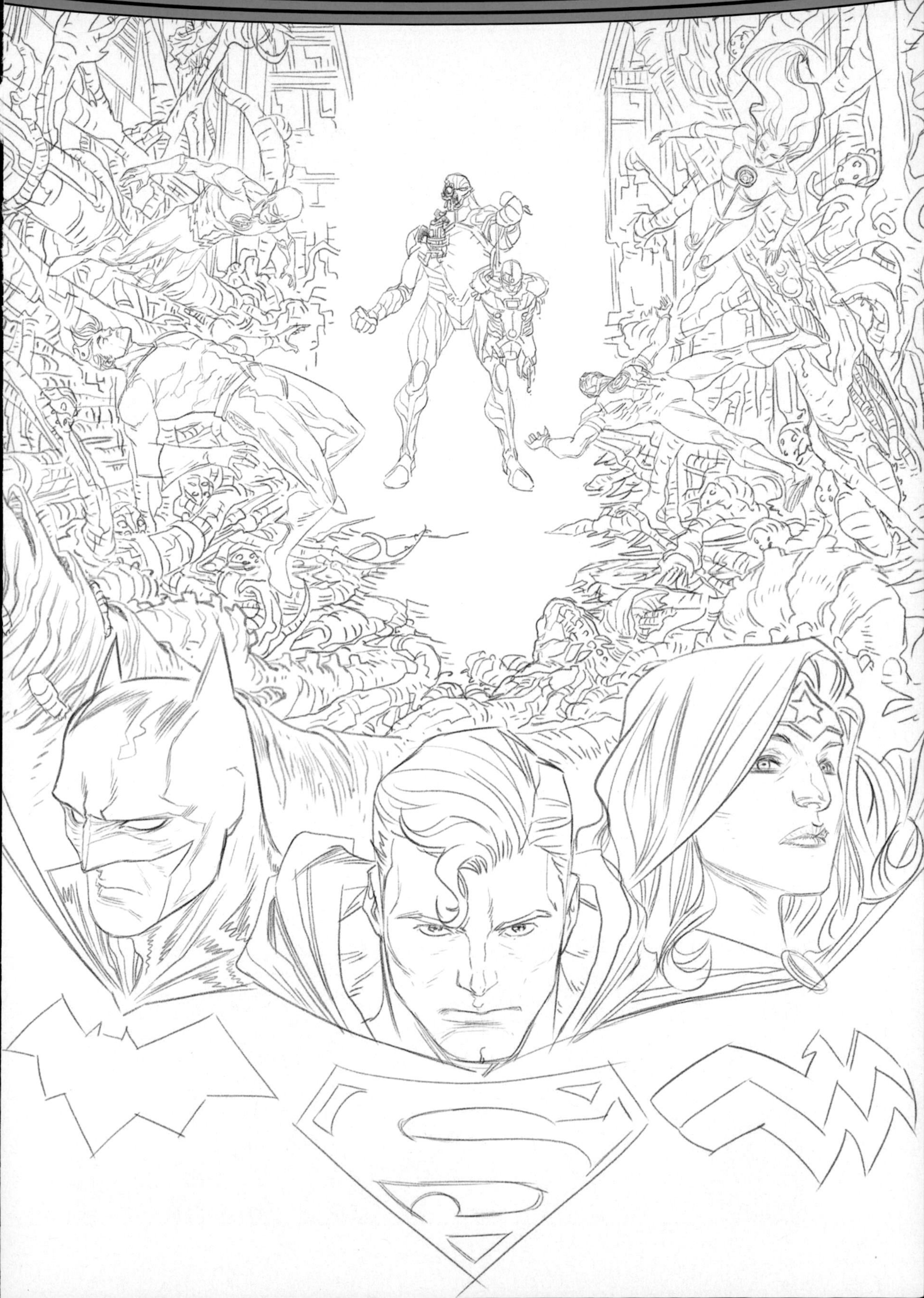

INKS FOR TRINITY #10 PAGE 12
by Francis Manapul

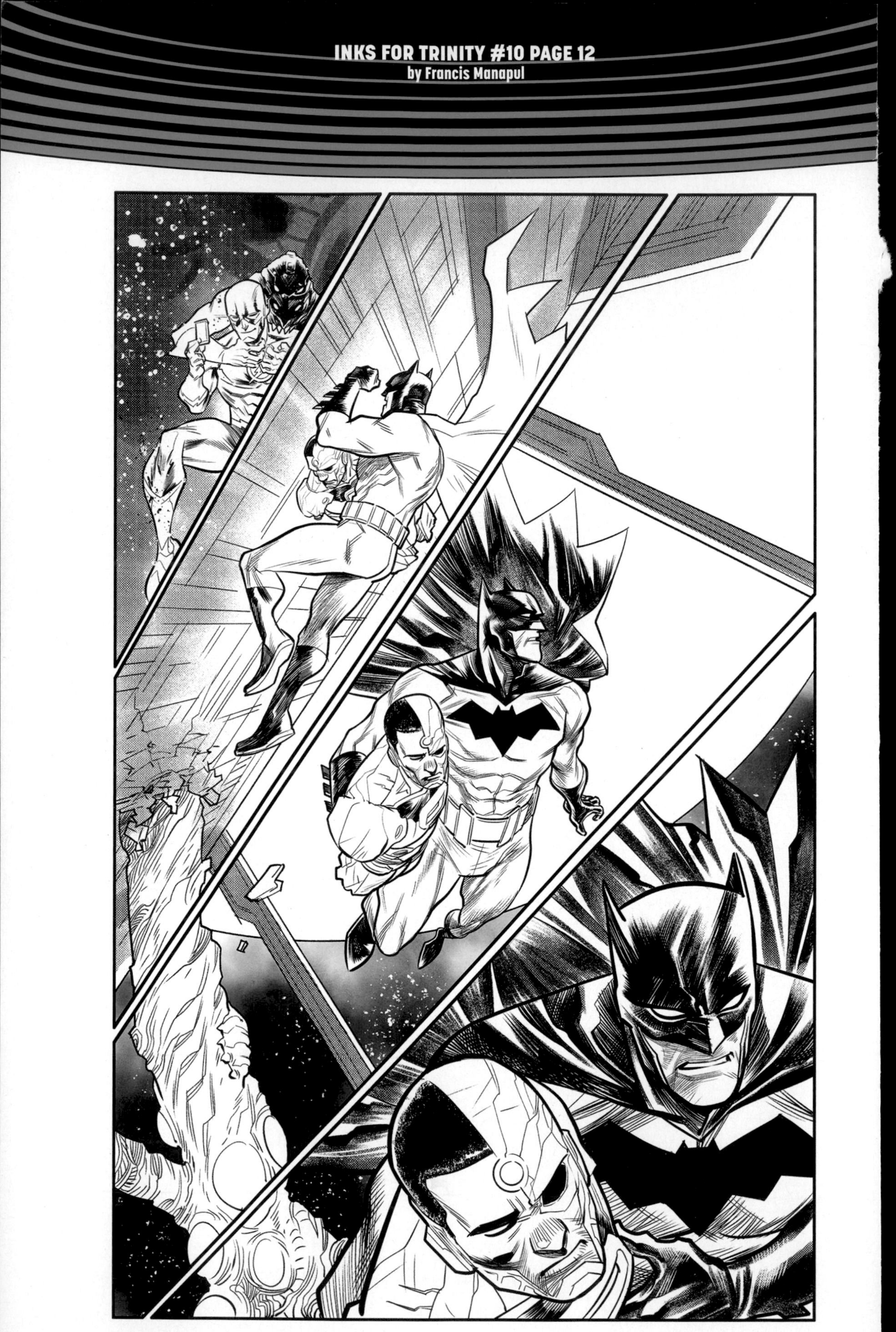

INKS FOR TRINITY #10 PAGE 13

by Francis Manapul

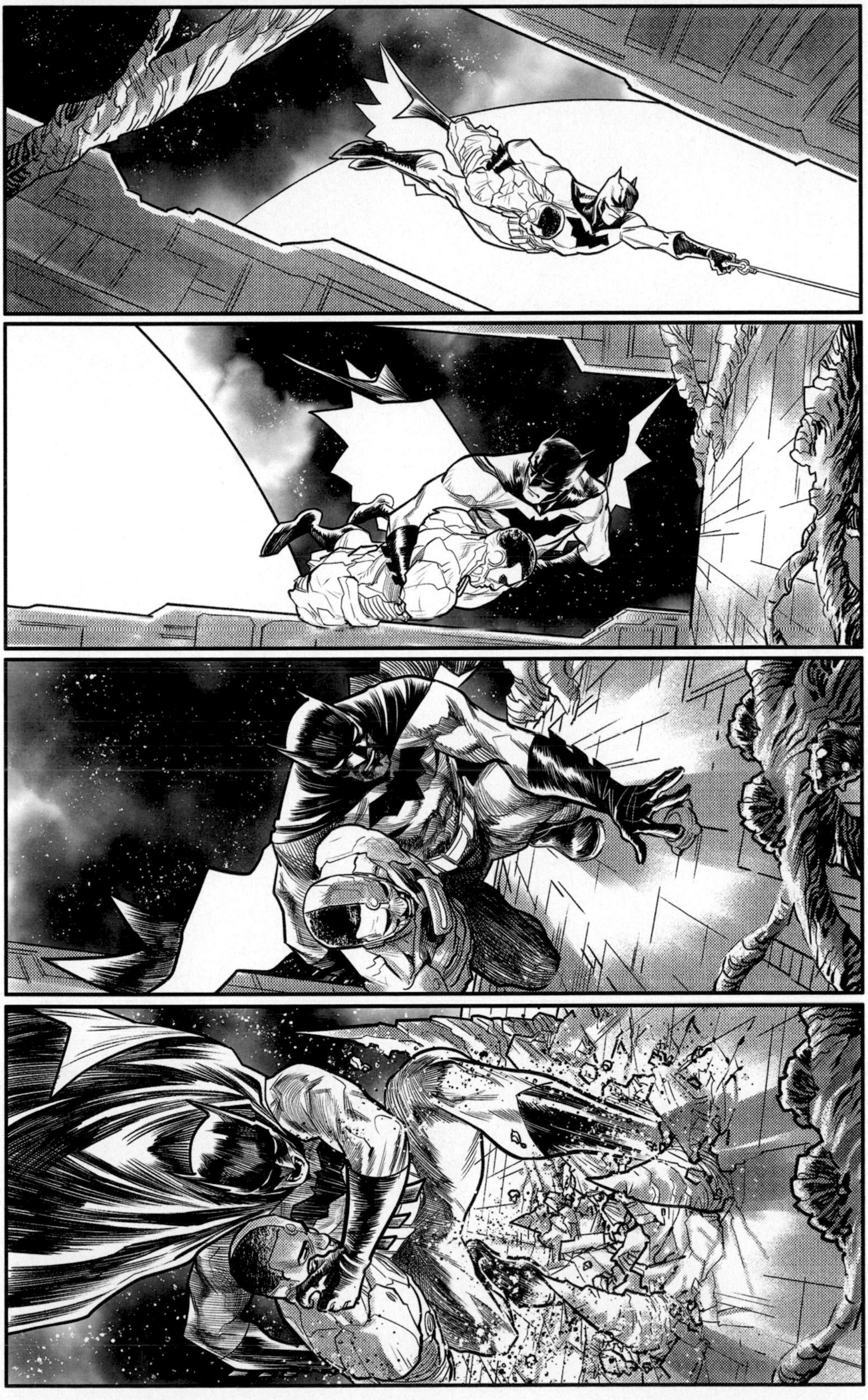

INKS FOR TRINITY #10 PAGES 14-15
by Francis Manapul

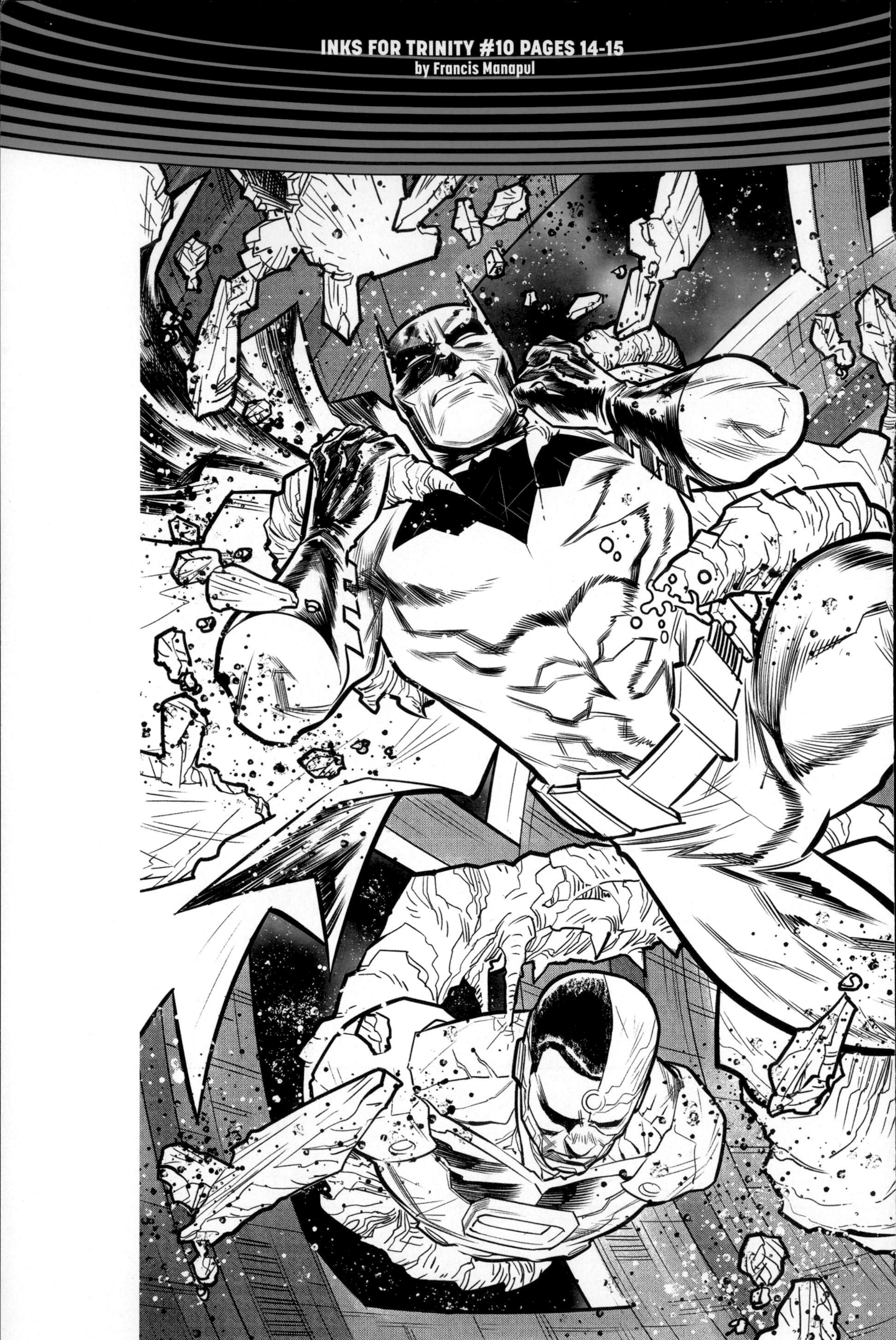

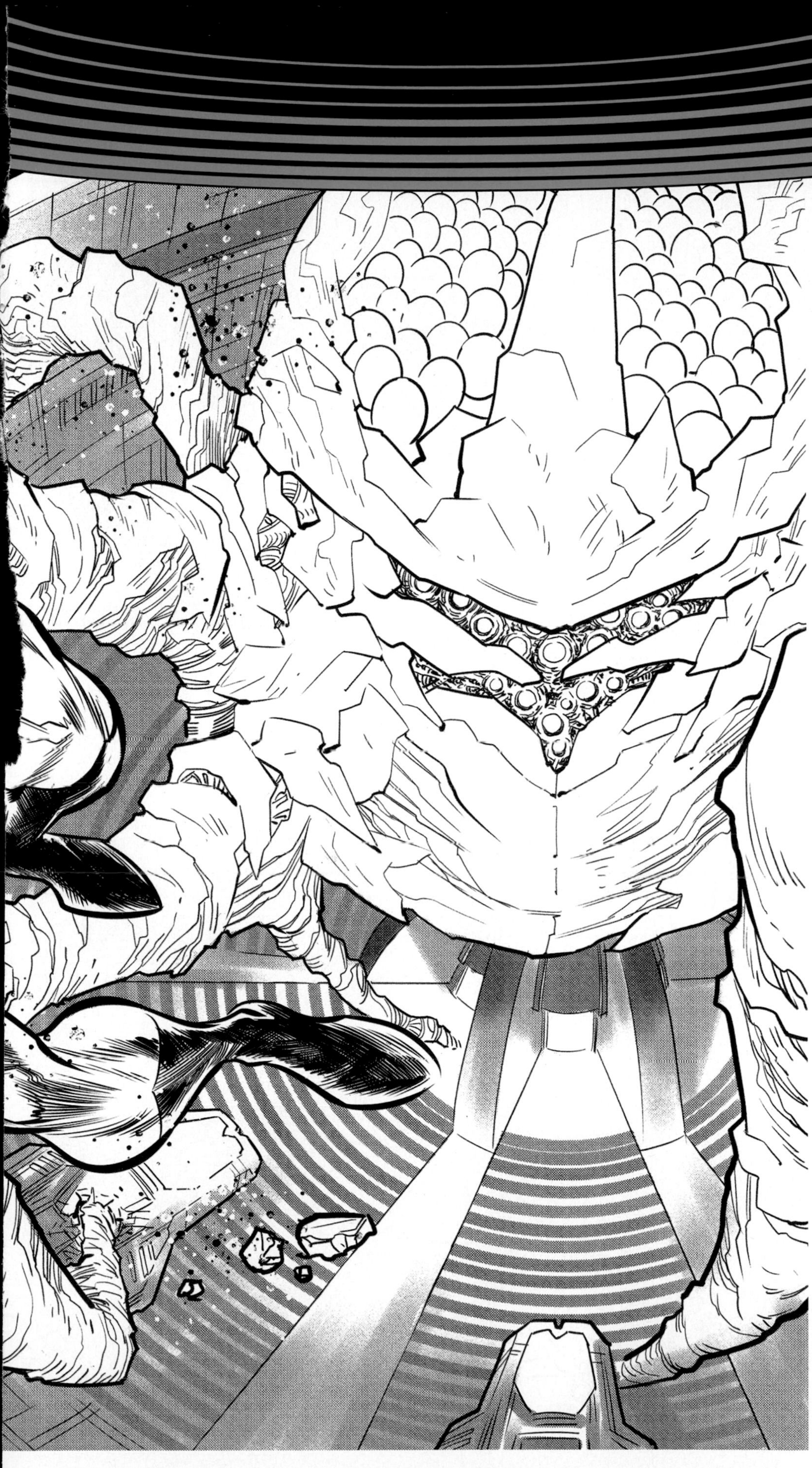

INKS FOR TRINITY #11 PAGE 1

by Francis Manapul

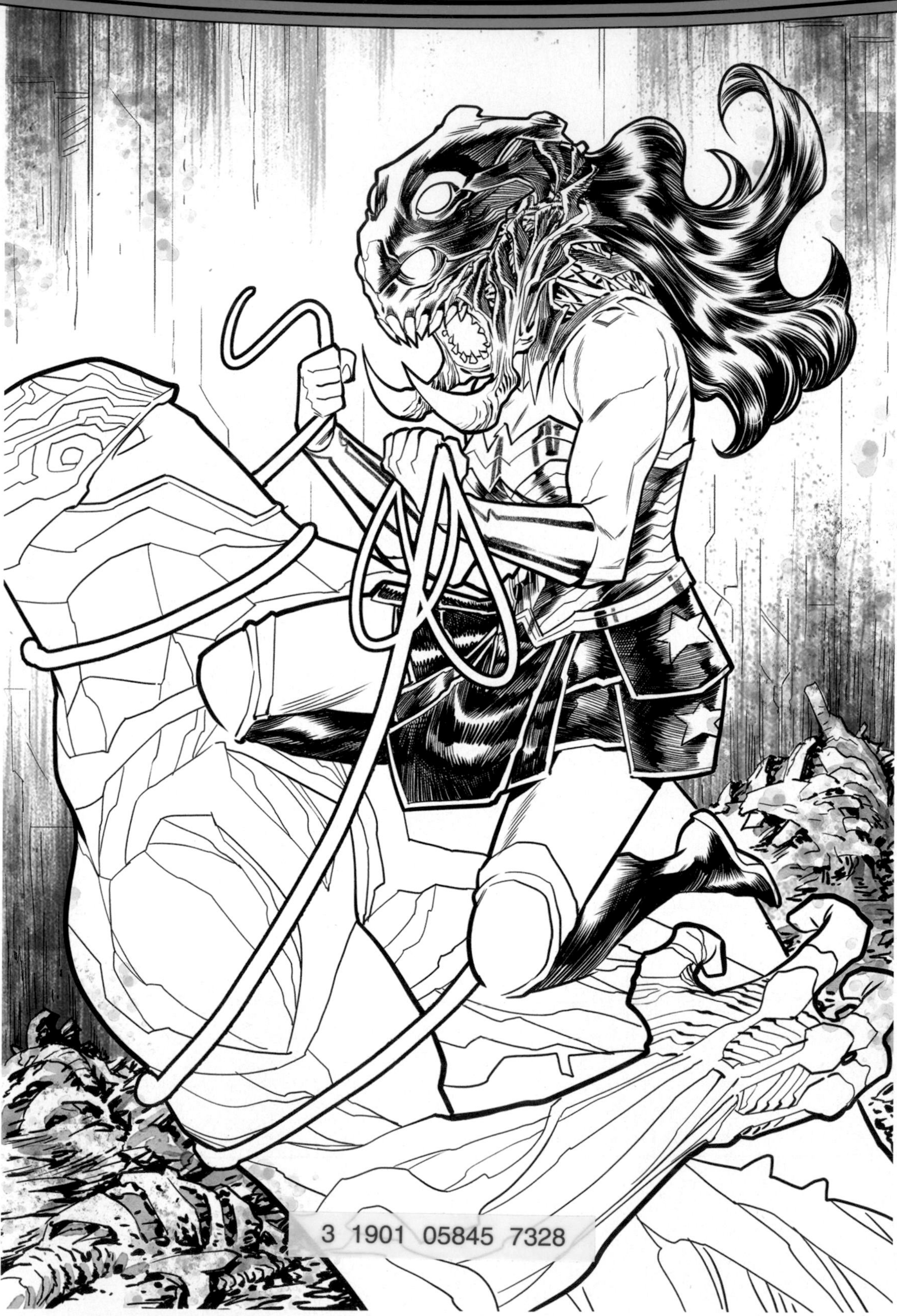